HARVARD STUDIES IN URBAN HISTORY

SERIES EDITORS   Stephan Thernstrom
Charles Tilly

Urban Growth and City-Systems in the United States, 1840–1860

Allan Pred

HARVARD UNIVERSITY PRESS
CAMBRIDGE, MASSACHUSETTS
LONDON, ENGLAND
1980

Library of Congress Cataloging in Publication Data

Pred, Allan Richard, 1936-
  Urban growth and city-systems in the United States, 1840-1860.

  (Harvard studies in urban history)
  Includes bibliographical references and index.
  1.   Cities and towns—Growth—United States—History.   2.   Urbanization—
United States—History.   I.   Title.   II.   Series.
HT123.P69   307.7′6′0973   80-12098
ISBN 0-674-93091-6

For Mary and Sol

Acknowledgments

This book would never have come about had I not been involved in a completely different project. For some years I have been trying to expand Torsten Hägerstrand's "time-geographic" conceptual framework and philosophical perspective; more specifically I have been attempting to deal with a wide range of issues concerning the interplay among the everyday experiences of the common individual, the structuring of activities by economic and noneconomic institutions, and social change. Had I not been collecting materials on the early impact of the telegraph on the structuring of institutional activities, and thereby on the daily (and lifelong) experiences of individuals, my path would not have intersected with certain materials and I would not have become aware of the variety of data available on the interurban flow of goods and economic information in the United States between 1840 and 1860. And, had I not noticed the data, I would not have been tempted to momentarily put aside my long-term commitment to "time-geography" in order further to pursue the themes developed in my previous contribution to the Harvard Studies in Urban History series, *Urban Growth and the Circulation of Information: The United States System of Cities, 1790–1840.*

I am once again very grateful to Adrienne Morgan, who did her usual superb job when drafting my maps and diagrams. Very special thanks also are due to Roger Miller, who, as graduate student and intellectual comrade, was willing to share both the sometimes fascinating reading and the frequent drudgery that were necessary for the compilation of the content analyses accompanying Chapter 6.

As ever, I am greatly indebted to Hjördis, Michele, and Erik for their patience, understanding, and love during the period in which I did research for and wrote this book.

Contents

Figures

Maps

Tables

Urban Growth and City-Systems in the United
States, 1840–1860

1

The Questions and Their Setting

The growth of a city normally cannot be separated either from the economic activities present in that place or from the interurban economic ties associated with those activities. Today the job-providing economic activities present in any American city or major metropolitan complex are intricately bound up with the job-providing economic activities of other cities and major metropolitan complexes through flows of goods, services, capital, and specialized information, and through the employment multiplier effects associated with such flows. Hence, the population size and economic well-being of the modern city or major metropolitan complex does not depend merely on its provision of goods and services to smaller places in its retailing and agricultural hinterland, as suggested by classical theory.[1] On the contrary, many of the most important economic linkages existing between U.S. urban centers are a consequence of the job-control, capital allocation, and decision-making activities occurring within the administrative units of large private-sector and government organizations. Moreover, most of the remaining key interurban economic ties in the United States arise from the input-output relationships that occur when production and distribution processes require the coordination of geographically separated establishments and facilities.

On the one hand, the headquarters and other administrative organizational units present in any U.S. metropolitan complex are, as a group, linked to a highly significant degree with three types of subservient units: those located in other larger and smaller metropolitan complexes both nearby and distant; those within the metropolitan complex itself and its traditionally defined trading hinterland (or primary sphere of economic influence); and those in nonhinterland smaller towns and cities. On the other hand, a large percentage of the economic activities and employment opportunities existing in any U.S. metropolitan complex is controlled by and linked to administrative units situated in other metropolitan complexes of varying size that are spread throughout the country.[2]

At the same time, the modern industrial technology used by profit-motivated corporations to turn out highly specialized products has necessitated the establishment of ever more elaborate physical input-output relationships. To put it another way: "Manufacturing has in-

creasingly become a matter of teamwork within vast [interorganiza-
tional] production systems, in which work has been divided between a
great number of component units specializing in one particular aspect of
[either] production" or service provision that is production related.[3] As
a result, at least half of the aggregate purchases and deliveries of the
manufacturing sector of even the largest and most economically diverse
metropolitan complexes are likely to occur nonlocally, involving, for the
most part, both nonhinterland metropolitan complexes of varying sizes
and locations and widely scattered nonhinterland smaller towns and
cities.[4]

The existence of intricate, crisscrossing economic relationships among
American smaller towns, cities, and metropolitan complexes means that
as a group all the urban units of the United States, or any of its component economic regions, may be regarded as a system of cities or city-
system. A system of cities may be defined as a national or a regional set
of urban units that are interdependent, or bound together by economic
interactions, in such a way that any significant change in the economic
activities, occupational structure, total income, or population of one
member unit will directly or indirectly bring about some modification in
the economic activities, occupational structure, total income, or population of one or more of the other members of the set.[5] Like any other
city-system, the national system of cities of the United States and each
of its component regional city-systems may be regarded as a particular
example of a complex social system. As such, each system is open: that
is, some of the units belonging to each system interact directly with
units outside its borders (urban units in other countries or regions), and
the system as a whole is frequently affected by events and processes unfolding elsewhere. Inasmuch as the U.S. (national) city-system and each
of its component regional city-systems are complex social systems, it
may be presumed that the total pattern of interdependencies, or economic ties, and associated information linkages between their units has
become increasingly complex with the passage of time.[6]

Despite the tangled web of economic relationships currently existing
among American small towns, cities, and metropolitan complexes, despite the supposed increase in the intricacies of those relationships over
the long historical run, despite clear shifts of regional economic fortune
that have occurred along with changing national and international demands for natural resources, goods, and services, and despite many recent cases of metropolitan stagnation and decline, particularly in the
"Snow Belt," the rank-size relations of major metropolitan centers
within the U.S. system of cities as a whole has been characterized in

some important, though limited, respects by regularity and stability ever since 1790.[7] (The so-called rank-size rule states that the population of any city should be roughly equal to the population of the country's or region's largest city divided by the national or regional population rank of the city in question.) Much more striking, the presently dominant units of regional sets of cities have been characterized by very long-term rank stability, experiencing either no shift in population rank whatsoever or an upward or downward shift of only one or two ranks ever since the period when each set began to function as a regional city-system. (By definition, the urban units of a region do not constitute a true system unless there is a significant level of economic interaction and interdependence among them; however, when a regional system is lacking, urban units may participate in the national system or function as "colonial" outliers of the city-system of another region.) In fact, if the United States is broken up into broadly defined economic-geographic regions, it is generally found that the metropolitan units presently occupying the very highest regional city-system size ranks were identified as regional leaders long before their populations reached as much as 1 or 2 percent of their present totals.[8]

THE QUESTIONS

Given the present-day complexity of city-system economic interdependencies, which presumably has its roots in the past, and the long-term regional rank stability of major metropolitan complexes, several interrelated questions may be asked concerning urban growth and city-system development processes during the nineteenth century in general and during the economically and politically pivotal 1840–1860 period in particular. How simple or complex were the economic interdependencies of major centers within the U.S. system of cities and its various regional city-systems during the 1840–1860 period? How did the economic interdependencies of that period interact with the feedback processes that apparently affected population growth within major centers and other individual cities? How can those same interdependencies be related to the ongoing processes of national and regional city-system growth and development? Why was major-center rank stability solidified or maintained during these two decades preceding the Civil War?

Although these questions are aimed at the antebellum period, it is not my intention to examine the urban growth and city-system development of the United States during that period as an end in itself, but as a means to the broader end of further illuminating the processes of growth and change that generally occur in systems of cities under different prevailing modes of production and capital organization. These types of questions are particularly appropriate to the years 1840–1860 because those twenty years witnessed the beginning of a major shift in the principal functions of most important urban centers, a related breakthrough in the importance of manufacturing in the national economy, and the two highest decennial rates of urbanization ever recorded in U.S. history. In the 1840s the registered urban population of the United States expanded by 92.1 percent, while the corresponding increase for 1850–1860 was 75.4 percent; by contrast, the total U.S. population increased only 35.9 percent during the 1840s and 35.6 percent during the 1850s.[9]

The 1840–1860 period also demands attention because a good deal less is known about city-system growth and change processes during that period than for the years prior to 1840 and subsequent to the Civil War. More specifically, the 1840–1860 period represents a critical gap in my own efforts to provide a conceptually consistent interpretation of past U.S. urban growth and city-system development. I have elsewhere contended at length that mutually related trade and information flows influenced both the growth of individual mercantile cities and the emerging characteristics of the infant city-system of the United States between 1790 and 1840. I also have interpreted the ways in which large-scale industrialization and transportation developments affected urban economic concentration and differential city growth in the United States between 1860 and 1914.[10] This book, then, is addressing particularly the processual bridges linking the rather different urban-growth circumstances of the early and late nineteenth century.

The strategy to be employed in seeking at least partial and tentative answers to the questions just put forth is as follows. In the next chapter the statistics and geographic distribution of 1840–1860 urban growth are scrutinized with particular emphasis on the extent to which such growth was or was not concentrated in both previously existing and newly emerging centers of national and regional significance. Then, in the third chapter, both conventional and recent views of antebellum urban growth and urban and regional economic interdependence are summarized critically in order to provide a contrast to subsequent chapters. Immediately thereafter, in chapter 4, a sample of the rich but highly fragmented empirical evidence available on 1840–1860 urban economic interdependencies is presented. The next chapter depicts a heuristic and probabilistic feedback model of 1840–1860 city-system growth and development, a model that also deals with the phenomenon of major-center rank stability by emphasizing the means by which the most important established channels of interurban growth transmission were likely to reinforce themselves. The sixth chapter presents evidence that illustrates the existence of strong geographic inequalities in the availability and circulation of specialized economic information, evidence that presumably lends credence to a key component of the model. One cornerstone of this evidence is the findings based upon content analyses of a sample of antebellum newspapers from selected cities. Finally, some summary and concluding observations are made regarding the evidence and arguments put forth.

The accumulation of migratory, investment, and other economic decisions is presumably fundamental to all urban growth and city-system change processes. Such decisions cannot be separated from the broad economic context in which they occur, for they both are influenced by that context and contribute to it.

THE ECONOMIC-HISTORICAL CONTEXT OF ANTEBELLUM URBAN GROWTH

The general contours of U.S. economic change and development between 1840 and 1860 are common knowledge (table A.1). The period began in the midst of a depression, which had started in 1839 and which lasted until 1843 and even longer in the South. In the mid-1840s a minor investment and industrial-output boom ensued. Westward settlement spread, and agricultural production was spurred by the existence of fertile lands, an expansionist public-land policy, the introduction of new agricultural implements, and the growing demand for wheat, flour, and corn. This demand arose first from European crop failures and famine conditions during 1846–1848 and later from the cutoff of Russian shipments to Europe during the Crimean War (1853–1856), as well as from burgeoning domestic urban requirements. Over the same period national territory and natural resources were extended greatly by a series of land acquisitions. Most of Texas and some nearby areas were obtained in 1845, the Oregon Territory in 1846, California and most of the Southwest in 1848, and the Gadsden Purchase in 1853. The mid-1850s saw a major boom, sparked not only by a surge in the export of western grains and southern cotton, but also by the continued expansion of a wide range of northeastern manufactures, a mounting influx of immigrants, and the gold-mining activities of California. This boom was terminated by the "crisis" of 1857, which was presaged by falling cereal prices after the Crimean War. The crisis was occasioned by the drying

up of foreign capital sources and the discouragement of new domestic
investments "by increasing evidence that profits on new projects were
not living up to expectations."[11] Following the crisis, with its associated
widespread failures of banks, railroads, factories, and commercial firms,
there were some indications of recovery and renewed growth, especially
in the Northeast. Business expansion, however, was somewhat damp-
ened by the political uncertainties and North-South tensions that were
to culminate in the Civil War.

The substantial increases in the total value added by manufacturing
and in the manufacturing value added per capita that occurred between
1840 and 1860, in combination with the significant increases in agricultural output during that same period (table A.1), were in some measure
synonymous with a pronounced geographic division of labor, a greater
but still rudimentary integration of the national economy as a whole,
and a more thorough integration of some of its component regional
economies. These associated output, specialization, and integration
changes were facilitated greatly by highly impressive transportation and
communications developments and improvements, which themselves
were an expression of the ongoing process of capital accumulation and
the seeking of wider markets.

Railroad trackage for the entire United States was well under 3,000
miles as of 1840, and total trackage, disjointed and unintegrated, was
still below 6,000 miles eight years later. Between 1849 and 1860, however, "the basic railroad network east of the Mississippi River" was
completed, total railroad mileage multiplied five times to over 30,600
miles, and a "strong tendency toward the combination of short lines
into larger systems" began to appear. Nevertheless, in 1860 there were
still more than three hundred independent lines in operation, and exchange of rolling stock was hindered by the use of eleven or more different gauges.[12] The utilization of the mushrooming railroad network
was encouraged by a general downward trend in freight charges per
ton-mile, which tended to lower the final cost of goods and thereby both
increase demand and discourage household manufactures. Railroad
usage was stimulated additionally by superior operating speeds, which
permitted quicker responses to altered market conditions and the shipment of perishable commodities with less spoilage. Another encouraging
factor was the ability of trains to operate on a year-round basis in parts
of the country where inland water transportation was obstructed either
by winter ice or by occasional low water levels during the summer.[13] In
the 1840s new canal routes in the West proliferated with unprecedented
swiftness, while steamboat tonnage on the western rivers and in the

Great Lakes and coastal carrying trades expanded substantially. As various forms of competition helped drive down the freight rates assessed by steamboats, the rapidly mounting tonnage volume of such vessels aided different levels of economic specialization and integration even more than is suggested by the tonnage growth figures. Technological improvements increased carrying capacity per measured ton, enabled faster operating speeds, and lengthened the average navigation season in the West to almost nine months, thereby allowing more annual round trips per steamboat in 1860 than in 1840.[14] In addition, the telegraph, which had no lines in operation before 1844, brought all but the westernmost settled sections of the country into direct informational contact with one another by the early 1850s. By 1860, when approximately 50,000 miles of lines were in operation, the telegraph had contributed to increased output, specialization, and integration, largely through permitting specialized business information and capital to circulate, turn over, and accumulate more rapidly than previously had been the case.[15]

No aspect of U.S. economic change and development between 1840 and 1860 was more important, in terms of its impact on urban growth (through the generation of employment opportunities) and on city-system interdependence (through the creation of specialized interurban goods flows), than the very rapid expansion of manufacturing. Although the United States remained a highly agricultural nation at the very end of the antebellum period, it had by then become the world's second-ranking industrial country. By 1860 its mills, factories, forges, and other manufacturing establishments were accounting for 32 percent of the total value of all commodity output, as opposed to some 17 percent twenty years earlier (table A.1). Among the outstanding attributes of pre–Civil War industrial growth were the thorough mechanization of all major branches of the textile industry and the application of the factory system and mass production techniques to the manufacture of such consumer goods as shoes, clothing, fur and woolen hats, clocks, watches, and sewing machines. The use of power-driven machinery and interchangeable parts also became associated with the fabrication of such diverse products as firearms, musical instruments, scales, stoves, and harvesters, reapers, and other agricultural implements. The growing employment of steam engines in factories and the nearly threefold multiplication of pig iron production (which was stimulated to a considerable degree by railroad demand)[16] went hand in hand with sharp upturns in the mining of anthracite and bituminous coals.[17] Furthermore, the rapid rise of standardized production in the metalworking industries was closely linked to the beginnings of the specialized machine tool industry. In fact, "the late 1840s and 1850s constituted one of the most significant periods of innovation in the development of American machine tools," with the initial producing of turret lathes, gear cutters, various milling machines, and other equipment that was essential to the mass output of metal goods.[18]

The blossoming of U.S. manufactures between 1840 and 1860 was generally associated with a major, but gradual, shift in the principal functions and sources of employment in most of the country's leading urban centers, as well as with the burgeoning of selected lesser towns and cities specializing in various industrial goods. This latter phenomenon was most common in the Northeast in general and in the immediate hinterlands of Boston, New York, and Philadelphia in particular, and to a lesser degree in parts of the Ohio valley. Until 1840 the growth of nationally and regionally dominant cities typically was fueled primarily by commercial activities, or a wholesaling-trading complex variously composed of four activity types: the coastal and interregional distribution of hinterland and local production; the hinterland and coastal distribution of interregional and foreign imports; the foreign export of hinterland and local commodities; and the reexport of carrying-trade commodities.[19] But the growth of such cities in the ensuing twenty years normally was propelled increasingly by the production of manufactured goods for domestic consumption. This changing situation was facilitated in no small part by the growing proclivity of wealthy merchants to invest excess accumulated capital in industrial ventures both locally and in satellite towns.[20] However, the functional transformation of existing and emerging major cities was neither uniform nor did it always involve the same mix of industries and the same set of market environment responses.[21] Recent evidence provided by Lindstrom convincingly demonstrates that in the case of Philadelphia the transformation began somewhat earlier. In Philadelphia "manufacturing rivalled commerce as the major source of urban income" by the late 1830s, largely as a result of the city's progress in four production categories: textiles; machinery; drugs, medicines, paints, and dyes; and precious metals.[22] More representatively, the functional transition of Boston to an industrially based economy apparently did not occur until after 1843; in 1840 the city's value of manufactures per capita was only 60 percent of Philadelphia's value.[23] In contrast, New Orleans, the country's fifth ranking city in 1840, did not significantly enter such a transition prior to the Civil War, still having but 3 percent of its population engaged in industrial pursuits in 1860.[24]

Regardless of the extent to which manufacturing had become the key to the growth of leading urban centers by 1860, it is clear that "the great era of the industrial city had not yet arrived,"[25] but was still awaiting the post–Civil War decades. Industrial capitalism had made its entrance in a very obvious way; but, as yet, it had not begun to dominate the urban scene. In more than half of the major cities of 1860 less than 10 percent of the population was employed in industrial activities. Even in those instances where the figure was substantially higher (for example, Philadelphia, 17.5 percent), manufacturing was not nearly so important in terms of occupational structure as it was to be by 1890. Likewise, the percentage of national value added by manufacturing contributed by the largest centers in 1860 was much less than it was to be by 1890, when only ten places could account for 38.5 percent of the national total.[26]

Put differently, despite the importance and magnitude of the manufacturing breakthrough, "the decades of the 1840s and 1850s witnessed only the beginning of modern industry" both in the United States as a whole and in its nationally and regionally dominant urban units.[27] In most places the manufacture of producers' goods was as yet insignificant. The facilities responsible for such goods normally turned out a highly diverse array of products, rather than one or a very few items. For example, in 1850, the famed Tredegear Works of Richmond, Virginia, were producing locomotives, "railroad wheels and axles . . . railroad chairs . . . marine and stationary engines [of] all sizes, sugar mills and engines, horse mills, and every kind of machinery usually required for the operations of the country," as well as bar iron in a multitude of sizes and shapes. Four years later, a British member of Parliament reporting on the fabrication of steam engines and machinery in New York, Philadelphia, Baltimore, Pittsburgh, Buffalo, Boston, and other American centers could comment: "there are large establishments . . . in almost every town of importance which combine various branches of manufacture . . . in some cases the manufacture of locomotives is combined with that of mill gearing, engine tools, spinning and other machinery. In others, marine engines, hydraulic presses, forge hammers, and large cannon were all being made in the same establishments . . . the practice doubtless arises, in addition to other causes, from the fact that the demand is not always sufficient to occupy large works in a single manufacture." And, in 1860, the Vulcan Iron Works of San Francisco were producing, among other things: general purpose steam engines, boilers, and steamboat machinery; saw, flour, and quartz mills; and pumping and mining machinery.[28]

Furthermore, the urban manufacturing establishments of 1860 were seldom bound up in extended "production systems," or chains of production, wherein the outputs of one establishment became the specialized inputs of another differently located establishment, where they in turn were combined with intermediate outputs from other production units to yield more complex outputs, which, after one or more additional stages of processing at yet other differently located establishments, were eventually assembled into a finished product.[29] Although there was a general shift toward larger-scale and more capital-intensive means of production during the 1840–1860 period, truly large-scale urban manufacturing facilities were still exceptional in 1860, being for the most part confined to a few branches of production. Admittedly, many large-scale urban manufacturing establishments can be identified. For example, a number of textile mills in New England, Philadelphia, and elsewhere employed 500 to 700 or more hands; some sugar refineries in New York City represented an investment of nearly one million dollars each; and a St. Louis tobacco-processing plant—the largest industrial unit of any type in that city—provided work for 500 people.[30] However, a more comprehensive examination of the sources available on 1860 manufacturing, such as that undertaken by Fred Bateman and Thomas Weiss, is apt to reveal a very different image characterized by proprietorships and close partnerships of small average size (but occasional monopoly potential). Manuscript samples extracted by Bateman and Weiss from the 1860 manufacturing census indicate that in only three of the nineteen states studied (Massachusetts, New York, and Maine) did the average employment per establishment of the twenty largest firms (ranked by value of total output) exceed 164, while in twelve states the figure was below 100. Even in the extreme case of the highly developed New England cotton textile industry considered as a whole, the 532 mills operating in 1860, though roughly twice the size of their 1840 predecessors, still only averaged 122 employees per establishment.[31]

In view of the specialization and scale attributes of manufacturing at the end of the antebellum era, it is evident that the industrially based interdependencies that emerged between cities during the 1840s and 1850s could not have been so complex as in later decades. Just how complex were these and other urban economic interdependencies? And what were the urban growth and city-system development implications of the various interdependencies that prevailed between 1840 and 1860?

2

The Pattern of Urban Growth, 1840–1860

Any examination and interpretation of city-system interdependencies and their consequences for growth and development during the 1840–1860 period first requires some determination of just which urban units grew most during those pivotal decades when the country's system of cities began to be transformed from a network primarily characterized by mercantile relationships to one dominated by manufacturing linkages.

At first glance, and as usually portrayed, the 1840–1860 pattern of U.S. urban growth as registered by census statistics is simple and the change dramatic. The total population of places with 2,500 or more inhabitants (the census definition of an urban place) grew at a pace never matched during any other period in U.S. history, increasing 3.4 times from over 1.8 million, or 10.8 percent of the total population, to in excess of 6.2 million, or almost 20 percent of the total population (table 2.1).

In 1840 the urban population pattern was highly concentrated both nationally and regionally. New York, Philadelphia, Boston, Baltimore, and New Orleans, the five largest urban centers in the United States, accounted for 49 percent of the nation's urban population. Most urban places were situated in a northeastern belt extending from Washington, D.C., to southeastern Maine; very few such places existed south of Virginia (map 2.1). The Northeast (the area due north of the Potomac, but excluding western Pennsylvania and Washington, D.C.) contained 72.6 percent of the total registered urban population. Within that region New York, Philadelphia, Boston, and Baltimore accounted for no less than 59.8 percent of the census-defined urban population.[1]

By the eve of the Civil War the pattern was somewhat more dispersed. The frontier of settlement had moved westward (maps 2.1–2.5). The share of the country's population, both rural and urban, residing in Ohio, Indiana, Illinois, Michigan, Wisconsin, Iowa, Missouri, and other states and territories entirely west of the Mississippi had reached 34.2 percent in 1860, as compared to 20.2 percent twenty years earlier. The five largest urban centers, which were identical with those of 1840, were now responsible for only 37.7 percent of all U.S. urban population. Although New England's degree of urbanization had increased significantly, the area's percentage share of the country's urban population

Table 2.1. Absolute population growth of major urban centers, 1840-1860.

U.S. total and location by group	Population			Absolute increase		
	1840	1850	1860	1840-1850	1850-1860	1840-1860
U.S. Urban total (places > 2,500)	1,845,055	3,581,439[a]	6,216,518	1,736,384	2,635,079	4,371,463
I New York[b]	360,323	654,429	1,092,791	294,106	438,362	732,468
Philadelphia[c]	220,423	340,045	565,529	119,622	225,484	345,106
Boston[d]	118,857	208,335	297,673	90,478	88,338	178,816
Baltimore	102,313	169,054	212,418	66,741	43,364	110,105
Albany[e]	33,721	50,763	62,367	17,042	11,604	28,646
(+Troy)[e]	19,334	28,785	39,235	9,451	10,450	19,901
Providence	23,171	41,513	50,660	18,332	9,153	27,485
Rochester	20,191	36,403	48,204	16,212	11,801	28,013
Hartford	9,468	13,555	26,917	4,087	13,362	17,449
II St.Louis[f]	16,469	79,061	164,766	62,592	85,705	148,297
Cincinnati	46,338	115,435	161,044	69,097	45,609	114,706
Pittsburgh[g]	31,204	73,341	93,359	42,137	20,018	62,155
Buffalo	18,213	42,261	81,129	24,048	38,868	62,916
Louisville	21,210	43,194	68,033	21,984	24,839	46,823
Detroit	9,102	21,019	45,619	11,917	24,600	36,517
Cleveland	6,071	17,034	43,417	10,963	26,383	37,346
III Chicago	4,470	29,963	112,172	25,493	82,209	107,702
San Francisco[h]	975	34,776	56,802	33,801	22,076	55,827
Milwaukee	1,712	20,061	45,246	18,349	25,185	43,534
IV New Orleans[i]	102,193	116,375	174,491	14,182	58,116	72,298
Richmond[j]	20,153	27,570	40,703	7,417	13,133	20,550
Charleston	29,261	42,985	40,552	13,724	(-2,433)	11,291
Mobile	12,672	20,515	29,258	7,843	8,743	16,586
V Newark	17,290	38,894	71,941	21,604	33,047	54,561
Washington, D.C.	23,364	40,001	61,122	16,637	21,121	37,758
New Haven	12,960	20,345	39,267	7,385	18,922	26,307

Lowell	20,796	33,383	36,827	12,587	3,444	16,031
Jersey City[k]	3,072	6,856	36,455	3,784	29,599	33,383
Syracuse[l]	—	22,271	28,119	22,271	5,848	28,119
Major center total	1,305,326	2,389,392	3,826,122	1,084,066	1,436,730	2,520,796
Major center total as percentage of U.S. urban total	70.75%	66.72%	61.55%	62.43%	54.52%	57.66%

Sources: U.S. Bureau of the Census, *Sixth Census or Enumeration of the Inhabitants of the United States . . . in 1840* (Washington, D.C., 1841); *Seventh Census of the United States: 1850* (Washington, D.C., 1853); *Eighth Census, Population of the United States in 1860* (Washington, D.C., 1864); *Census of Population: 1960* (Washington, D.C., 1961), vol. I, part A; Roger W. Lotchin, *San Francisco 1846–1856: From Hamlet to City* (New York: Oxford University Press, 1974), 8.

a. The U.S. urban population total for 1850 as given here does not coincide with the normally reported figure, as given in table A.1 This is partly due to the inclusion of San Francisco's 1852 population. (The normally reported figure treats San Francisco as if it did not exist, since the 1850 census returns for that city were destroyed by fire.) A smaller portion of the discrepancy results from the fact that the population of some cities includes subsequently annexed units whose 1850 size was under 2,500.

b. Including Brooklyn (1840, 1850, 1860). This inclusion, as well as those specified in the following notes, is based on the argument that urban population growth should be measured for functionally integrated urban units rather than for politically defined units.

c. Including Northern Liberties, Southward, Kensington, Spring Garden, and Moyamensing (1840, 1850). All of these places were incorporated into Philadelphia in 1854. If Philadelphia's 1850 population had included all the territory that was to be incorporated into it in 1854, the total would have amounted to 408,762, not 340,045.

d. Including Charlestown, Roxbury, Cambridge, and Dorchester (1840, 1850, 1860); and also Chelsea, North Chelsea, Somerville, Brookline, and West Roxbury (1850, 1860).

e. Albany and Troy, which are today part of the same Standard Metropolitan Statistical Area (SMSA), may be considered as a single urban complex during the 1840–1860 period because of their extremely close proximity (only a few miles separated their respective cores), their linking ferry serves, and, most important, their shared transfer and transshipment functions in conjunction with the Erie Canal. However, in order to provide as much detail as possible they are listed separately in this and most subsequent tables.

f. Including Carondelet (1860).

g. Including Allegheny (1840, 1850, 1860); Lawrenceville and Birmingham (1850, 1860); and East Birmingham and Manchester (1860).

h. The 1840 population of San Francisco was probably considerably lower than 975, an estimate made for 1848 shortly before the city began to explode in size as a consequence of the Gold Rush. The population given for 1850 actually applies to 1852 (see note a).

i. Including Algiers (1860).

j. Including Manchester (1860).

k. Including Hudson (1860).

l. Although some village population existed at the site of Syracuse in 1840, the city was not incorporated until 1848, when three separate communities were joined.

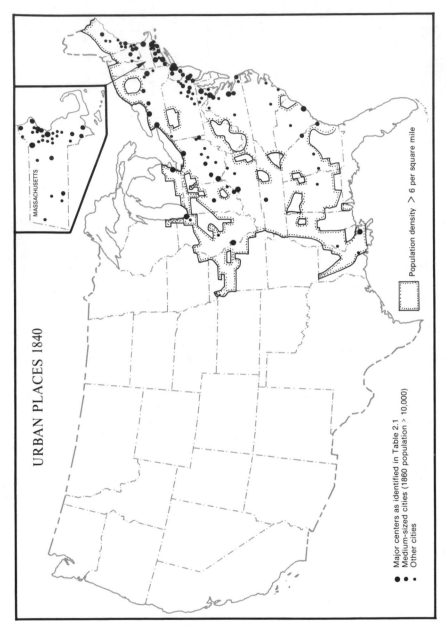

URBAN PLACES 1840

MASSACHUSETTS

• Major centers as identified in Table 2.1
•• Medium-sized cities (1860 population > 10,000)
• Other cities

▫ Population density > 6 per square mile

Map 2.1. The total pattern of urban places (population > 2,500) existing in 1840. For this map and maps 2.2–2.5 the sources are identical with those cited in table 2.1.

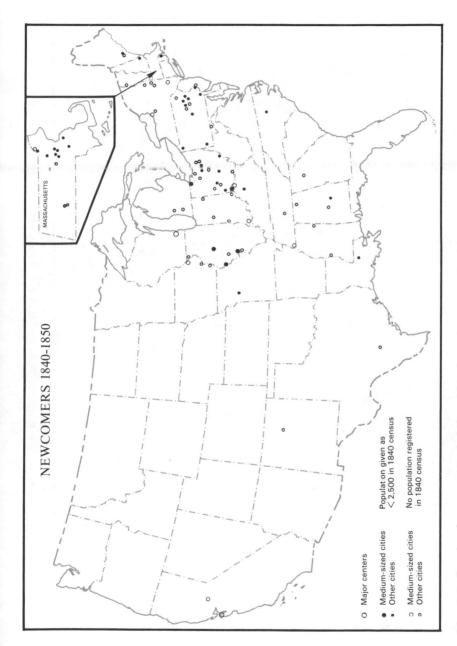

NEWCOMERS 1840-1850

MASSACHUSETTS

○ Major centers

● Medium-sized cities
• Other cities

Populat on given as
<2,500 in 1840 census

○ Medium-sized cities
○ Other cities

No population registered
in 1840 census

Map 2.2. Previously enumerated and previously unenumerated urban newcomers, 1840–1850.

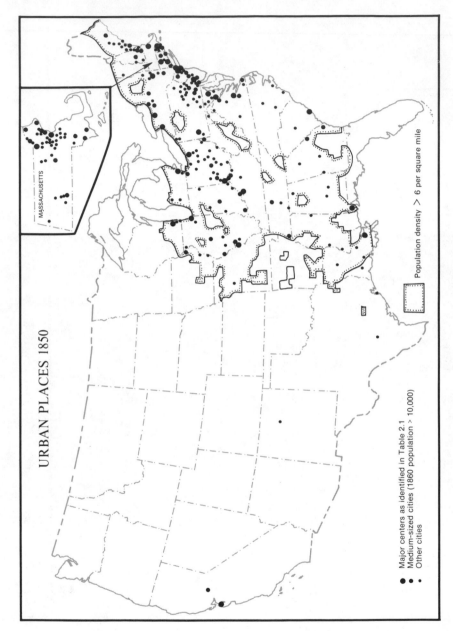

URBAN PLACES 1850

MASSACHUSETTS

- Major centers as identified in Table 2.1
- Medium-sized cities (1860 population > 10,000)
- Other cities

Population density > 6 per square mile

Map 2.3. The total pattern of urban places (population > 2,500) existing in 1850.

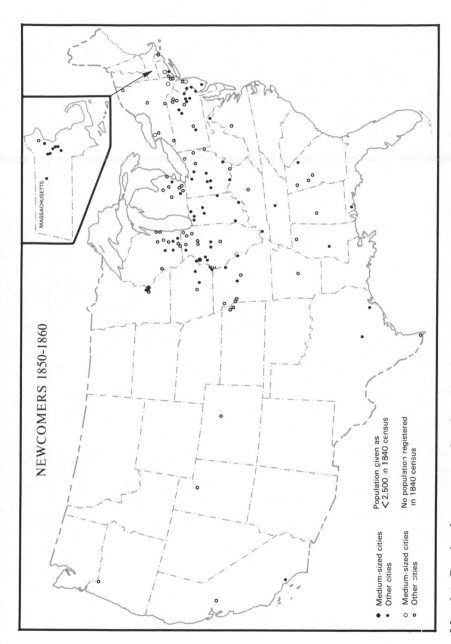

NEWCOMERS 1850-1860

MASSACHUSETTS

● Medium-sized cities
• Other cities
○ Medium-sized cities
◦ Other cities

Population given as
<2,500 in 1840 census

No population registered
in 1840 census

Map 2.4. Previously enumerated and previously unenumerated urban newcomers, 1850–1860.

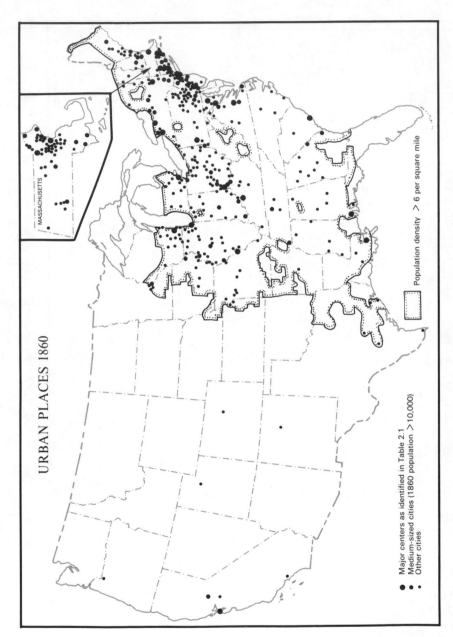

URBAN PLACES 1860

MASSACHUSETTS

● Major centers as identified in Table 2.1
●● Medium-sized cities (1860 population > 10,000)
● Other cities

☐ Population density > 6 per square mile

Map 2.5. The total pattern of urban places (population > 2,500) existing in 1860.

had dropped from 23.5 in 1840 to 18.5 in 1860. And, by the latter date, the portion of the national urban population held by the entire Northeast had diminished to 63.3 percent, while New York, Philadelphia, Boston, and Baltimore had fallen to 55.1 percent of that region's registered urban population total.[2]

As soon as one examines the 1840–1860 pattern of urban growth in any detail, however, a somewhat less clear and differently shaded picture emerges. This is especially true if one attempts to determine how the total increment of urban population between 1840 and 1860 was allocated among different types of places and, more specifically, the extent to which that increase was concentrated in previously existing plus newly emerging urban centers of national or regional importance.

ABSOLUTE AND PERCENTAGE POPULATION GROWTH OF MAJOR URBAN CENTERS: THE SURFACE PATTERN

The absolute increases and the percentage increases recorded between 1840 and 1860 by major urban centers (all those places that had attained a population of about 27,000 or more by the end of the observed period) are shown in tables 2.1 and 2.2. In those tables the twenty-nine places that had neared or crossed the threshold of 27,000 have been divided into five groups.

Group I includes the nationally important centers of New York, Philadelphia, Boston, and Baltimore, as well as four other northeastern centers that had become regionally significant before 1840. By 1840 these centers had acquired size rankings within their regional city-system that were either identical to or little different from the regional rankings held by their 1970 metropolitan-area descendants. The first three members of the group each recorded larger absolute gains than any other single city in the country. Substantial absolute gains were also tallied by some of the remainder of the group, especially by Baltimore. But the percentage increases of the members of this group for 1840–1850, for 1850–1860, and for the entire 1840–1860 period, with but one exception (Hartford 1850–1860), were consistently below the corresponding percentage increases for the total official urban population. And, in the case of Albany (excluding Troy), whose function as a canal transfer and transshipment point was beginning to be challenged by the railroads, the 1840–1860 rate of population gain was little more than one-third of the 1840–1860 percentage increase for all places defined as urban.

Group II in tables 2.1 and 2.2 comprises seven centers that, prior to 1840, had assumed positions of dominance within two regional city-sys-

Table 2.2. Percentage population growth of major urban centers, 1840-1860.

U.S. total and location by group	Percentage increase		
	1840-1850	1850-1860	1840-1860
U.S. urban total (places > 2,500)	94.11[a]	73.66[a]	236.93
I New York[b]	81.62	66.98	203.28
Philadelphia[c]	54.27	66.31	156.57
Boston[d]	76.12	42.20	150.45
Baltimore	65.23	25.65	107.62
Albany[e]	50.53	22.86	84.95
(+Troy)[e]	48.88	36.30	102.93
Providence	79.12	22.05	118.62
Rochester	80.29	32.42	138.74
Hartford	43.17	98.58	184.29
II St. Louis[f]	380.06	82.97	900.46
Cincinnati	149.12	79.65	247.54
Pittsburgh[g]	135.03	27.29	199.19
Buffalo	132.04	91.97	345.45
Louisville	103.65	57.51	220.76
Detroit	130.93	117.04	401.20
Cleveland	180.58	154.88	615.15
III Chicago	570.31	274.37	2,409.44
San Francisco[h]	3,466.77	63.34	5,725.85
Milwaukee	1,071.79	125.54	2,542.87
IV New Orleans[i]	13.88	49.93	70.75
Richmond[j]	36.80	47.64	101.97
Charleston	46.90	(-5.66)	38.59
Mobile	61.82	42.62	130.89
V Newark	124.95	84.97	315.56
Washington, D.C.	71.21	52.80	161.61
New Haven	56.98	93.01	202.99
Lowell	60.53	10.32	77.09
Jersey City[k]	123.18	431.72	1,086.69
Syracuse[l]	—	26.26	—
Major center total	83.05	60.13	193.12

Sources: See table 2.1.

a. The percentage increases for the urban population as a whole differ somewhat from those mentioned in chap. 1 at note no. 9 because the 1850 total used here coincides with that indicated in table 2.1, rather than with that conventionally given in census publications. See note a to table 2.1.

b–l. See corresponding notes to table 2.1.

tems—one around Lake Erie, the other centered in the valleys of the Ohio and the upper Mississippi—that were to merge subsequently into a larger midwestern city-system. Two of these cities, St. Louis and Cincinnati, accumulated the fourth and fifth largest absolute population increases between 1840 and 1860. Even Detroit, the city in this group with the most modest 1840–1860 absolute increment, expanded by more than 36,500. The percentage increases acquired by the members of this group during the 1840s were in every instance greater than the official percentage gain for all urban places as a whole. With the exception of Pittsburgh and Louisville, which fell short by differing degrees, this was also true for the 1850s and for the 1840–1860 period in its entirety.

The third and smallest group includes but three places: Chicago, and San Francisco and Milwaukee, two centers whose 1840 populations were below the official urban threshold. These three cities not only recorded impressive absolute gains, but they also showed 1840–1860 percentage increases that were higher than those of any of the other major urban centers. The three places are classed together not only because of their phenomenal relative expansion but also because none of them had been really integrated into a well-articulated regional city-system before 1840.

Although they had functioned as comparatively major urban centers some time before 1840, the four southern cities making up the next group were not participants in a very well articulated large regional city-system by either 1840 or 1860. By the population-growth standards then prevailing, none of these places fared extremely well during the score of years preceding the Civil War. New Orleans booked the eighth largest absolute increase in the country for 1840–1860, but its percentage increase for the full twenty-year span was less than that for all urban places during either the 1840s or the 1850s. Charleston had the lowest 1840–1860 absolute and percentage gains of any of the observed major centers, and it actually lost population during the 1850s. This loss was associated with the mass selling of slaves in response to the demand for slave labor created by high cotton prices. During the 1850s the slave population of Charleston tumbled from 18,532 to 13,909, while the white population actually increased by over 3,000, or 16.81 percent. Mobile and also Richmond, which differed from its three southern sisters in not being a major cotton port and in being more industrially oriented, expanded somewhat more rapidly. All the same, they still fell far short of the percentage increases recorded both for all registered urban places and for most major urban centers outside the South. In fact, only two of twenty-five nonsouthern major centers had smaller 1840–1860 percentage increases than Richmond.

The final group in tables 2.1 and 2.2 consists of six special northeastern centers. This miscellaneous group had rather mixed growth records. Significant absolute increases and high percentage gains were attained by Newark and Jersey City, which in many respects were already bound closely enough to New York to be thought of as parts of the same emerging metropolitan complex. In contrast, Lowell—which is today part of the Boston metropolitan complex and was then closely linked to that city—had a very slow rate of growth during the 1850s and comparatively little population expansion for the 1840–1860 period as a whole. Washington, D.C., had a record of absolute and percentage population increases that was in keeping with the first group of major northeastern centers, but it is considered separately because its growth was rooted primarily in political rather than economic functions. Syracuse is also a special case because, unlike cities belonging to the first northeastern group, it had not achieved any degree of regional dominance, or rank stability, before 1840.[3] Syracuse, in fact, was not incorporated until 1848, and therefore its 1840–1850 and 1840–1860 percentage increases cannot be used comparatively. Finally, New Haven had an above-normal 1850–1860 percentage increase but an 1840–1860 gain that was somewhat below that for all places officially classified as urban. This northeastern city was assigned to group V because its present-day regional importance is not commensurate with that of the places included in group I.

ABSOLUTE AND PERCENTAGE POPULATION GROWTH OF MAJOR URBAN CENTERS: THE HIDDEN PATTERN

Despite the very substantial absolute population increases of the four largest northeastern centers, as well as St. Louis, Cincinnati, and Chicago, and despite the tremendous percentage increases accumulated by the cities in groups II and III, the most striking impressions created by the tables are these: (1) the failure of the major northeastern centers (group I) to keep pace with the 1840–1850, 1850–1860, and 1840–1860 percentage gains recorded for all urban places; and (2) failure of all twenty-nine major centers as a group to keep up with the same set of percentage gains.[4] When these two impressions are considered together, it appears that both the previously existing and the newly emerging urban units of national and regional importance grew more slowly than did the urban population as a whole. However, it can be argued that this joint impression is deceptive because the data are distorted by the effect of urban "newcomers" to the 1850 and 1860 censuses and also by the emphasis on percentage increases. This emphasis is so misleading as to suggest the need for some other measure of comparative urban growth.

Distorting Effects of Urban Newcomers. The 1840–1860 period was unquestionably one of unmatched relative increases in the registered urban population of the United States. But it was also a period when the official (census) rate of entry of commercial and industrial centers into the national system of cities was at an unsurpassed peak that was to carry over into the 1860–1870 decade and decline thereafter (table 2.3). This circumstance led to a significant overstatement of the abso-

Table 2.3. Number of previously existing and newcomer urban places (population > 2,500) in the U.S. system of cities, 1790-1970.

Decade	(A) Number of urban places at beginning of decade	(B) Number of newcomer urban places during decade	(B/A) Rate of newcomer entry into the city-system
1790-1800	24	9	37.50
1800-1810	33	13	39.39
1810-1820	46	15	32.61
1820-1830	61	29	47.54
1830-1840	90	41	45.55
1840-1850	131	105	80.15
1850-1860	236	156	66.10
1860-1870	392	271	69.13
1870-1880	663	276	41.63
1880-1890	939	409	43.56
1890-1900	1,348	392	29.08
1900-1910	1,740	526	30.23
1910-1920	2,266	459	20.26
1920-1930	2,725	454	16.66
1930-1940	3,179	306	9.63
1940-1950	3,485	592[a]	16.99
		1,279[b]	36.70
1950-1960	4,764	1,277	26.81
1960-1970	6,041	1,021	16.90

Source: U.S. Bureau of the Census, *Census of Population: 1970, Number of Inhabitants—United States Summary* (Washington, D.C., 1971), pp. 46–47.
a. According to urban definition in effect through 1940 (unincorporated places excluded).
b. According to urban definition in effect since 1950 (unincorporated places included).

lute increases in the total registered urban population for both the 1840s and 1850s and consequently to an exaggeration of the corresponding percentage increases for those decades. In particular, the high rate of new entrants into the national city-system helped to distort the absolute and percentage increases in question largely through two mechanisms: the use of an arbitrary threshold to define urban places; and the frequent failure to recognize any place as urban unless it had become legally incorporated.[5]

The urban population of the United States in 1840, 1850, and 1860, as defined by census authorities, included all those incorporated places with 2,500 or more inhabitants. Such a definition implies that tightly clustered settlements with fewer than 2,500 people were not urban in either form or function. Yet places with fewer than 2,500 residents that carried on retailing, wholesaling, service, or manufacturing activities were common in New England, Pennsylvania, Ohio, and elsewhere. Accordingly, some antebellum authorities recognized places with certain functions and at least 2,000 inhabitants as urban "towns," and one observer, Israel Andrews, went so far as to regard "towns and villages of over 200 inhabitants" as urban. (Recently, Edward Muller, in identifying nineteenth-century Ohio and Indiana urban centers, has included settlements with populations as low as 100.)[6] Regardless of how far below the 2,500 level the population of a primarily urban settlement actually stood at any given census date (t_1), it should be apparent that its crossing of the 2,500 threshold at a subsequent census date (t_2) could only have yielded an absolute urban population increase equal to the difference between the t_2 and t_1 totals. Yet, in the census statistics on total urban population the absolute increase for such places includes the actual t_2 total, as if the places had had no previous existence.

Between 1840 and 1850 at least thirty-seven previously enumerated places joined the urban ranks as a consequence of passing the arbitrary threshold set by census authorities. These newcomers were most highly concentrated in Massachusetts, Pennsylvania, and Ohio, rather than at the fringes of spreading settlement as might be expected if one were to mistakenly regard all city-system additions as completely new urban units (map 2.2). The census credits these places with adding over 139,-000 people to the total registered urban population, whereas in reality their 1840–1850 absolute increase was well under half that figure (table 2.4, columns A and B).

In the same threshold-crossing way, at least another sixty-nine previously enumerated settlements were officially added to the national system of cities between 1850 and 1860. This set of newcomers was well

	Number of places, 1850[a]	(A) Contribution to registered absolute increase in total urban population, 1840-1850	(B) Actual absolute increase, 1840-1850	(C) Place category percentage increase, 1840-1850	(D) Share of registered absolute increase in total urban population, 1840-1850	(E) Share of combined actual absolute increase of place categories III and IV, 1840-1850
Place category						
I Newcomers listed in 1840 census as having a population < 2,500	37	139,088	66,118	110.36%[b]	8.00%	—
II Newcomers not listed in 1840 census	54	236,397	[c]	[c]	13.59	—
III Major centers listed in tables 2.1 and 2.2[d] (excluding four southern centers)[f]	29	1,086,753	1,084,066	83.05	62.49	79.66[e]
	25	1,043,587	1,040,900	91.22	60.01	76.49
IV All other previously existing urban places > 2,500 in 1840	113	276,833	276,833	51.29	15.92	20.34[g]

Sources: See table 2.1.

a. The total number of places listed in this column does not coincide with the 1850 figure given in table 2.3 because of the way in which New York and other major centers have been defined (see notes to table 2.1) and because of certain inconsistencies in census enumeration.

b. See discussion in text of the inordinate impact of modest absolute population gains on the percentage increase of smaller places.

c. Increase cannot be determined.

d. Including San Francisco's 1852 population, as in table 2.1.

e. Would be 80.52% if spillover growth were included for Elizabeth, N.J., Camden, N.J., Alexandria, Va., and New Albany, Ind. See text.

f. Group IV in tables 2.1 and 2.2.

g. Would be 19.48% without the spillover growth centers mentioned in note e.

represented in western states such as Illinois, Iowa, and Wisconsin (map 2.4). But there were also concentrations in Massachusetts, Pennsylvania, and Ohio, which once again contradicts what might be expected if this set of places were erroneously regarded as being made up of totally new urban units. The census suggests that these sixty-nine new centers added more than 275,000 individuals to the total registered urban population, whereas in fact their total 1850–1860 absolute gain was about 115,000 below that figure (table 2.5, columns A and B).

Between 1840 and 1850 another fifty-four newcomers were added to the officially defined urban category, but these had not been enumerated previously as separate entities. Consistent with the westward spread of settlement, such newcomers to the national city-system were much more numerous in the area west and southwest of Ohio than were the previously enumerated newcomers in the same general area (map 2.2). However, in complete contradiction to any logic built on settlement spread, a fair balance existed between previously enumerated and previously unenumerated newcomers in Ohio and the Northeast as a whole, with New York having six centers of the latter type but none of the former. This contradiction arises because, in the vast majority of instances, urban newcomers to the 1850 census that had not been specifically enumerated in the 1840 census were not completely new places. Instead, such units typically had been in existence prior to 1840 but either had not become legally incorporated or had not otherwise gained an independent identity until some time during the 1840s. Their 1840 populations had thus been included in the townships, districts, parishes, hundreds, or other larger jurisdictional units to which they belonged.[7] In many cases long-existing but previously unenumerated newcomers had considerable populations by 1850, thereby suggesting that they had passed the 2,500 mark by 1840, if not earlier. For example: Oswego, New York, which began as a trading post about 1722, entered the official urban ranks with 12,205 inhabitants; Poughkeepsie, New York, which had been settled as early as 1698, made its official urban debut with 11,-511 residents; Memphis, Tennessee, which was platted and settled in 1819, made its urban entrance with a population of 8,841; and Burlington, Vermont, which had been established in 1773, formally became recognized as a city when it held 6,110 people.[8] Given these circumstances, as well as the census practice of including the entire population of every previously unenumerated newcomer in its computation of total urban population increases, it is quite plain that the 1840–1850 absolute increase of over 236,000 attributed to such newcomers is exaggerated sig-

Table 2.5. City-system newcomers and urban population growth, 1850-1860.

Place category	Number of places, 1860[a]	(A) Contribution to registered absolute increase in total urban population, 1850-1860	(B) Actual absolute increase, 1850-1860	(C) Share of registered absolute Place category percentage increase, 1850-1860	(D) Share of combined actual absolute increase in total urban population, 1850-1860	(E) Increase of place categories III and IV, 1850-1860
I Newcomers listed in 1850 census as having a population < 2,500	69	275,793	160,125	138.48%[b]	10.47%	—
II Newcomers not listed in 1850 census	70	326,563	[c]	[c]	12.39	—
III Major centers listed in tables 2.1 and 2.2[d] (excluding four southern centers)[f]	29	1,436,730	1,436,730	60.13	54.52	70.68[e]
IV All other previously existing urban places > 2,500 in 1850[g]	25	1,359,171	1,359,171	62.29	51.58	66.86
	204	595,993	595,993	50.00	22.62	29.32[h]

Sources: See table 2.1.

a. The total number of places listed in this column does not coincide with the 1860 figure given in table 2.3, for reasons given in note a, table 2.4.

b. See note b, table 2.4.

c. Increase cannot be determined.

d. See note d, table 2.4.

e. Would be 72.66% if spillover growth were included from Elizabeth, N.J., Hoboken, N.J., Camden, N.J., Alexandria, Va., Covington, Ky., Newport, Ky., New Albany, Ind., and Alton, Ill.

f. Group IV in tables 2.1 and 2.2.

g. The 204 places in this category are synonymous with the 113 places in category IV of table 2.4, plus the 91 places in categories I and II of that table.

h. Would be 27.34% without the spillover growth centers mentioned in note e.

nificantly (table 2.4, column A). Unfortunately, published sources do not allow a precise determination of the extent of this exaggeration.

A similar distortion appears in regard to the previously unenumerated urban newcomers of the 1850s. The census of 1860 reveals seventy urban units that had been unlisted ten years earlier. In keeping with the general westward shift of population, significant numbers of these cities were found in Illinois, Wisconsin, and in the lower Mississippi valley (map 2.4). Furthermore, several of the more peripheral of these newcomers, for example, Minneapolis–St. Paul, Denver, Salt Lake City, and Portland, Oregon, were already establishing the highly ranked, regionally dominant positions held by their present-day descendants, despite the fact that their 1860 populations were usually far less than 1 percent of those of their 1970 Standard Metropolitan Statistical Area (SMSA) counterparts.[9] Nevertheless, almost half of the previously unenumerated newcomers to the 1860 census were in Michigan, Ohio, and the Northeast (New York alone had ten such centers). This again reflects the fact that most of the places in this category were not completely new, but had actually existed within larger jurisdictions at the time of the 1850 census. Here too, the relatively large size of some of these long-existing newcomers suggests that they had topped a population of 2,500 before the previous (1850) census. For example: Newburgh, New York, which was settled by 1709, did not become officially recognized as a city until its population reached 12,578; New Brunswick, New Jersey, which was colonized by the English as early as 1681, had 11,256 inhabitants when it finally obtained urban stature; Lockport, New York, which had been in existence some four decades earlier when the Erie Canal was under construction, was admitted to the urban category with 10,871 residents; and Scranton, Pennsylvania, which was initially settled around 1788, officially joined the urban classification when its population was 9,223.[10] In view of all this, the 1850–1860 absolute urban population increase of over 325,000 supposedly contributed by previously unenumerated places must be regarded as an exaggeration of indeterminable dimensions (table 2.5, columns A and B).

If both previously enumerated and previously unenumerated newcomers are momentarily dropped from consideration because of their distorting influences, it becomes evident that, as a group, the twenty-nine major urban centers listed in tables 2.1 and 2.2 had a growth rate (percentage increase) during the 1840s that was higher than that for all other previously existing urban places by about 32 percent (table 2.4, column C). During the 1850s, the percentage increase of these nationally and regionally dominant cities as a group still exceeded that for all other earlier acknowledged urban places by more than 10 percent (table 2.5, column C), even though the ranks of the latter group now were swelled considerably by the newcomers of the 1840s, many of which were growing rapidly. (In both decades the comparative performance of the major centers is noticeably enhanced if the somewhat sluggish and regionally less well integrated southern cities of New Orleans, Richmond, Charleston, and Mobile are eliminated.) Moreover, whereas table 2.2 showed the percentage increases of individual major northeastern centers consistently falling short of the total urban percentage increases registered by census authorities, a slightly different image emerges when all newcomers are ignored and a growth-rate comparison is made only with the group of places (row IV in table 2.4) that had been recognized as urban in one or more earlier censuses but that were not major centers and therefore did not qualify for tables 2.1 and 2.2. This latter group of places grew just over 51 percent between 1840 and 1850, a rate surpassed by New York, Philadelphia, Boston, Baltimore, Providence, and Rochester, but not by Albany plus Troy or Hartford. However, the same expanded group of places (row IV in table 2.5) grew exactly 50 percent between 1850 and 1860, a percentage increase that was exceeded in the Northeast only by New York, Philadelphia, and Hartford (table 2.2).

Percentage Increases Versus the Share of Absolute Increase Captured. Although they are conventionally used and easily understood, percentage increases are a rather crude measure of comparative urban growth. This is especially so because they give inordinate weight to the relatively modest absolute gains acquired by smaller places. As a case in point, any newcomer urban unit belonging to place category I in table 2.5 whose population grew by 2,500 during the 1850s would, by definition, have experienced a percentage increase ranging anywhere from a minimum of 100 to a much higher figure (for example, 500 percent for a place that went from a population of 500 to 3,000), whereas Albany, which added over 11,600 to its population during that same decade, underwent a "slow" increase of less than 23 percent.[11]

Given the highly misleading quality of intercensal percentage increases in urban population, there is a clear need to employ some alternative measure of the 1840–1860 growth of major urban centers vis-à-vis the growth of other urban places. Neither the objectives of this book nor the readily usable sources make it feasible to give detailed consideration to the interplay of migration, mortality, and fertility in antebellum urban growth in general or in the population growth of particular cities during that period. However, some general observations on the combined role of those demographic forces will suggest a simple alternative measure of growth.

The broad evidence available on immigration and internal migration has led John Sharpless to assume "that the growth of cities in the nineteenth century was due largely to migration and not self-generation." Jeffrey Williamson and Joseph Swanson similarly have contended that "natural population growth within the [mid-nineteenth-century] city [was] a minor source of incremental labor supply."[12] How can such assertions be made? For one thing, it has been suggested that natural increase could not have accounted for a very substantial share of urban growth in early- and mid-nineteenth-century U.S. cities because those places had both high mortality rates and low fertility rates, fertility rates that were perhaps only two-thirds of those in rural areas.[13] Furthermore, during the 1840–1860 period unprecedented numbers of immigrants arrived from Europe on U.S. shores (over 1.4 million during the 1840s and about twice that number during the 1850s), and many of them temporarily or permanently settled in New York (the major port of entry), in other entry ports, or in a variety of cities throughout the country. In 1850, for example, foreign-born whites constituted almost one-half of New York's population, about one-third of the population of Philadelphia and Boston, and roughly one-fifth of Baltimore's inhabitants. Ten years later, foreign-born whites accounted for 60 percent of St. Louis's inhabitants and around 50 percent of the populations of Cincinnati, Chicago, Buffalo, Detroit, Cleveland, Milwaukee, and San Francisco.[14] In addition, the recent analysis of "persistence rates" indicates that the antebellum native-born and foreign-born populations of the United States were highly mobile, not only in their propensity to migrate from one rural area to another rural area or to a city, but also in their propensity to migrate from cities, presumably to other cities in most instances. In fact, although late-twentieth-century Americans tend to think of themselves as highly mobile, "compared with someone living in the [mid-] nineteenth century, a person today is less likely to have been a migrant within the last five years." It is noteworthy that in those cities where factory capitalism was taking firmest hold, employment turnover was particularly apt to induce in- and out-migration. Mid-nineteenth-century factories often were notorious for their short-notice hiring and firing of workers, due to competitive pressures on wage rates, periodic business-cycle crises, limited worker organization, and the unplanned and uneven character of operations.[15]

In view of this broad evidence, it also is assumed here that migration was the primary demographic contributor to urban growth between

1840 and 1860. (According to one calculation, the net number of migrants arriving in Philadelphia between 1840 and 1850 corresponded to about two-thirds of the city's population growth for the decade, with much of the remaining growth apparently stemming from migrants' natural increase.)[16] In other words, the degree of success that cities of that era had in expanding their populations presumably depended mostly on the extent to which the ever changing supply of employment opportunities in their local economies permitted them both to attract migrants and to hold in-migrants and potential out-migrants away from other competing cities.[17] If this somewhat oversimplified position is taken, then it follows that comparative urban growth performances for the 1840–1860 decades ought to be measured in terms of the captured share of the total absolute increase in urban population, or, more roughly speaking, in terms of the captured share of the total volumes of rural-to-urban migration, interurban migration, and immigration.

As indicated in table 2.4 (column D), during the 1840s the 29 major centers captured almost 62.5 percent of the total absolute increase in urban population *as registered by census authorities,* while the three other place categories answered for varying portions of the remainder. By almost any standard this represents an impressive record of attracting and holding migrants, who had at least 233 urban destinations from which to choose. But because the total absolute increase in urban population as registered by census authorities is exaggerated as the result of the way in which they have determined the urban growth contribution of both previously enumerated and previously unenumerated newcomers, it is useful to compare the aggregate growth performances of the 29 major centers with that of the 113 other places officially given urban status for 1840. Such a comparison reveals that the 29 major centers as a group captured very close to 80 percent of the combined absolute population increase of the two place categories (table 2.4, column E). Not only did this group succeed in capturing far more migrants than the much larger group of previously recognized urban places, but the four leading northeastern dominants—New York, Philadelphia, Boston, and Baltimore—alone rang up an absolute increase (roughly 571,000) that was more than twice that accumulated by the group of 113 places. This absolute increase also exceeded that of the entire latter group added to whatever was the combined actual absolute increase of newcomer place categories I and II in table 2.4.[18]

Between 1850 and 1860 the share of the official total absolute increase in urban population captured by the 29 major centers was nearly 55 percent, or somewhat less than during the 1840s (table 2.5, column D).

Nevertheless, this still represents a formidable record of attracting and holding migrants, for such city-bound individuals then had at least 372 urban alternatives to select from. The comparative growth performance of the 29 major centers can be brought into even sharper focus by disregarding the exaggerated absolute-increase contributions of both the previously enumerated and the previously unenumerated newcomers. A comparison of the 1850–1860 absolute increases of the 29 major centers with those of 204 other places officially designated as urban for 1850 shows the former group capturing almost 71 percent of the absolute increment of the two place categories combined (table 2.5, column E). Once again, and contrary to the impression of poor relative growth performance created by table 2.2, the four largest northeastern centers alone acquired a far greater absolute increase than the entire group of previously recognized urban places (other than major centers), even though that latter group had increased its membership by 91 cities. In fact, the absolute increase of New York, Philadelphia, Boston, and Baltimore as a group (approaching 800,000) was more than 1.33 times greater than that for the group of 204 previously recognized places, despite the considerable underenumeration that apparently occurred in the first three major northeastern centers.[19] The 1850–1860 combined absolute increase of New York, Philadelphia, Boston, and Baltimore also exceeded by about 40,000 the absolute increase of the same group of 204 places added to that of the 69 previously enumerated newcomers (table 2.5, column B).

The comparative growth performance of the twenty-nine nationally and regionally dominant cities during the 1840s and 1850s becomes even more striking when notice is taken of the growth that spilled over from some of those major centers, either to break-in-bulk ports and railroad-terminal cities on river banks opposite the centers, or to proximate cities that were attractive to major-center businessmen seeking manufacturing outlets for excess accumulated capital. If attention is limited to spillover growth that occurred in opposite-bank break-in-bulk ports and railroad-terminal cities that also qualified for official urban status by an earlier census, then the 1840–1850 absolute population increases in Elizabeth, New Jersey (opposite New York), Camden, New Jersey (across the Delaware from Philadelphia), Alexandria, Virginia (opposite Washington, D.C.), and New Albany, Indiana (across the Ohio from Louisville) would have to be taken into consideration. For the 1850–1860 decade the same would be true of the absolute increase of those same four places as well as Hoboken, New Jersey (opposite New York), Covington and Newport, Kentucky (opposite Cincinnati), and

Alton, Illinois (across the Mississippi and a few miles upstream from St. Louis).[20] When the spillover growth occurring in these cities is acknowledged, the share of absolute urban growth associated with the twenty-nine major centers mounts to over 80.5 percent of the 1840–1850 combined total for these major centers and all other previously recognized urban places, and close to 73 percent of the corresponding 1850–1860 total. Obviously, the inclusion of spillover growth of the nearby manufacturing investment variety would even further enhance the share of absolute urban population increases captured by the twenty-nine major centers.[21] However, the absolute increases of such places as Paterson, New Jersey (spillover from New York), Lynn, Salem, Quincy, and numerous other eastern Massachusetts cities (spillover from Boston), and Norristown, Pennsylvania (spillover from Philadelphia) are not included here in any separate absolute-growth share computation. This is partly because the importance of spillover growth has already been stressed, and partly because any decision as to the distance beyond which manufacturing investment spillover growth was no longer of consequence would be purely arbitrary. (One recent analysis of urban growth in the mid-Atlantic states suggests that spillover growth resulting from manufacturing investment during the 1840s probably extended as much as thirty-five miles outward from New York and Philadelphia.)[22]

It may legitimately be asked whether each one of the twenty-nine major centers, which as a group did extremely well in capturing and holding absolute numbers of migrants, actually captured shares of the total urban population increases of the 1840s and 1850s that were commensurate with its initial size. One answer to this question is provided by table 2.6, which does not include previously enumerated and previously unenumerated newcomers in its calculations because of their distorting influences.[23] For each of the last two antebellum decades the table indicates an absolute growth quotient (Q) for each city. The quotient can be expressed as follows:

$$Q = \frac{P_{t2} - P_{t1}/U_{t2} - U_{t1}}{P_{t1}/U_{t1}} \tag{2.1}$$

where P_{t1} is the population of a major center at the decade's outset, U_{t1} is the total population of all those urban places—major or otherwise—having more than 2,500 residents at the decade's outset, P_{t2} is the population of a major center at the decade's termination, and U_{t2} is the decade-end total population of all those places included in U_{t1}.[24] In those circumstances where the quotient exceeds one, the share of total absolute growth captured by a major center is more than commensurate

Table 2.6. Absolute growth quotients of major urban centers, 1840-1850 and 1850-1860.

Location	Percentage of 1840 urban population (all places >2,500) (Pt_1/Ut_1)	Share of 1840-1850 absolute growth of population (exclusive of newcomers)[a] (Pt_2-Pt_1/Ut_2-Ut_1)	Absolute growth quotient (Q), 1840-1850 $([Pt_2-Pt_1/Ut_2-Ut_1]/Pt_1/Ut_1)$	Percentage of 1850 urban population (places >2,500) (Pt_1/Ut_1)	Share of 1850-1860 absolute growth of urban population (exclusive of newcomers)[a] (Pt_2-Pt_1/Ut_2-Ut_1)	Absolute growth (Q), 1850-1860 $([Pt_2-Pt_1/Ut_2-Ut_1]/Pt_1/Ut_1)$
New York[b]	19.53	21.61	1.11	18.27	21.56	1.18
Philadelphia[c]	11.95	8.79	0.61	9.49	11.09	1.17
Boston[d]	6.44	6.65	1.03	5.84	4.35	0.75
Baltimore	5.55	4.90	0.88	4.72	2.13	0.45
Albany[e]	1.83	1.25	0.68	1.42	0.57	0.40
(+Troy)[e]	1.05	0.69	0.66	0.80	0.51	0.64
Providence	1.26	1.35	1.07	1.16	0.45	0.39
Rochester	1.09	1.19	1.09	1.02	0.58	0.57
Hartford	0.51	0.30	0.59	0.38	0.66	1.74
St. Louis[f]	0.89	4.60	5.16	2.21	4.22	1.91
Cincinnati	2.51	5.08	2.02	3.22	2.24	0.70
Pittsburgh[g]	1.69	3.10	1.83	2.05	0.98	0.48
Buffalo	0.99	1.77	1.79	1.18	1.91	1.62
Louisville	1.15	1.62	1.41	1.21	1.22	1.01
Detroit	0.49	0.88	1.80	0.59	1.21	2.05
Cleveland	0.33	0.81	2.45	0.48	1.30	2.71

Chicago	0.24	1.87	7.79	0.84	4.04	4.81
San Francisco[h]	—	2.48	—	0.97	1.08	1.11
Milwaukee	—	1.35	—	0.56	1.24	2.21
New Orleans[i]	5.54	1.04	0.19	3.25	2.86	0.88
Richmond[j]	1.09	0.55	0.50	0.77	0.65	0.84
Charleston	1.59	1.01	0.64	1.20	(-.12)	(-.10)
Mobile	0.67	0.58	0.87	0.57	0.43	0.75
Newark	0.94	1.59	1.69	1.09	1.63	1.50
Washington, D.C.	1.27	1.22	0.96	1.12	1.04	0.93
New Haven	0.70	0.54	0.77	0.57	0.93	1.63
Lowell	1.13	0.92	0.81	0.93	0.17	0.18
Jersey City[k]	0.17	0.28	1.65	0.19	1.46	7.68
Syracuse[l]	—	1.63	—	0.62	0.29	0.47

Sources: See table 2.1.

a. For 1840–1850: share of actual absolute population increase for place categories III and IV in table 2.4 (including San Francisco, Milwaukee, and Syracuse). For 1850–1860: share of actual absolute population increase for place categories III and IV in table 2.5.

b–l. See corresponding notes in table 2.1.

with its initial size. Conversely, the share captured by a place is less than commensurate with its initial size when the quotient falls below one.

According to table 2.6, except for the South's four regionally unintegrated units, major centers generally captured shares of absolute growth that were more than commensurate with their initial population for either one or two decades. Among the exceptions to this generalization were Washington, D.C., which came extremely close to obtaining size-commensurate absolute growth shares for both the 1840s and 1850s; Baltimore and Albany plus Troy, each of which had significant absolute increases in both decades (table 2.1); and Lowell, which had an absolute increase of 12,587 between 1840 and 1850, or enough to clearly surpass the absolute growth achieved by any of the 113 places with an 1840 population over 2,500 that are not specified in table 2.6. Although the failure of these four urban entities to acquire anticipated absolute increases in both decades is not to be dismissed completely, and although the inability of other major centers to attain size-commensurate absolute growth shares for a single decade also is not to be entirely ignored, these shortfalls ought not to be divorced from the following line of summary reasoning. First, it has just been seen that between 1840 and 1850 the major centers of table 2.6 (and their nearby spillover growth satellites) were as a group attracting (and holding) more than four out of five of the migrants settling either in such places or in all other previously recognized urban places. Second, it has also been observed that the corresponding figure for 1850–1860 was close to three out of four migrants. Therefore, it follows that the failure of any single major center to capture less than its size-commensurate share of absolute population increases was more likely to reflect a competitive loss of migrants to rival centers of national or regional importance than a competitive loss of migrants to smaller previously recognized urban places.

In summary, then, a pattern of antebellum urban growth that was not immediately apparent has come into focus. The absolute population increases associated with U.S. urban growth during the 1840s and 1850s were highly concentrated in a limited number of major centers (and their surrounding spillover growth satellites), most notably in and around the long-established dominant cities of the Northeast, but also to a significant degree in already identified and emerging dominant units in the Midwest and California. Although it was not always commensurate with initial city size, this concentration of absolute growth in major centers was particularly striking because it occurred despite the addition to the national city-system of at least 230 newcomers situated not only in frontier areas but also in Massachusetts, New York, and the Northeast in general, as well as in Ohio and other older portions of the Midwest. The high share of absolute increases captured by major centers runs counter to the impression of a poor growth performance for those centers (as a group) that is obtained when their percentage increases for the antebellum decades are compared, in a conventional manner, to the percentage gains of all places registered as urban—a comparison that is distorted by the considerably inflated increases ascribed to newcomers. On the other hand, this concentration of absolute population increases is compatible with the more elaborate and differently oriented growth-rate analyses of Sharpless, who concludes: "The very largest cities [greater than 46,000] were—on the average— capturing 2½ times their 'just' share of the total increase in the nation's urban population in the decades immediately prior to the Civil War."[25]

3

Antebellum Urban Growth and Regional Interdependence: Conventional and Recent Views

The importance of the questions raised in chapter 1 with respect to major center growth, regional rank stability (outside the South), and city-system development has been underlined by the finding that antebellum absolute urban growth was quite concentrated in previously existing and newly emerging centers of national and regional significance. Though they are important, these questions concerning urban interdependence and city growth during a period of pivotal urban economic transformation are not normally raised within the terminology and systems framework employed here. All the same, there is a very considerable body of closely related literature in urban history, economic history, and urban and historical geography. Given its great volume and variety, one may wonder in what ways that literature can help to answer the questions posed on the economic interdependencies of major centers, the feedback processes affecting population growth within individual cities, and the antebellum processes of city-system growth and development. A critical assessment of the possible contributions to be offered by the literature is probably best made by considering the works belonging to three thematic categories: traditional and modern urban biographies and related studies of urban rivalries and hinterland competition; analyses and interpretations of interregional trade patterns; and more recent conceptual contributions.

URBAN BIOGRAPHIES AND URBAN-RIVALRY STUDIES

Commencing in the 1930s, academic historians began to produce a number of books dealing with some of the major individual cities considered here and covering the 1840–1860 period either in whole or in part.[1] Many of these urban biographies, such as those on Chicago, Washington, D.C., Milwaukee, and Rochester, have attempted to produce a comprehensive or definitive view.[2] (Somewhat less scholarly ancestors of the sweeping urban biography are to be found in the bulky tomes of historical miscellanea compiled by newspapermen and librarians in the late nineteenth century for Philadelphia, Baltimore, St. Louis, and other cities.)[3] Other efforts, such as some of those concerning

New York, Boston, Philadelphia, Newark, Cincinnati, and Pittsburgh, have been somewhat more limited in their topical or temporal scope.[4] Urban biographies of both the sweeping and the more narrowly focused types have varied in their emphasis, with topics ranging from the traditionally treated items (municipal institutions, local manufactures and commerce, transportation services and utilities, and leading political and entrepreneurial figures) to issues reflecting the concerns of present-day social scientists (changes in internal urban spatial structure, the social experiences of ordinary and unexceptional people, and the antecedents of such modern urban problems as the ghetto, violence, and poverty).

Although the urban biographies centering on traditional subject matter have been criticized for their neglect of general economic and social processes and their strictly narrative approach,[5] they often include many bits of information on the local economy and its external trade. But when the informational fragments of any single work are juxtaposed and placed in a larger context, they normally can provide only secondary assistance in answering questions on antebellum urban growth and city-system relationships. This is so because these writings seldom include any data in tabular or other organized forms.[6] In addition, in those uncommon instances where the forces behind local urban growth are considered, the composition of economic linkages with non-hinterland cities customarily is given little or no attention; that is, city-system relationships are almost completely ignored.

For the most part, more recent scholarly efforts dealing with the past of an individual city are not subject to criticism for disregarding general processes. Such efforts normally focus upon one of several interrelated processes: social and geographic mobility, class formation and class conflict; adjustment to the urban environment; or the interplay among occupation, ethnicity, and residence. In so doing they often yield insights into the workings of the local economy of a major city. However, few of these works show any explicit or implicit concern with the interurban flows of goods, services, capital, and specialized information, and thereby the interurban channeling of employment multiplier effects. In short, they have little to say about antebellum processes of national and regional city-systems growth and development.[7]

A much smaller, but highly relevant, set of books and articles at least partly touching upon the 1840–1860 period has considered the commercial rivalries that developed between single pairs of cities. Both in the Northeast and in newer settled areas west of the Appalachians, fierce intercity rivalries developed for the markets, agricultural exports, and natural resources of hinterland areas, with the competing groups of urban merchants attempting to establish control mainly through the promotion, development, and utilization of railroads, regularly scheduled steamboat services, and canals. Among the better documented accounts of struggles between major cities for hinterland expansion and dominance are James Livingood's examination of the Philadelphia-Baltimore rivalry and Wyatt Belcher's inquiry into the Chicago–St. Louis rivalry.[8] The pages of this somewhat dated set of works contain much that is helpful in gaining insights into the economic growth of particular cities and the relationship of that growth to the establishment, maintenance, and usurpation of economic interdependencies with smaller hinterland centers. Nevertheless, such urban-rivalry studies are generally disappointing because they either neglect totally or only mention perfunctorily the contributions to the growth process made by interdependencies with nonhinterland cities. In other words, just as many urban biographies treat the individual city as if it were a closed system, so most urban-rivalry studies in effect tend to portray each competing pair of cities and their overlapping hinterlands as a closed system.

THE LITERATURE ON INTERREGIONAL TRADE

Until relatively recently, interpretations of U.S. economic development before the Civil War stressed the importance of cotton cultivation and other forms of regional specialization as well as the domestic market spawned by that specialization through the promotion of interregional trade. In essence, the so-called Callender-Schmidt-North thesis proposed that each of the country's three great regions—the East (or Northeast), the South, and the West—"tended to devote itself more exclusively to the production of those commodities for which it was best able to provide." Consequently:

> There was fostered a mutual economic dependence between sections and the establishment of predominant types of industry in each which were in turn dependent on foreign commerce. The South was thereby enabled to devote itself in particular to the production of a few plantation staples contributing a large and growing surplus for the foreign markets and depending on the West for a large part of its food supply and on the East for the bulk of its commerce and banking. The East was devoted chiefly to manufacturing and commerce, supplying the products of its industries as well as the imports and much of the capital for the West and the South while it became to an increasing extent dependent on the food and fibers of the two sec-

tions. The West became a surplus-grain livestock-producing kingdom, supplying the growing deficits of the South and East.[9]

This once popular view, also referred to as the cotton-staple theory of growth, has been subject to a crescendo of criticism for well over a decade. Several detailed inquiries have called into question the South's large-scale importation of western foodstuffs, maintaining instead that between 1840 and 1860 most of the South was self-sufficient with respect to wheat, corn, peas, beans, and pork.[10] Albert Fishlow, in fact, has argued that "the trade between the West and South was always of limited importance to both regions: the South was neither a major market for western produce nor in dire need of imported foodstuffs." And Diane Lindstrom has been more geographically specific in her contention that southern "deficient areas, primarily the urban centers and the coastal tidewater, could not consume the available surpluses of the upper South (Kentucky, North Carolina, and Tennessee), much less buy from the Old Northwest."[11]

The validity of the Callender-Schmidt-North thesis has also been challenged because it apparently overstates the role of the South's cotton-based aggregate demand as a factor encouraging antebellum industrial development in the Northeast. Based on quantitative estimating procedures, Lawrence Herbst has asserted that while "aggregate southern expenditures on interregional commodity exports from the north[east] were large, and growing at a significant rate" in 1839, the "market for northern manufactures *directly due to cotton income* in the South [ran] a poor fourth compared to the markets in foreign countries, the four great seaports of the North[east], or the West." Paul Uselding similarly has proposed that in 1840 the entire southern market could only account "for something in the range of 20 to 25 percent of the transportable manufacturing output of the North[east]."[12] Moreover, by the late 1850s the western market for northeastern manufactures presumably was on a more or less equal footing with the entire southern market for such goods.[13]

In terms of providing some understanding of the urban growth and city-system problems addressed here, the Calender-Schmidt-North thesis (and much of the literature critical of it) suffers from two additional major deficiencies.

First, it does not acknowledge that almost always, regardless of the quantity and direction of antebellum interregional goods shipments, such flows either were wholly interurban (originating and terminating in cities) or contained an important interurban component. At some point in their journey from ultimate origin to ultimate destination, even agricultural products and raw materials usually moved either from one port or terminal city to another or from an urban collection center to an urban distribution center. More precisely, most trade between the Northeast and the South included a leg between New York, Boston, Philadelphia, or Baltimore, at one end, and New Orleans, Richmond, Charleston, Mobile, Savannah, Norfolk, or lesser ports at the other end. And trade between the West and other regions of the country usually involved both: (1) the assembly or breakdown of shipments either at places such as Cincinnati, St. Louis, Detroit, and Chicago, or at lesser "interior entrepôts"; and (2) the receipt or forwarding of goods via one of three "natural avenues and gateways." The first avenue extended from Buffalo eastward over the Hudson-Mohawk Valley route, with New York its customary terminus; the second spanned the Appalachians from Pittsburgh and Wheeling on the Ohio River to Philadelphia and Baltimore; and the third passed along the Mississippi to and from New Orleans.[14]

Second, and by extension, the literature related to the Callender-Schmidt-North thesis does not acknowledge that whether or not interregional commodity flows were completely or partly interurban, they always had growth implications for the involved centers. This was partly the case because such flows meant more employment opportunities, either in conjunction with output-exporting and input-importing manufacturing or in association with the provision of transportation, financial, and mercantile services, as well as storage, local cartage, and cooperage. Furthermore, additional employment opportunities came about as a consequence of local multiplier effects promoted by those activities. Inasmuch as different cities in the Northeast (or South or West) were more engaged with some interregional commodity flows than were other cities in the same region, it follows that any patterns or changes in interregional trade observed at the aggregate regional level did not have the same growth (or decline) ramifications for all urban centers in the sending or receiving region. In short, whatever the virtues of various interregional trade arguments, they only permit implicit and very general observations about city-system interdependencies. Certainly their three geographically extensive units of observation are "too heterogeneous to serve as meaningful units of analysis and comparison" for the purposes of this book.[15]

Because both the proponents of the Callender-Schmidt-North thesis and many of their recent detractors ignore the economic heterogeneity of the Northeast, West, and South, they are also vulnerable to criticism for failing to acknowledge the possibility that a growth-inducing role was played by intraregional demand and the intraregional commodity and capital flows stemming from that demand. A full understanding of the past growth determinants of a broadly defined economic region requires some comprehension of the extent and nature of the internal economic interactions, or interdependencies, that occurred between the urban units of that region.[16] This is especially so since virtually all past intraregional trade—like virtually all interregional trade—was apt either to be fully interurban or to include an important interurban component. In other words, at some juncture in their shipment from ultimate origin to ultimate destination, antebellum intraregional commodity flows conceivably could have moved from one major center to another, from a less populous hinterland urban place to its dominant major center, from a hinterland town or city to a more distant major center, or between lesser urban places either within the same major-center hinterland or within two different such hinterlands.

There are many indications that intraregional flows were highly significant between 1840 and 1860. Fishlow has estimated that between 1839 and 1860 the exports from the Northeast, West, and South "to other regions and abroad increased in importance" from 13 to 19 percent of the gross national product. That the bulk of the remainder entered intraregional trade rather than being locally consumed is suggested by an 1843 estimate that set goods consumption at the place of production at $500 million, or 33.3 percent of total U.S. goods output.[17] It has already been mentioned that New York, Philadelphia, Boston, and Baltimore were major markets for northeastern industrial production. Likewise, in the West, the 1840–1860 rise in significance of both agriculturally based manufactures and industrial activities associated with the geographically specialized extraction of lead, copper, iron, and timber strongly suggests the mounting occurrence of interurban trade—and related urban employment-opportunity generation—within that region.[18] Finally, Lindstrom's findings indicate that during the 1840s Philadelphia's trade linkages with other major northeastern centers and with cities and towns in its own hinterland were much more important than the sum of its economic ties with the West and the South.[19]

A recurrent theme in writings on antebellum interregional trade is the geographic reorientation of goods shipments between the West and the Northeast that came about as a result of the burgeoning railroad construction of the 1850s, the earlier proliferation of western canals, and the associated dramatic decline in freight rates along interior waterways caused by intense route competition during the 1840s.[20] At the outset of the 1840–1860 period most agricultural trade between the West and the Northeast (and overseas) that did not go via the Erie Canal moved instead down the Mississippi and was forwarded from New Orleans. By the end of the period the relative importance of the Mississippi as a conduit of agricultural flows from the West to the Northeast was considerably diminished (table A.2). By 1849, largely because of rail and canal feeders to Lake Erie, the older northern parts of the West were fairly free of agricultural-shipment bonds to New Orleans. This pattern had become further entrenched by 1851 when the New York Central and Erie railroads were completed between New York City and Lake Erie, and when Boston and Ogdensburg, New York (at the easternmost end of Lake Ontario), were linked by the Northern Railroad (completed in 1850) and the Vermont Central. Also, the tide already had begun to turn in other parts of the West by the late 1840s. For example, when the Illinois and Michigan Canal between Chicago and the Illinois River was completed in 1848, it quickly reoriented agricultural goods that previously had been shipped southward on the Mississippi. However, it was the provision of through eastward service from the Ohio Valley by the Pennsylvania and Baltimore and Ohio railroads in 1853 that perhaps exercised the most critical redirection influence. Once Ohio, Indiana, and Illinois began to be crisscrossed by feeders to these two trunk lines (maps 3.1–3.3), increasingly large quantities of agricultural commerce ("whose more profitable previous alternative lay with the southward flowing rivers that drained the West") were siphoned off directly to the Northeast, sometimes moving at first by steamboat up the Ohio and then continuing by rail.[21]

The westward thrust of railroad construction during the 1850s also decreased the relative importance of the Mississippi as a channel for western agricultural shipments to the Northeast by reaching recently settled areas within which new commercial crop production was stimulated to expand quite rapidly. Thus, the Chicago, Burlington & Quincy, as well as other railroads that penetrated northern Illinois, southern Wisconsin, and eastern Iowa, allowed corn, wheat, and other new surplus production to move directly eastward, whereas it otherwise would have been shipped to St. Louis and thence onward to New Orleans before finding its way to northeastern (or foreign) markets. It was this new swelling output facilitated by the railroads that, in accord with the logic of Johann Heinrich von Thunen's agricultural location theory, "put pressure on farmers in areas of Ohio" and western New York to shift to other types of production.[22] It should not be assumed, however, that the railroad routes to new surplus areas were carrying much

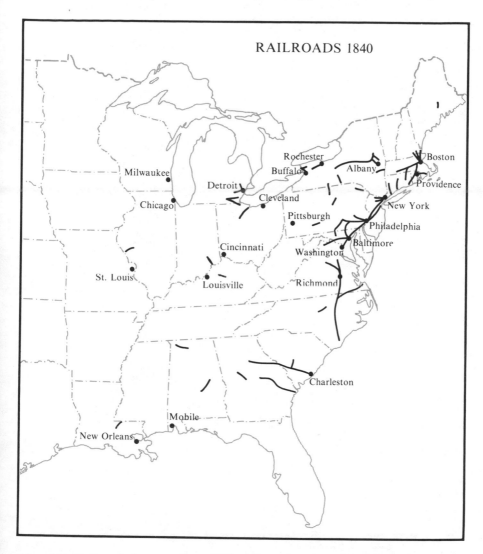

Map 3.1. Railroads in operation, 1840. Adapted and modified from Charles O. Paullin, *Atlas of the Historical Geography of the United States* (Washington, D.C.: Carnegie Institute of Washington and the American Geographical Society of New York, 1932), plate 138L.

through traffic to the Northeast, other than livestock (year-round) and flour (during the winter when ice hindered traffic on the Great Lakes and their tributary canals). Because of the nature of jointly falling rail and water freight rates and because of rail coordination problems, most

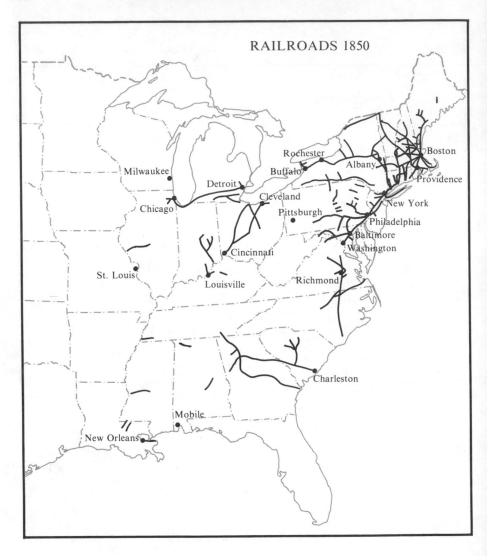

Map 3.2. Railroads in operation, 1850. Adapted and modified from Paullin, *Atlas,* plate 139A.

train shipments originating on these new railroad lines were unloaded at western Great Lakes ports and forwarded by large-capacity vessels to either the Erie Canal or to the terminus of the New York Central, Erie, or Northern Railroad.[23]

As a result of the interurban character of interregional trade, whatever geographic realignment took place in the flow of commodities be-

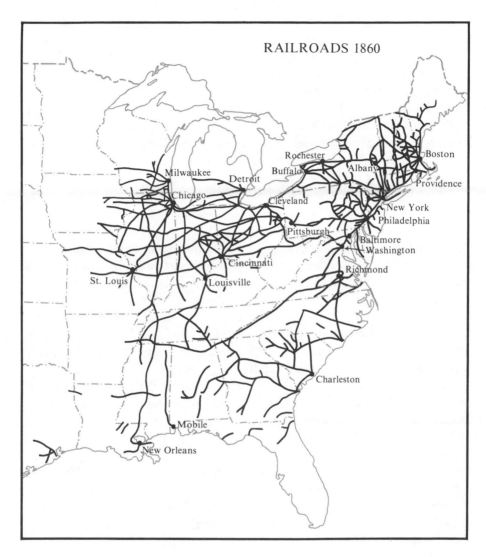

Map 3.3. Railroads in operation, 1860. Adapted and modified from Paullin, *Atlas,* plate 139B.

tween the West and the Northeast during the twenty years preceding 1860 also expressed itself in the form of new and altered city-system interdependencies—a point not normally emphasized in the literature. Such emerging and modified interdependencies, and their selective growth consequences,[24] not only affected major centers like New Orleans, Chicago, Cincinnati, Pittsburgh, Buffalo, New York, Boston, Philadelphia, and Baltimore, but also an uncountable number of lesser urban places that acted on a smaller scale as points of collection, distribution, processing, and consumption.

In consonance with the neglect of intraregional relationships that characterizes the great majority of works for and against the Callender-Schmidt-North thesis, the literature on trade reorientation does not pay sufficient attention to the intraregional-flow consequences of 1840–1860 transportation developments. For one thing, as some urban-rivalry studies have clearly shown, antebellum railroad and canal developments led to the reshaping of major-center hinterlands within the West and Northeast, that is, to the realignment of intraregional commodity traffic moving back and forth between large and small places. (The composition of traffic between major center and hinterland also was altered by the specialization encouraged by new transportation facilities and lower shipping costs.)[25] In addition, although the expanding railroad and canal networks had stripped the Mississippi River system (including the Ohio) of "much of its interregional orientation," shipping activity "on that system continued to increase throughout the ante-bellum period" and "became increasingly [intra]regional in character."[26] Perhaps most important, the transportation developments occurring between 1840 and 1860 contributed to the initial binding together of a new regional city-system in the Midwest and, by definition, the emergence of new interurban economic linkages, or interdependencies, especially between the largest cities of that region.

Prior to the 1840s, the principal streams of commodity movement were such that one could talk of a separate Lake Erie regional system of cities (dominated by flows between Buffalo, Cleveland, and Detroit) and a distinct Ohio and upper Mississippi valley regional system of cities (dominated by flows between Pittsburgh, Cincinnati, Louisville, and St. Louis). Almost completely unnoticed by the writers on interregional trade reorientation is the fact that, in conjunction with the 1840–1860 extension of transport routes, these two systems began to merge into a larger midwestern city-system, which also included Chicago and Milwaukee and a number of other urban newcomers. More specifically, while the old main channels of commodity movement continued to be highly important, new intraregional trade patterns between major centers were encouraged as a consequence of new routes. These new routes included: the Mahoning, or Pennsylvania and Ohio, Canal (completed in 1840), which connected the Mahoning River and the Ohio Canal, thereby tying Pittsburgh and Cleveland via Akron; the Cleveland and Pittsburgh Railroad (completed 1851), which helped to further bind those two cities; the Miami Extension Canal (completed 1845), which connected the Miami and Wabash & Erie canals and permitted Cincinnati and Buffalo to be linked via Toledo; the Mad River & Lake Erie Railroad (completed 1848), which also linked Cincinnati and Buffalo with the aid of lake vessels sailing to and from its northern terminus at Sandusky; the Cleveland, Columbus & Cincinnati Railroad (completed 1851), which linked Cleveland and Cincinnati by cooperating with the already exisiting Columbus & Xenia and Little Miami railroads; the Pittsburgh, Fort Wayne and Chicago Railroad (last leg completed 1858), which joined the major Pennsylvania and Illinois centers included in its title; the Michigan Central (completed 1852), which tied Detroit and Chicago together; and the Chicago, Alton and St. Louis (completed 1857), which provided a more direct link between Chicago and St. Louis than that previously existing (since 1853) via the Chicago and Mississippi, Illinois Central, and Chicago and Rock Island railroads.[27]

RECENT INTERPRETATIVE VIEWS

A variety of concepts and ideas introduced in relatively recent works by economic historians and geographers can be quite useful in answering several questions regarding the economic interdependencies of major cities and the processes of antebellum urban growth and city-system development. This is so either because those works actually provide insights, or because their shortcomings suggest paths of reasoning that are to be avoided. Only a few of the most positively or negatively helpful of these works will be discussed.

In a monograph on 1820–1870 urban growth in the Northeast, Jeffrey Williamson and Joseph Swanson sought to explain and model variations in city growth rates. They did so by first testing the validity of the hypothesis that large cities grow at the expense of smaller urban places because of increasing "urban scale economies"—economies that are mostly external to the manufacturing plant or commercial facility but internal to the city unit. They also systematically estimated "the impact of 'hinterland' on city growth," and attempted to quantify both the advantages of manufacturing and "the disadvantage of age on city growth."[28] The efforts of Williamson and Swanson by their own admission are somewhat disappointing because "only a very small percentage of the variation in city growth" is explained.[29] These efforts have come under severe attack by Robert Higgs.[30] Among other things, Higgs criticizes Williamson and Swanson for their assumption of a single long-run cost curve for all cities when proposing a regression model to test their own urban-scale-economy hypothesis, which argues that growth rates should fall off in cities exceeding some curve-determined optimum size. Such an assumption is regarded as indefensible since: "Cities produce a variety of goods and services, and in general no two cities produce the same *assortment* of goods and services."[31]

To put the matter somewhat differently from Higgs, the two authors are to be strongly criticized for implicitly denying both that different activities produce different immediate local employment multipliers and that different mixes of activities yield different levels of external economies (and long-run growth potential) for one another.[32] Moreover, throughout their monograph Williamson and Swanson treat each city as an isolated unit rather than as a member of a regional or national city-system. In so doing they overlook the fact that activities producing different goods and services will generate their own different nonlocal employment multipliers—thereby affecting the growth of other cities—and that the size of those activities is influenced by nonlocal multiplier effects originating in other cities, both inside and outside the hinterland of the place in question. (Even when considering hinterland impacts on urban growth Williamson and Swanson do not recognize that cities are affected by interurban employment multipliers and economic exchange, for they measure the growth stimulus provided by hinterland demand solely by "the rate of growth of [the] rural population of the state in which the city resides.")[33] This neglect of the crucial feedbacks by which local employment opportunities are created and maintained is difficult to understand because the authors' assumption (like mine) is that antebellum urban growth depended primarily on the ability of the local economy to attract and hold migrants. In fact, other limitations of the Williamson-Swanson effort (including the way in which their simply derived growth rates mask the expansive growth performance of large cities[34] and their frequent use of highly questionable data)[35] seem minor in comparison with this oversight of basic process relationships.

On the basis of his own empirical work on a portion of the middle Ohio valley, and in response to the shortcomings of the work of Williamson and Swanson, as well as others, Edward Muller has proposed a generalized model of selective urban growth in newly settled, moderately sized North American regions.[36] The descriptive model strives to take specialization and shifts in economic function into account and to consider transportation developments insofar as they affect each city's accessibility to major regional activities and its pattern of exchange within and beyond the region. Three periods of development are proposed.

(1) During the "pioneer periphery period" most urban centers provided "little more than basic goods and commercial services for localized areas" because of "the sparsely distributed population, meager purchasing power and low volume of interregional trade." An urban hierarchy of three levels began to appear as a result of the interplay of central-place, or local-demand, forces and mercantile, or long-distance-trade, forces. The greatest amount of urban growth took place in the major entrepôt cities located "at nodal points resulting from the intersections of the early interregional transportation arteries with regional routes. These new centers handled the regions' external commercial relations, processed (if necessary) agricultural products into transportable forms, serviced immigrants and produced some consumer goods." The lowest level of urban place "arose with the spread of rural settlement into the interior of the region, producing local services and periodic commercial connections with the regional entrepôt[s]." Intermediate-level cities, or "district trade centers," evolved because "the difficulty of intraregional movement" and localized rapid settlement growth "at substantial distances from the entrepôt city supported the development of some professional and artisan activities as well a commercial services at a few intermediate points." Selective urban growth in this context depended largely on "differential access to local hinterlands of varying extent and density of settlement"; it depended little on manufacturing since "both artisan-style consumer good production and agricultural processing activities were nearly ubiquitous."[37]

(2) During the "specialized periphery period," expansion and specialization of cash crops and related processing industries resulted from the higher agricultural prices facilitated by improved transport links to interregional markets and "the expansion of the [intra]regional circulation network." However, since the internal improvement network developed unevenly, new staple production and attendant new rural settlement were allocated unevenly withing the region. Agricultural specialization and an accelerated influx of migrants "greatly expanded demands for [commercial services and] both imported and locally produced manufactured goods." Under these circumstances:

> The established regional entrepôt[s] concentrated much of the increase in interregional commerce. The pattern of growth among other towns again primarily related to the distribution of nodality on the expanding transportation network within the region and the corresponding access to expanding or intensifying local hinterlands. While rapidly growing new centers [newcomers] accompanied the spread of

settlement into previously undeveloped areas, the superiority of improved routes in longer settled areas both aggrandized the nodality of or shifted nodality to their major nodal points at the expense of formerly important centers in nearby areas without such access. Large-scale processing operations also frequently developed at the nodal centers of these transportation facilities, further enhancing their nodal position and their growth of population. Moreover, [a new level was inserted in the regional urban hierarchy when] a few interior urban centers developed subregional nodality [within and beyond] their own immediate hinterland [thereby gaining] access to sufficiently large market thresholds for the development of a variety of specialized services and locally manufactured foods in competition with some of the imports and industries of the regional entrepôt[s].[38]

(3) In the final "transitional periphery period" developments were marked by further integration with the national railroad and water-borne transportation system "and full elaboration of connectivity within the region." By further reducing market delivery costs, transportation improvements were likely to strengthen the region's position as a specialized producer of old or new (zonally expanded) primary goods.[39] But transportation improvements could also spur the diversification of manufacturing by permitting some industries to "capitalize on the large scale of production made possible by . . . newly accessible markets," while at the same time the railroads made formerly protected small-scale local manufacturers and artisans highly vulnerable to intraregional and interregional competition. Hence, one of two developments could occur during this period:

If the region continued to specialize in primary staple commodities without subsequently industrializing, the urban system retained essentially the same structure with selective growth among the centers reflecting shifts in the nodality of the revised circulation network (or in the service demands of a new staple production). Although dramatic locational changes sometimes occurred, the nearly ubiquitous provision of railroad service tended to reinforce the extant distribution of nodality . . . Direct links with interregional trunk routes benefited a few interior centers as some trade shifted away from the original entrepôt. At the same time, the reduction of transport time and costs further concentrated many functions at nodal points at the expense of more localized district trade centers. Thus, towns with subregional nodality enjoyed both the centralization of district functions and decentralization of some interregional commerce . . .

The alternative course [firstly meant that] the regional entrepôt

turned its attention to expanding its varied industries ... The urban
centers with subregional nodality also enlarged their already emerging consumer-oriented manufacturing activities or, in the case of a
dramatic nodal shift, developed new ones. Additionally, these same
centers and a few smaller ones proximate to the regional entrepôt developed some producer good manufactures which depended on that
latter city's growing industries for their market. In contrast, the district centers which did not improve upon or suffered diminished nodality within the region maintained their dependence upon their local
hinterlands and agricultural processing operations, failing to develop
large or diverse manufactures while concomitantly losing artisan activities.[40]

Muller's densely expressed model is commendable for the way it
weaves together conceptual and emipirical stands from the works of
others. It incorporates one of the more valid components of classical
central-place theory (the relationship among rural population levels, accessibility patterns, and the intraregional distribution of consumer
goods and services) while at the same time relying heavily upon James
Vance's perceptive mercantile model of pioneer settlement. Vance re-
jects the notion that "towns grow up [solely] to care for central-place
functions,"[41] emphasizing instead the early-established importance of
regional entrepôts (usually at break-of-bulk locations) that acted as
wholesaling and trading links with older and distant major centers before much of the surrounding territory was either widely and intensely
settled or well integrated.[42] Vance's model also focuses on the subsequent growth and development of trade between regional entrepôts and
those smaller commercial towns within their hinterland that initially
both collected agricultural goods or resources and further distributed
imports. In addition, it stresses the linear alignment of intraregional and
interregional trading relationships, rather than a highly "nested" structure of trading relationships wherein the market areas of cities of a
given size and "order" of goods and service provision are hierarchically
meshed into the market areas of cities of successively larger size and
higher order.[43] Finally, in the tradition of Adam Smith, Vance points to
the increasing specialization of production and wholesaling activities
that accompanies mounting trade volumes, a condition that suggests
the development of more intricate city-system interdependencies with
the passage of time.

The Muller model additionally builds upon Michael Conzen's analysis
of nineteenth-century transportation connectivity and accessibility in
the Midwest, a study that (like Vance's) concludes that metropolitan

dominance over hinterland territory "operated to a large degree independently of those forces that created central place patterns within the framework of nested hierarchies."[44] In his further elaboration of the model, Muller enriches it by dealing both with the concept of "initial advantage" and (in passing) with the interrelated processes of innovation diffusion and information circulation.[45]

The Muller model is also especially appealing for its consideration of the simultaneous progress (or lack thereof) made by urban places of different sizes and functions. Furthermore, extension of the model to regions larger than those treated by Muller (more precisely, the Midwest as a whole rather than a portion of the middle Ohio valley) would suggest that, because of the constant westward spread of settlement between 1840 and 1860, different phases of city-system interdependence and development were unfolding concurrently throughout that twenty-year interval.

Yet, despite its integrative accomplishments and the understanding it provides, Muller's model leaves something to be desired on a number of counts. Although he stresses intraregional relationships and at the same time focuses on transportation improvement, thereby avoiding the errors of many interregional trade authors, Muller does not pay adequate attention to major-center economic interrelationships either within larger regional city-systems or in the nation as a whole. He also tends to place excessive emphasis on temporally distinct periods, or development phases. Put otherwise, Muller's model does not represent an integrated city-system framework since it neither simultaneously deals with the urban units of different regions in a meaningful way, nor explicitly allows the cities of different intraregional (or interregional) areas to be in different phases at the same time. Moreover, the model is insufficiently dynamic, being incomplete, imprecise, and rather loose in its treatment of many key feedbacks. Nothing really specific is said of nonlocal employment multipliers, and both the diffusion of growth-inducing innovations and the other consequences of specialized information circulation are treated fleetingly.

Lindstrom's "Eastern [or Northeastern] demand model," though concerned principally with the period 1810–1840 and only secondarily with the period 1840–1850, provides a relevant conceptual framework that applies to the internal workings and economic interdependencies of a region larger than the one covered by Muller's model.

According to Lindstrom's model, the antebellum per capita incomes achieved in the Northeast were the highest of any region in the country primarily because of the two parallel means by which that area ("extending from Maine to Maryland and west to the trans-Appalachian barrier") created a demand for its own goods. First, "nodes of economic activity expanded as the major urban centers extended the coastal and internal hinterlands that were dependent upon them for commercial and financial services. These enlarged hinterlands reciprocated by producing an abundance of agricultural, extractive and in some cases manufacturing commodities for the [major] urban center." (Or, to translate this into the language of city-systems, major cities intensified their interdependencies with smaller collection and distribution centers that had previously fallen within their hinterlands while also developing new interdependencies with smaller urban places that had not formerly been within their hinterlands.) Second, through exploiting sectoral diversification and geographical proximity, the subregions centered around the commercially dominant seaport cities "increased the quantity of trade among themselves." (Or, through the exchange of local and hinterland products the degree of large-city interdependence increased.)[46]

In commenting upon her simple model, Lindstrom further points out: "Bourgeoning [intraregional] commerce, both within and among [sub]regions, facilitated further specialization and division of labor [or additional goods flows and higher levels of urban interdependence] which ultimately led to high rates of growth and rapid structural change." The role of the agricultural sector in all of this is depicted as having been of some importance, even though the lead, or pull, role is assigned to rapidly growing cities. For as the coal-fired steam engine and other factors facilitated the expansion of manufacturing in the major seaports as well as in newer industrial towns, and as the "urban demand for foodstuffs and industrial raw materials" swelled rapidly, "farmers specialized in a limited range of products [thereby creating specialized interdependencies between smaller collection centers and major centers] and used their growing money incomes to purchase goods they had formerly made in their households." The latter circumstance further fueled both "the demand for urban manufactures and services" and the need for specialized urban interdependencies, especially among the leading seaports that acted as shipment focal points as well as production centers.[47]

If Lindstrom's model can be lauded highly because of the city-system relationships and growth processes it explicitly and implicitly touches upon, it also can be faulted for not being conceptually precise and sufficiently elaborate about those relationships and processes. Through regarding the "coastal" and "internal" hinterlands of major urban centers as aggregate entities, she fails (as Muller does not) to distinguish be-

tween the flows and linkages associated with hinterland towns of different sizes and functions.[48] In other words, her model intentionally or unintentionally suggests that the expansion of interdependence between
major centers and their hinterland towns was uniform in relative magnitude if not in kind, and that there was nothing in the way of economic
interaction or interdependence among hinterland urban places. Also
overlooked are the more intricate interdependencies that can arise
when smaller cities and towns are situated in the overlapping hinterlands of two major centers.[49] The question of the presence or absence of
more complex interdependencies, or interurban channels of growth
transmission, is further avoided because the model does not specify interdependencies between centers in different subregions except for those
between the leading seaports.[50] Moreover, although Lindstrom acknowl-
edges that her model "does not gainsay the contribution to Eastern
[Northeastern] growth stemming from the expansion of Western and
Southern markets," she does not even suggest what types of urban interdependencies occurred in conjunction with the increased interregional sale of northeastern goods.[51] In a not unrelated vein, Lindstrom
does not indicate whether her model of intraregional demand and interurban relationships is applicable in part or in full to the intraregional
pattern of exchange that developed in the Midwest in association with
the emergence of a larger, regionwide system of cities in that part of the
country between 1840 and 1860. Finally, her model in effect confines the
interurban growth transmission occurring within a region to the multipliers directly generated by production and trade activities. Consequently, the model unrealistically denies that antebellum urban growth
and city-system development processes were at all affected by subpro-
cesses involving either the diffusion of growth-inducing (or job-providing) innovations between major centers and within hinterlands, or the
influence of specialized information circulation on the economic actions
and locational decision-making of urban merchants, investors, and manufacturing entrepreneurs.

In stark contrast to Lindstrom's omission, one group of authors in recent years has portrayed the past and present occurrence and spread of
growth within city-systems largely or entirely in terms of the "filtering,"
or "trickling down," of economic innovations and related "growth impulses" "downward through the urban hierarchy."[52] In most of these
conceptualizations and interpretations, which are derived from Walter
Christaller's central-place theory, economic innovations are required to
be initially adopted in the largest metropolitan unit of the national or
regional city-system in question, with their subsequent diffusion paths

being determined by the size order of cities and interurban distances. Because, in building upon Christaller, the models suggest directly or indirectly that the diffusion of economic innovations is channeled by already exisiting urban interdependencies (and the specialized information flows necessary to their maintenance), they may be regarded as providing insight. However, these strict hierarchical diffusion formulations contain too many flaws to be applied without question to the interpretation of 1840–1860 urban growth and city-system development processes.

To begin with, proponents of these models ignore the possibility of any diffusion or interurban growth transmission occurring from a city of given population to urban places of comparable or larger size. At the same time, since they are relying on Christaller, these scholars allow only the interdependencies associated with market-oriented retailing and service activities to influence the paths of interurban diffusion. Thereby, they implicitly deny that a similar influence can be exerted either by manufacturing, wholesaling, financial, and insurance activities or by administrative functions and other specialized economic activities within the private or public sector. Yet if it is maintained that existing urban interdependencies, or interurban economic linkages and their accompanying information flows, steer the diffusion of innovations and growth, then there is no logic in confining the argument to one subset of relationships rather than extending it to the complete set.

Hierarchical diffusion interpretations of growth occurrence and transmission within city-systems are further marred by two crucial and interrelated omissions. First, those who espouse hierarchical diffusion, or assert that "impulses of economic change" are transmitted sequentially from higher to lower centers in the urban hierarchy, either underestimate or totally neglect the significance of nonlocal employment multiplier effects of both the backward linkage and the forward linkage variety. (Backward linkage effects would occur when the demand for goods or services generated by a local innovation justified job additions at nonlocal supplying units. Forward linkage effects would occur when the output of goods or services resulting from a local innovation induced nonlocal facilities to increase their level of consumption and employment.) Second, champions of the hierarchical-diffusion view fail to consider the growth-transmission ramifications of postadoption events and the accumulation of day-to-day decisions relating to input acquisition, pricing, marketing, and a host of other operational matters. Just because a specific growth-inducing innovation diffuses through all or part of a national or regional city-system, it will not necessarily survive or succeed (and provide employment) at the same scale in all cities of adoption. Except possibly where threshold-level or market conditions are critical, the degree of success associated with each adoption of an economic innovation, regardless of city location, will usually depend in some measure on the accumulation of a wide range of operational decisions by the adopting entrepreneur, firm, or governmental unit.

There are also empirical grounds for questioning the applicability of the hierarchical-diffusion perspective to 1840–1860 developments in the United States. Not a single advocate of hierarchical diffusion has specified or documented a hierarchical sequence of linkages through which adoption-influencing information has been passed from city to city. Instead, supporters typically have arrived at a heirarchical conclusion by merely plotting dates of initial local acceptance against city-size and calculating moderate to good—but far from perfect—correlations between the two.[53] These dubious conclusions are rebutted by more painstaking studies that specify nonhierarchical information and influence components in the diffusion of a number of economic innovations in the United States between 1790 and 1840, and by a great variety of contrary evidence pertaining to more recent phenomena in Canada, France, Sweden, Denmark, and the United States.[54]

A CLOSING OVERVIEW

The need for closely examining and carefully interpreting the growth and development consequences of interdependencies within the U.S. system of cities and its component regional city-systems during the 1840–1860 period should now be apparent. So-called urban biographies usually can be of no more than secondary assistance in establishing the character of urban interdependencies since, at best, they provide tidbits of information rather than a broad-ranging picture of economic relationships. Urban-rivalry studies, though explicitly concerned with the economic interrelationships of pairs of major cities, have little or nothing to say of the interdependencies between those cities and nonhinterland urban places. The literature on interregional trade and economic development, whether for or against the Callender-Schmidt-North hypothesis, has been found wanting in most instances becasue it fails to acknowledge the following three points. First, antebellum goods shipments almost always were either wholly interurban or contained an important interurban element. Second, interregional commodity flows always had growth implications for the involved urban centers. Third, intraregional economic relationships also played a growth-inducing role.

Similarly, the related literature on the pre-Civil War geographic reorientation of interregional goods shipments that resulted from transportation improvements has been found deficient on two counts: it largely neglects the new and altered city-system interdependencies that accompanied reorientation; and it pays inadequate attention to the consequences of 1840–1860 transport developments for intraregional goods flows and urban interdependence patterns.

In addition, recent conceptual contributions treat cities as isolated units, rather than as members of a regional or national city-system (Williamson and Swanson). They also give insufficient treatment to certain types of city-system interdependencies (those between major centers within larger regional city-systems and the nation as a whole in the case of Muller, and those associated with hinterland towns of different size and function as well as those at the subregional and interregional levels in the case of Lindstrom), and they deny the possibility of nonhierarchical city-system interdependencies (the literature on growth via innovation diffusion). Finally, recent conceptual contributions inadequately consider, or fail to consider, nonlocal multiplier effects and the influence of specialized information circulation on the diffusion of growth-inducing innovations and on economic actions and day-to-day operational decisions. In other words, recent contributions do not fully recognize the ways in which interdependencies between cities enter into the processes of urban growth and city-system development.

4

Snapshots of Antebellum
City-System Interdependence

In view of the shortcomings in the literature of antebellum urban growth and regional interdependence,[1] it is clearly necessary to consider more fully the development of interdependencies involving major centers during the urban economic transformation that occurred from 1840 to 1860. Only in this way is it possible to soundly interpret the concentration of absolute growth in major centers and the development of the U.S. city-system, and to gain some clues to the rank stability of regionally dominant urban centers.

THE REPRESENTATIVENESS OF THE INTERDEPENDENCIES TO BE EXAMINED

Though a close examination of the 1840–1860 interdependencies involving major centers is easily justified, one basic reality must be faced. The information about economic "exchange and interaction" that is necessary "to argue process" within the mid-nineteenth-century U.S. system of cities[2] is only available in piecemeal form. It is not possible, for any year or time period within the 1840–1860 interval, to reconstruct the full set of economic flows moving between all the distinctly separate urban units within the national city-system as a whole or within any of its regional city-systems. (This would require filling in the cells of a three-dimensional interaction matrix, with one of the axes indicating flows of goods, services, and capital on a sector-by-sector basis, as in figure 4.1.)[3] Nor is it possible to assemble an 1840–1860 time series of the total array of economic flows for any one large center, although in a few instances it is feasible to construct reasonably detailed time series of the movement of a particular commodity to or from a single place, such as the cotton shipments from New Orleans. It is not even possible to put together a comprehensive version of all the trade flows of a single major city for any single year between 1840 and 1860.

Despite these impossibilities, it is far from true that there is an "absence" of "flow data measuring [or indicating] . . . commodity movements between cities" during the final antebellum decades.[4] On the contrary, the data and unquantified sources available on 1840–1860

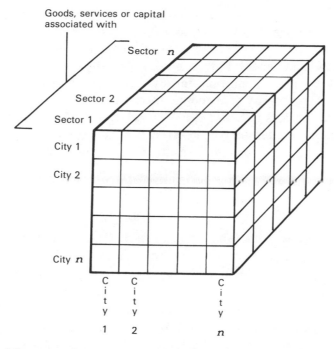

Figure 4.1. The sector-by-sector economic flows occurring within a national or regional system of cities.

city-system interdependencies are quite rich in their variety and occasional detail, though they are highly fragmented. In fact, the volume of information obtainable on major centers is so great that it is impractical to present more than a fraction of it in a book of this length. Unfortunately, the data and other plentiful materials in question are not neatly collected or arranged in a few locations.

Because of its widely scattered character, the information cannot be systematically sampled or stratified in terms of commodity class, type of major center, or date. Instead, representativeness in these areas can only be sought by making somewhat arbitrary selections on the basis of a general familiarity with the assortment and quality of the data and other materials available, and on the basis of prior acquaintance with the place-to-place variations in functional specialization prevailing between 1840 and 1860. Although there is no way of conclusively demonstrating the point, it is assumed that the snapshots of interdependence presented in this chapter for Boston, Philadelphia, Buffalo, Cincinnati, and Charleston are representative in terms of the criteria just mentioned—commodity class, type of major center, and date. It is hoped that they are also representative in terms of the spectrum of intraregional and interregional major-center city-system relationships they cover, and of the types of city-system relationships revealed for intermediate- and smaller-sized urban places. The last aspect of representativeness is especially important, for although this chapter is focused on the mix and complexity of economic interdependencies that existed between major centers (because 1840–1860 absolute urban growth was highly concentrated in such centers), it is aimed at conveying at least some elementary understanding of the workings of entire city-systems in general.

FORMS OF ANTEBELLUM URBAN INTERDEPENDENCE

In many respects, the urban interdependencies of the period 1840–1860 can be easily understood from a late-twentieth-century vantage point. Agricultural commodities, in processed or unprocessed form, typically moved from collection or import centers either to domestic distribution and consumption centers or to export ports, often being transferred from one carrier to another at some intermediately situated break-in-bulk center. With or without similar transshipment, lumber, coal, ores, and other natural resources normally were freighted in a processed or unprocessed state from places where they had been extracted or assembled for shipment to places where they were to be either utilized for construction, heating, or manufacturing purposes, or forwarded abroad. Manufactured goods were transported from importing or producing cities to those cities where they either were ultimately consumed by other manufacturing establishments or by the household sector, or were shipped overseas. Banks in smaller urban places held correspondent relationships, or deposit accounts, with banks in larger cities.[5] Investment capital sometimes moved from the city where a lending bank or risk-taking entrepreneurs were located to another place where the borrowing individuals or institution were to apply it to a job-providing facility of some kind or a transportation construction project. Fire, marine, and other insurance services occasionally flowed from the urban centers where insurance companies were based to other cities where policyholders resided or did business. However, this seemingly straightforward group of interurban relationships was further enlarged and made somewhat more complicated by the fact that agricultural and industrial goods moving beyond local or very nearby markets were quite likely to become involved in one or more of a variety of middleman transactions that had growth implications for the cities where those transactions occurred.

Especially in many areas of the West and more remote parts of the Northeast, local general-store keepers of the early 1840s did much of their business with farmers in the form of barter, accepting produce payments that eventually were sent in lots "to a central market [or city of varying size], where they were consigned to a commission [general produce] merchant or to the merchant's wholesale supplier," either for local sale or for forwarding to yet other middlemen at a more distant location.[6] As such areas became more densely settled or more easily served by transportation, the pattern came to resemble that already existing in other sections of the West and Northeast, with local buyers replacing general-store keepers as the principal purchasers and forwarders of surplus farm products. However, the general-store keeper of small and medium-sized western and northeastern towns continued his role as purchaser of butter, eggs, cheese, and a wide variety of minor products. And, by the 1850s, he still "dealt with the same produce merchants in the larger cities with whom other local produce dealers traded." But there was an increasing tendency for contacts with commission merchants to be more specialized than previously had been the case and to occur in major cities and involve institutions such as the Chicago Board of Trade and Milwaukee Corn Exchange.[7] In the South, large and small planters commonly shipped their cotton from a local river landing or town directly to factors in a major Gulf or Atlantic port, who "arranged for storage, insurance, freight, drayage, weighing, and selling" to the representatives of other middlemen from northeastern ports or from England.[8]

Although more direct selling practices were beginning to emerge, wholesale jobbers, or brokers, intervened in a very large share of the interurban traffic in manufactured goods during the 1840–1860 period. It is "likely that dry goods jobbers still distributed at least 80 per cent of all [such] goods sold in the United States in 1860, and the figure may well have been higher." Jobbers were also a dominant element in the interurban movement of shoes, hardware, drugs, plumbing and building materials, and other industrial items. This was so because they facilitated matters in several ways: by "collecting the individual small orders of dispersed customers and transmitting them ... as large individual orders [to selling houses or other middlemen, as well as manufacturers]; by guaranteeing payment [to the supplier, by extending credit—often long-term—to the purchaser]; and by maintaining contact with the expanding market area."[9]

Urban manufacturers also frequently conveyed their products to other cities or acquired inputs from other centers with the direct assistance of commission merchants (and selling houses) that specialized in the buying and selling of a particular product and actually stocked that product, or samples of it. Such specialized selling-house operators and their traveling agents, who largely had replaced the general wholesale merchant of earlier decades, appealed to the manufacturer in a variety of ways. They enabled him to reduce risk and to avoid the bookkeeping and management inconveniences of maintaining numerous small accounts by dealing instead with a limited number of customers. They often supplied him with the working capital necessary for expansion. In addition, commission merchants could provide specialized information on distant market conditions and other relevant matters at no additional cost. By offering a variety of items in the same or related lines, and thereby providing an opportunity for choice at time of purchase, the specialized commission merchants also were useful to village and small-city retailers who made annual or semiannual trips either to New York and other major coastal ports or to interior centers such as Cincinnati, Chicago, and St. Louis in order to acquire manufactured products and other goods. (Retailers on purchasing trips could also initiate the interurban flow of manufactured articles by dealing with middlemen who were either importing merchants or sellers by auction.)[10]

In only a few branches of manufacturing did producers more or less completely eliminate the need for middlemen and deal directly with their customers, thereby making for more direct interurban transactions and flows. This type of marketing linkage, which became the prevalent form for the interurban distribution of producers' goods in a later era, was most characteristic of the railway supply industry during the 1850s. That industry had little need for wholesale jobbers or commission merchants since it catered to a market in which demand was generated by "a small number of readily identifiable customers," and since the managements of the consuming railroads strove to minimize material costs and rationalize "the flow of goods by assigning purchasing to a specialist or specialized department" of their own. Furthermore, few middlemen possessed the technical background to keep up either with the increasingly complex technology of railroad equipment or with such issues as the durability of wheels and rails, engine design and capabilities, and car capacities. In addition, a small number of textile and other producers apparently sent out their own traveling sales agents, as opposed to the more frequently used traveling agents of wholesale selling houses. All the same, as of 1860, outside of the rapidly expanding railway supply industry, various types of "independent wholesalers, using traditional mercantile techniques, still controlled the distribution of more than 95 per cent of all manufactured products sold in the United States."[11]

BOSTON'S CITY-SYSTEM INTERDEPENDENCIES

The variety and complexity of Boston's antebellum interdependencies are reflected by source materials pertaining to that city's trade in boots and shoes, cotton goods, ice, musical instruments, and flour and grains, as well as by information on insurance and railroad investment activities based in that city.

The Boot and Shoe Trade. For many major antebellum cities an important set of city-system interdependencies arose from the wholesaling and shipping of hinterland manufacturing specialties. This is perhaps nowhere better illustrated than in the case of Boston's boot and shoe trade.

The scholarly attention justifiably given to the cotton textile industry often obscures the significant stature that the boot and shoe industry had acquired by the time the Civil War began. In 1860 the manufacture of boots and shoes was the country's first-ranking industry in terms of employment (providing work for over 123,000 people), and its third-ranking industry in terms of value added: the industry's total of $49.2 million, up from $30.1 million in 1850, was only $5.5 million behind cotton textiles and $4.4 million behind lumber milling.[12] To an increasing extent the rapidly expanding output of boots and shoes had become concentrated in parts of Boston's hinterland. Between 1846 and 1855 production in Massachusetts alone burgeoned from 20.9 million pairs worth $14.8 million to 33.2 million pairs worth $37.5 million.[13] By 1860 Massachusetts (most notably the eastern half), southern New Hampshire, and southwestern Maine were accounting for close to 57 percent of the nation's value of boot and shoe production (table A.3). What is more, Boston's hinterland was almost certainly responsible for an even larger percentage of that portion of U.S. boot and shoe production that was exported beyond places of production. This must have been the case for at least two reasons. First, a significant, but unspecifiable, fraction of antebellum footwear demand was satisfied by shoemaking shops of the traditional local-market orientation kind, that were claimed in 1859 to be found "in every city, town, and hamlet of the Union." (The 1860 census acknowledged the existence of close to 12,500 boot- and shoe-making establishments.) Second, up to 1860 the only other areas where some, but not all, boot and shoe producers served nonlocal markets were in and around Philadelphia and New York and in northern New Jersey.[14]

The magnitude of boot and shoe production in Massachusetts, New Hampshire, and Maine was such that, by 1858, it could justify the presence in Boston of no less than 218 specialized commission merchant and jobbing houses that sold (mostly on credit) to wholesalers and general-store retailers visiting from elsewhere. This production also supported a Boston Shoe and Leather Exchange that since 1854 had allowed hinterland manufacturers and local wholesalers to bargain daily between noon and two o'clock. (Practices adopted by Boston boot and shoe wholesalers around 1829 had compelled "the market to come to their doors" to make binding purchases rather than to remain at home and receive shipments on consignment.)[15]

The collection of boots and shoes in Boston for wholesaling and eventual shipment brought that city into economic interchange with numerous hinterland urban places of varying sizes, in which production had become concentrated for a number of reasons. These reasons included: (1) the early establishment of comparatively large-scale production (and cost advantages) based upon a strict division of labor among artisans working in their homes or in central shops that evolved into factories; (2) a wide range of production innovations, such as "separate lasts for left and right shoes, tin patterns instead of wood, and standardization of sizes, which was a prerequisite for large-scale marketing"; (3) pioneering efforts made between 1840 and 1860 to increase productivity by the use of sole pressing and cutting machines, other mechanical devices for cutting and rolling leather, pegging machines, and stitching machines (table A.4); (4) local specialization in particular lines, such as coarse "brogans," higher grade men's boots, and women's shoes (which probably brought some hinterland towns into interdependence with one another); and (5) the availability of a local and rural outwork labor force, derived from sailors' families along the coast and, more generally, from seasonally idle farmers' families. These highly competent workers, who helped hinterland urban capitalists supplant traditional artisan production, had "learned to do rapidly and perfectly single things, such as heeling ... without knowing much about other [shoemaking] operations," and they passed their skills down from generation to generation.[16]

Lynn, which reached a population of more than 19,000 by 1860, was clearly the most important supplier of Boston's boot and shoe wholesalers. The city, which specialized in cheaply priced women's and children's shoes, produced about 6 million pairs in 1860 (the year of the "great shoemakers strike"), well over twice what it had turned out fifteen years earlier but substantially below the level attained before the crisis of 1857 brought the industry as a whole to a standstill (table A.5). Worcester was the only Massachusetts city larger than Lynn to ship boots and shoes to Boston in significant quantities. The other Massachusetts urban places with important boot-and-shoe linkages to Boston (1855 production over 100,000 pairs) had 1860 populations ranging from below 2,500 (34 of 51 major supplying places) to close to 10,000 in the case of Haverhill (table A.5). In other words, for most of the major supplying towns, boots and shoes were the only goods sold in quantity to Boston for either wholesaling and forwarding or for local consumption. Therefore, the employment and population levels of these small towns in some measure depended upon the effectiveness, capital resources, and business acumen of Boston's wholesaling houses. At the same time, the jobs in Boston associated with those houses and with transportation and other activities ancillary to the boot and shoe trade depended upon the scale of production in the small towns and the few larger cities that acted as suppliers. (These employment multiplier effects are not permitted by those theorists who either see all growth impulses as descending downward through the urban size hierarchy, or see interurban growth transmission as something that spreads to, never from, hinterland places.) In this connection, it should also be recognized that the hinterland boot and shoe industry supported a sizable hide and leather business in Boston (106 establishments had sales of $25.6 million in 1858),[17] which resulted in additional employment multipliers and leather shipments moving outward from Boston to its hinterland over the same routes by which boots and shoes flowed inward.[18] This business, too, brought interdependencies with those centers, particularly New York, Baltimore, and Philadelphia (table A.6), through which leather was purchased from wholesalers who had acquired hides and processed skins from a variety of domestic and foreign sources.

The configuration of interurban linkages that had emerged by the late 1850s in conjunction with the shipment of boots and shoes beyond Boston was striking in three respects, as the data for 1859 show (tables A.7 and A.8; map 4.1).

First, in 1859, when Boston wholesaled more than $43 million worth of boots and shoes (as compared with $50 million in 1856, before the economic crisis), over 25 percent of all domestic shipments destined for points outside New England went to New York City, where much was acquired by wholesale houses that resold their purchases to merchants

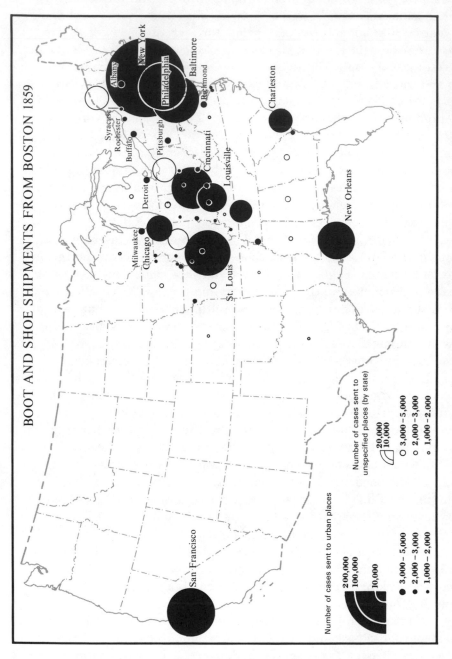

BOOT AND SHOE SHIPMENTS FROM BOSTON 1859

Map 4.1. Shipment of boots and shoes from Boston to points outside New England, 1859. Solid circles are proportional either to the actual values or to the mean of the range values given in tables A.7 and A.8. Open circles are proportional to the total approximate number of cases sent to all unspecified places within the same state.

from the West and South.[19] Close to another 17 percent went to Baltimore and Philadelphia together. If shipments to Albany plus Troy,
Rochester, and Syracuse are added to those to New York, Philadelphia,
and Baltimore, and if some allowance is made for the "frequent and numerous" (but unspecified) shipments to Providence, Hartford, and
lesser New England centers, it may be estimated that almost 50 percent
of all the domestic shipments of boots and shoes forwarded from Boston had initial destinations within the Northeast.[20] In short, as a group
the most important direct city-system interdependencies stemming from
domestic footwear exports were those between Boston and major intraregional centers of much larger of comparable size. This pattern,
which is clearly incompatible with those views that depict all city-system interdependencies as hierarchical, reflected a geographical specialization of labor within the boot and shoe industry inasmuch as cheaper-
grade pairs from Boston's hinterland were sold in Philadelphia at the
same time that producers in the latter city were widely marketing their
fine-quality footwear. By the same token, incidentally, specialized high-
quality products, such as "ladies' gaiter boots with heels," occasionally
were brought in from New York and sold in Boston.[21]

A second impressive feature of Boston's wholesale trade in boots and
shoes was the extent to which the overall pattern, both interregionally
and intraregionally, was characterized by large-city interdependence. In
fact, in 1859 shipments to major centers were well in excess of 80 percent of all footwear marketed outside New England (table A.7). The
predominance of this type of city-system interdependence in conjunction with the trade had been in evidence for some time. In the 1840s
western footwear dealers based in regionally dominant centers were
largely dependent upon Boston boot and shoe supplies, a condition encouraged by the fact that in Chicago and elsewhere "many of the pioneer shoe jobbers were men from Massachusetts who had learned the
business there."[22] The linkage with New Orleans was also of long stand-
ing—on one 1850 trip a packet carried a few hundred thousand dollars'
worth of boots and shoes to the Louisiana city—as was that with Richmond, where one wholesaling house spent $400,000 for shoes from Bos-
ton in 1850. Moreover, large annual shipments to San Francisco had occurred from the very outset of the gold rush, and the press of that city
deemed the trade important enough to give occasional accounts of the
Boston Boot and Shoe Market.[23]

A third striking aspect of Boston's boot and shoe wholesaling in 1859
was the extent to which shipments went directly to distant nonhinterland cities of intermediate and small size (table A.8). It is not particu-

larly surprising that significant quantities of pairs were wholesaled either to Nashville, Memphis, Savannah, and Norfolk, each of which controlled limited wholesaling hinterlands within the uncoordinated South, or to Indianapolis, Dayton, and Columbus, each of which was emerging as a subregional dominant (city of the second-highest regional order) with the aid of railroads that enhanced its nodality. Nor is it especially surprising that shipments of 100,000 pairs or more went to Alton, Illinois, and New Albany, Indiana, since they may be regarded as spillover growth centers for St. Louis and Louisville respectively.[24] But the direct wholesales to the thirteen other cities listed in table A.8 (as well as the direct smaller shipments to several hundred other lesser urban places in the South and West),[25] are so unexpected and complex that conventional theories of urban interdependence would not even acknowledge such relationships. (Christaller's central-place theory would only allow a good to move interregionally to a small [or large] center if it came from the largest unit in the national city-system, in this case New York.[26] And the mercantile model of pioneer settlement would normally require shipment through the hands of a wholesaler in one of the receiving region's principal "unraveling points," or major centers.) In addition, the quantity of boots and shoes arriving at the thirteen cities in question also suggest the existence of intraregional city-system interdependencies. In view of the populations of those cities, it would appear that wholesalers there must have been in the habit of making another round of fairly widespread sales to other larger, comparably sized, and smaller urban places.

Cotton Goods. Somewhat less detailed data on the wholesaling and shipment of cotton textiles, another of Boston's well-known hinterland manufacturing specialties, provides a snapshot of city-system interdependencies that are in some respects similar to those associated with the shipment of boots and shoes beyond Boston.

As of the mid-1840s, the cotton textile mills of Lowell, Massachusetts, of Manchester and Nashua, New Hampshire, and of a great number of other producing centers of varying importance in Massachusetts, Maine, and New Hampshire followed the earlier established practice of shipping most of their output to Boston. Although Lowell and Manchester had 1850 populations of 33,383 and 13,932 respectively, most of the remaining cotton-mill towns forwarding to Boston had 1850 populations under 2,500, and as a consequence usually were especially strongly linked to Boston in relative terms.[27] Once in Boston, cotton goods were marketed with the assistance of specialized wholesale jobbers, who often had provided the investment capital for textile mills and who either dealt with merchants from elsewhere in the United States or arranged for export abroad.

In 1846 the domestically bound coastal shipments channeled through Boston wholesalers fell almost entirely into four categories (table A.9). The first of these categories, shipments to the major northeastern centers of New York, Philadelphia, and Baltimore, completely dominated the picture, accounting for over 80 percent of the total identifiable flows to domestic points. Interregional, rather than intraregional, large-city interdependencies characterized the second category of shipments, since the major southern centers of New Orleans, Charleston, Richmond, and Mobile acquired over 18 percent of Boston's sales of cotton goods to coastal points. (Additional flows, not indicated in table A.9, are very likely to have gone directly to western major centers, as opposed to indirectly via New York, Philadelphia, and Baltimore commission merchants. These would have moved by way of the Boston and Worcester and Western railroads, which provided a connection to Albany and to the canal and railroad termini of that city.)[28] Shipments within the third category, those going directly to the southern ports of Norfolk, Savannah, Galveston, and especially Apalachicola (1850 population less than 2,500), though not aggregately amounting to very much, are noteworthy because they included nonhinterland cities of medium and small size and are not covered by the prevailing theories of urban interdependence.[29] Finally, less than 1 percent of shipments went to hinterland cities and towns within New England.[30] However, given the relative density of rail lines radiating outward from Boston [see map 3.2], it is highly probable that the volume of hinterland distribution was much greater than is suggested by table A.9.

In subsequent antebellum years, the destination mix of coastal cotton goods shipments from Boston apparently was altered in two significant ways. First, soon after the gold rush the array of large-city interdependencies associated with those shipments was increased by the rise of San Francisco as a city of major importance. (In 1853, the California city received over 6,500 bales and cases of cotton goods from Boston.)[31] Second, and more important, between 1847 and 1849 an even larger share of the total flow began to move to New York, "whither [many of] the selling agencies were transferred . . . consequent upon the establishment in that city of more direct communication and better facilities for transacting trade with the South and West." In fact, through the use of steamboats on Long Island Sound and "little packet schooners around Cape Cod," New York began to obtain cotton goods directly from places within Boston's hinterland, other than those places in Rhode Island and the Connecticut valley that had earlier dealt directly with the nation's largest city.[32]

Obviously, the shipment of cotton goods from hinterland mill towns to Boston necessitated the movement of unprocessed cotton in the opposite direction. This, in turn, led to a considerable amount of economic interaction between Boston and the leading cotton ports of the South (including Savannah), to the relatively small-scale acquisition of reshipments from other major centers in the Northeast, and to direct links with a variety of smaller places, most notably Apalachicola, that presumably were within the hinterlands of major southern centers (table A.10). The adoption of steam engines in some hinterland textile mills, especially after the mid-1840s, also occasioned both the movement of coal from Boston to the new and previously existing mill towns where such innovation diffusion had taken place, and an intensified interdependence between Boston and the sources of coal, principally Philadelphia.[33]

The Ice Trade. A highly significant set of city-system interdependencies associated with most major U.S. cities between 1840 and 1860 was derived from the wholesaling and shipping of hinterland agricultural specialties and natural resources. Boston's hinterland provided nothing substantial in the way of agricultural surpluses that could be marketed and forwarded elsewhere, although the city's coastal tributary area allowed some of its wholesalers to develop an active interurban trade in cod, mackerel, shad, salmon, and other kinds of seafood.[34] Few shipment statistics are available on Boston's fish trade, or on its commerce in conventional hinterland natural resources such as lumber, granite, and lime, but some data do exist on its trade in another hinterland natural resource of somewhat surprising importance—ice "harvested" from ponds.

By the middle of the 1840s, Boston's ice trade, which dated from 1806, had assumed quite noticeable dimensions. Ice was useful as a return ballast in the holds of coasting vessels that had delivered cotton, coal, and flour to Boston; and the growing demand for ice to preserve meat and other perishables that were to be sold in the market places of major cities led to the establishment of "ice depots" in connection with those market places. Boston's ice trade also began to flourish because of the increasing popularity of household refrigerators ("ice boxes"), and the development by Boston business interests of cost-reducing innovations, such as horse-drawn ice cutters, ice plows and ice scrapers, devices for raising blocks from the water, and machines for distributing blocks in the icehouses were they were stored before shipment.[35]

As is to be expected with a commerce of this sort, the most important domestic (as well as foreign) shipments went to places where there was demand but no supply. Thus, the largest domestic recipients in the mid-1840s were not major centers in the Northeast, as was the case with boots and shoes and cotton goods, for these centers normally had access to local or nearby ice sources. Instead, New York and Baltimore obtained relatively minor quantities,[36] and three major southern centers—New Orleans, Mobile, and Charleston—acquired roughly 95 percent of the domestic total in 1845 and about 90 percent in 1846 (table A.11). All of the remaining shipments were noteworthy inasmuch as they created direct economic relationships with southern urban places that were then either of intermediate size (Savannah and Norfolk) or close to it (Wilmington, North Carolina),[37] or that in 1850 were still below the 2,-500 mark. The mix of smaller southern cities and towns receiving minor ice shipments varied from year to year. For example, in 1844 direct shipments had gone to the North Carolina ports of Edenton, Washington, and New Bern; and in 1847 these places were joined by Fredericksburg, Petersburg, and Portsmouth, Virginia, by Fayetteville, North Carolina, the Georgia river cities of Augusta and Macon, the remoter locations of Columbus, Mississippi, and Thibodeaux, Louisiana, and by Galveston.[38]

The preponderance of interregional large-city interdependencies in Boston's ice trade was amplified as its domestic volume expanded to about 62,600 tons in 1852, and as its total volume surpassed 146,000 tons in 1856. Richmond, another major southern center, became a customer, and San Francisco established itself as a significant importer (2,232 tons in 1852) until ice harvests in the foothills of the Sierra Nevada began to offer competition in the late 1850s. Sacramento, in the hinterland of San Francisco, also occasionally acquired smaller direct shipments until that time. In addition, limited (but unspecified) quantities of ice accompanied shipments of seafood from Boston to Buffalo and other major centers.[39]

Despite the cumbersomeness of ice blocks, the hinterland interdependencies of Boston's ice trade were not confined to Wenham, Medford, Woburn, and other towns in its immediate vicinity with workable ponds. The Fitchburg Railroad, which reached fifty miles to the northwest and was fed by other lines extending into Vermont and New Hampshire, was by 1850 bringing 100,000 tons annually to Boston for both local consumption and further shipment.[40] Moreover, since sawdust had to be used to protect southbound shipments from melting, linkages for the acquisition of that waste product were maintained with various sawmill towns on the Penobscot River in Maine.[41]

Pianos and Musical Instruments. As the Civil War approached, the city-system interdependencies of most major centers included to an increasing degree some local, as opposed to hinterland, manufacturing specialties. One of Boston's principal interdependence-generating industrial specialties was the manufacture of pianos and miscellaneous musical instruments. By 1850, when the pianoforte was gaining increasing popularity with the growing urban upper and middle classes throughout the United States, Boston had established itself as the leading producer of those instruments. The Boston industry then held a share of the nation's total piano-producing employment that was more than nine times greater than the city's share of all national manufacturing employment; or, in more technical terms, Boston had a "location quotient" of 9.23. Five years later the Boston output had risen to more than 6,100 pianos per year. And by the census of 1860, when piano manufacturers were still the city's third most important industrial employers, the value of their production represented approximately 28 percent of the national total. Although no precise shipment data are available, it is known that the quality of Boston pianos—and particularly those of the Chickering Manufactory—was such that they were much in demand in New York, which was just assuming national leadership in piano production, as well as in Philadelphia and Baltimore, which had piano manufacturers of their own. The apparent prevalence of shipments to major centers both inside and outside the Northeast is suggested by the frequent advertisements for Boston pianos that appeared in the newspapers of major centers as far away as Chicago.[42]

Insurance and Railroad Investments. Although insurance and nonlocal investment were not common activities in antebellum major centers, a significant volume of Boston's city-system interdependencies was based on the provision of insurance services and the movement of investment capital.

Boston was one of the country's earlier insurance centers, providing fire and marine as well as life insurance. One of its firms, the New England Mutual Life Insurance Company, had been chartered in 1835 and consequently laid claim to being "the oldest American mutual life assurance company."[43] By 1855 this company had established branch offices or stationed agent representatives in thirty-eight places outside Boston (map 4.2). Although the provision of life insurance services was directed at the household sector, and therefore may be presumed to have had a local and hinterland orientation originally, only fifteen of

Map 4.2. Location of offices and agents representing the New England Mutual Life Insurance Company, 1855. Derived from *American Railroad Journal and General Advertiser (ARJ)*, 28 (1855), 670.

these places, including Providence, Lowell, New Haven, and Hartford (itself an important insurance center), were situated in New England. Moreover, five of these fifteen New England places were located either along Long Island Sound or in the Connecticut valley, either within New York's sphere of primary economic influence or within an area where the hinterlands of New York and Boston overlapped to a considerable degree.[44] In numerical terms, at least, the most important recipients of New England Mutual's insurance services were other major centers both inside and outside the Northeast. Intraregionally, the Boston company's services were available in New York, which had the largest office outside Boston, as well as in Philadelphia, Washington, D.C., Rochester, and Albany plus Troy. Interregionally, agents were making policy sales in the southern major centers of Charleston and Mobile, and, with the exception of Pittsburgh, in every major center of importance around the Great Lakes and in the valleys of the Ohio and upper Mississippi. Finally, the direct nonhinterland interdependencies spawned by New England Mutual were complex insofar as they involved cities of medium and small size that were within the hinterlands of other major centers, such as Galena (Chicago), Columbia (Charleston), Lansing (Detroit), and Ford du Lac (Milwaukee).[45]

Because of the uncertainties involved in making investments at a distance and "the absence of institutions designed to effect the transfer of funds," capital was not particularly mobile in the 1840s and 1850s.[46] All the same, during that period Boston businessmen began to invest heavily in railroads outside New England in an effort "to improve the connections of [the city] with outlying regions, more especially with trade routes from the trans-Allegheny West." These investors were principally merchants who had accumulated capital in the China trade and businessmen who prior to the 1840s had placed their savings in New England railroads. Boston investment in railroads beyond the Alleghenies was facilitated by the fact that, following the collapse of state-backed internal improvement projects, business interests from the West actively sought funds in the Massachusetts city, knowing full well the extent to which railroad investment know-how already had accumulated there.[47]

Boston's placement of capital in rail routes toward and within the West largely involved the movement of its funds to major centers, or large-city interdependencies. Boston capitalists had been active in financing the construction of the Attica and Buffalo Railroad (completed in 1842) and of the Auburn and Rochester Railroad (completed in 1841), which were consolidated to form the New York Central in

1852–1853.[48] These two projects in essence involved the movement of capital to Buffalo and Rochester. Investments made in 1845 in the Little Miami Railroad and the Mad River and Lake Erie Railroad meant that Boston capital flowed to Cincinnati, which was to be connected to Lake Erie via those lines. Larger-scale commitments that were made during 1846 to the Michigan Central, which eventually linked Detroit with Chicago, in effect required the flow of Boston funds to Detroit. Most important, heavy investments placed during the 1850s in the Illinois Central (which became the world's largest railroad in that decade), and the Chicago, Burlington & Quincy resulted in capital movements from Boston to Chicago.[49]

Although the railroad investment activity of Bostonians had a distinct western bias during the final antebellum decades, it also involved intraregional flows of capital to Philadelphia and Baltimore. The Philadelphia-based Reading Railroad, in which Boston capitalists already had acquired a significant interest during the 1830s, attracted additional Boston financial resources in the early and mid-1840s in order to pay for double-tracking and operating equipment and to help relieve the road's debt. Consequently, by 1847 Bostonians supposedly owned about one-third of the Reading. And when the Philadelphia, Wilmington and Baltimore Railroad ran into financial difficulties in the late 1840s, investors from Boston and elsewhere in New England scented "a promising opportunity for profit." They therefore "purchased four-fifths of the existing common stock of the road and took over the floating debt, which they converted into new shares."[50]

All this emphasis on the intraregional and interregional movement of Boston railroad investments to large centers should not obscure the fact that between 1840 and 1860 Boston capital also moved to hinterland centers of less importance in connection with the expansion of New England railroads (see maps 3.1–3.3). Relatively speaking, however, Boston's most important contributions to New England railroads had come in the 1830s when rail links were built between textile centers and the Bay State's leading city. Moreover, the new railroads that were of local importance "depended upon local [non-Boston] subscription," and during the 1840–1860 period New York capital also played a significant role in financing New England railroads, especially those in southern New England.[51]

Flour and Grains. In one form or another, flour and grains, especially corn, were essential elements in the diet of mid-nineteenth-century urban dwellers. This fact, and the growing European market for basic foodstuffs that followed Great Britain's repeal of the Corn Laws and the continental crop failures of the mid-1840s, meant that every major U.S. center had an important set of city-system interdependencies based on flour and grain flows and their related wholesaling activities. In each instance these flows could take several forms. They could involve the assembling of crops or flour from hinterland centers and the forwarding of shipments to places elsewhere in the country, or the breaking-in-bulk of flour and gains acquired from nonhinterland sources and the further domestic forwarding of most of those edibles. They also could include the nonhinterland procurement of foodstuffs, either for local consumption or for foreign export. In was these last two flow categories—the nonhinterland procurement of foodstuffs for both local consumption and foreign export—and their attendant wholesaling linkages that characterized Boston's flour- and grain-based interdependencies.

The most striking element in Boston's incoming flour shipments was the dominance of arrivals from intraregional major centers. For the scattered years shown in table A.12, New York, Philadelphia, and Baltimore, along with the second-order major center of Albany and its Western Railroad connection, together accounted for between 42.24 percent (1852) and 75.52 percent (1841) of the barrels of flour shipped to Boston for both local consumption and export.[52] Initially, New York, whose wholesalers and shippers forwarded shipments from Albany and the Erie Canal, was responsible for close to half of the overall total, but this situation changed rapidly in 1842, the first full year of operation of the Western Railroad. That line enabled significant quantities of flour to move by an all-rail route from Albany to Boston, rather than to be floated by sloop over the more circuitous route that passed down the Hudson River and through Long Island Sound.[53] As the quantities of flour being carried by the Western Railroad peaked in the late 1840s,[54] and as European demand simultaneously shot up, the amount of flour arriving from Philadelphia and Baltimore fell off in relative importance. By 1860, however, there was a considerable absolute and relative increase in shipments from Philadelphia and Baltimore, because the hinterland production of those major centers was supplemented by perhaps a million barrels of western flour arriving by the Pennsylvania Railroad and by the Baltimore and Ohio Railroad, which had reached Wheeling in 1853.[55]

A second element in Boston's flour trade was the combined supply shipped from two major southern centers, New Orleans and Richmond, which amounted to between 7.66 percent (1860) and 38.14 percent (1849) of its total flour receipts. The height reached in 1849 appears to have been attributable to "the considerable supplies" accumulating at

New Orleans, "the [exceptionally] low rate of freights" then being offered from that place, and the dissatisfaction that merchants had experienced the previous year with the delays and bottlenecks of the Western Railroad.[56] The sharp decline of New Orleans by 1860 is in keeping
with the general geographic reorientation of western foodstuff shipments caused by the new railroad and steamboat services of the mid-
and late 1850s.[57] The shipments coming from Richmond's hinterland,
which were significant in quantity from 1849 onward, are noteworthy insofar as they contradict the Callender-North-Schmidt image of the
South as a foodstuff-deficient area.[58]

Shipments from nonhinterland centers of intermediate and small size
were a third element in Boston's flour trade. During the 1840s these
more complex expressions of city-system interdependence never exceeded more than 7.23 percent (1842) of Boston's total flour receipts.
During that decade the shipments came primarily from southern ports
(again contrary to the Callender-North-Schmidt image), especially from
Fredericksburg, Virginia, which had an 1850 population just over 4,000.
However, in the 1850s the focus shifted to Ogdensburg, in upstate New
York, whose 1860 population surpassed 7,400. Ogdensburg was within
the hinterland of New York City and served both as a terminus for the
Northern Railroad and as a break-in-bulk center for western flour mov-
ing through the Great Lakes.

The final subset of city-system interdependencies stemming from
Boston's flour trade involved hinterland centers. At first, in a conventional manner, a few such places were shipping to Boston locally milled
flour surpluses in rather insignificant quantities: about 0.5 percent of all
receipts in 1841.[59] A much more complex situation arose in the 1850s
when hinterland centers began to account for a substantial share of
Boston's flour acquisitions (30.49 percent in 1860), primarily by trans-
shipping and forwarding interregional shipments. Thus, the northern
termini of the Boston and Maine and Fitchburg railroads supplied western flour that had come via the Great Lakes or Canada,[60] while the
southern end points of the Boston and Providence Railroad and the
Fall River Railroad provided western flour that had been forwarded via
either New York or Albany. Most impressively, by 1860, wholesalers in
Portland, Maine, were sending over 217,000 barrels of flour per year to
Boston. This flour came to Portland over the Grand Trunk Railroad,
which passed through Montreal and Ontario to Detroit, "where it had
'a complete and independent connection with the Western States.' "[61]
Because all five of these railroads, as well as the Western, made stops at
hinterland cities and towns that needed flour, they limited the number

of economic linkages developed by Boston as a flour redistribution center.[62]

Corn, which was used as a food in a great variety of ways during the mid-nineteenth century, was quantitatively the second most important foodstuff of those recorded as arriving in Boston for local consumption and export.[63] With one major exception, the city-system interdependencies connected with Boston's corn trade resembled those generated by its flour trade. First, for the years indicated in table A.13, corn shipments were dominated by the intraregional centers of New York, Philadelphia, Baltimore, and to a lesser extent, Albany (including the Western Railroad). These places together answered for from 51.95 percent (1845) to 64.13 percent (1860) of Boston's corn receipts.[64] Second, although New Orleans's position was unstable during the early 1840s, in general that leading southern center served as a major source of western corn at least as late as 1852, only to fall off by 1860 in accord with the overall reorientation of interregional trade.[65] Third, the corn-based interdependencies between Boston and nonhinterland urban places of small and medium size were more important than structurally similar interdependencies based on flour. Approximately one-third of all corn shipments to Boston came from this group of places in 1841, 1844, and 1845. A portion of these flows was associated with places that were unquestionably within Philadelphia's immediate hinterland: more specifically with Salem, New Jersey (1860 population less than 2,500) and with unnamed Delaware ports. Furthermore, insofar as these flows originated in Fredericksburg and Norfolk, as well as in other ports in Virginia and North Carolina, they also are incompatible with the Callender-North-Schmidt depiction of southern foodstuff dependency. Only in one respect, the apparent failure of the fourth category of cities and towns, those in Boston's own hinterland, to act as rail forwarders of western production, did the corn-based interdependencies of Boston differ markedly from its flour-based interdependencies.

Other Observations and Evidence. The most persistent impression to emerge thus far from the consideration of Boston's city-system interdependencies is the prevalence of linkages with centers of national or regional significance both in the Northeast and in other parts of the country. If all the large-city interdependencies that already have been specified for Boston during the 1850s are combined schematically with other identifiable Boston relationships during that decade, the pattern presented in figure 4.2 is obtained.[66] This figure inadequately restates the importance of intraregional as opposed to interregional economic relationships; but it gives graphic substance to the argument that ante-

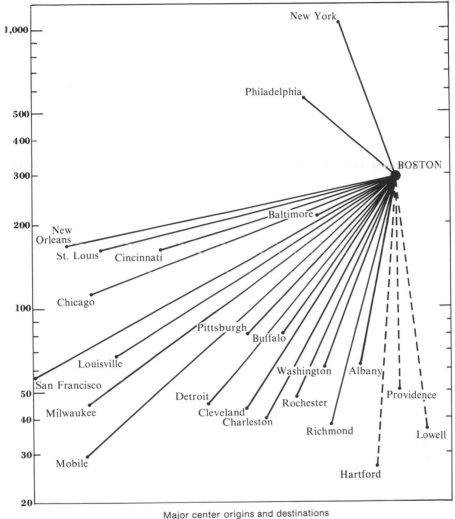

Major center origins and destinations

Figure 4.2. Boston as an origin and destination of goods and capital flows involving other major centers during the 1850s. (Flows to and from the undiscussed centers of Syracuse, Newark, Jersey City, and New Haven are not indicated.) Based on sources cited in tables A.6–A.13 and note 66 to this chapter.

bellum interregional trade was either wholly or partially interurban. Moreover, although in some instances the volume of goods moving between Boston and another major city may have been small, it is clear from the diagram that most of the interdependencies between Boston and major centers would not be acknowledged by those who employ Christaller's central-place theory in order to depict city-system growth. For example, according to central-place theory, Boston would not have received goods or services from Providence, Lowell, and Hartford, since they were less populous and within Boston's hinterland.[67] Nor would that theory allow the sending of goods or services from Boston to the more populous cities of New York and Philadelphia. Nor, again, would that theory permit either Boston's acquisition of goods or services from any of the eighteen other diagrammed major centers (since Baltimore was comparably sized and the rest were smaller), or Boston's provision of goods and services to the same places (since New York was larger and closer to all of them).[68]

Another important observation to be made is that direct interdependencies between Boston and nonhinterland urban places of small and intermediate size appear time and time again in relation to many other kinds of goods. For example, direct city-system interdependencies between Boston and places in the primary-influence spheres of other major centers occurred in connection with Boston's receipt of naval stores (from North Carolina ports), pork (from "interior New York towns"), cheese (from towns in western and northern New York), white pine (via Ogdensburg and various southern places), iron and iron products (from Coatesville, Pennsylvania, and other Pennsylvania and Maryland locations), and oats (from Salem, New Jersey, and various Delaware and Virginia ports).[69] Interdependencies of this more complex form also occurred in conjunction with the shipment from Boston of products as diverse as locomotives and cabinetware (to lesser Ohio, Indiana, and Illinois centers), and a host of other manufactured goods, most of which had been forwarded to the Massachusetts capital for wholesaling purposes from cities and towns within its own hinterland.[70]

Finally, it should be emphasized that for several reasons the intensity and variety of interdependencies between Boston and urban places in its own hinterland were greater than the intensity and variety of interdependencies between most other major antebellum centers and urban places within their respective hinterlands. The first reason for this difference was that the average density of population within a radius of about fifty miles of Boston was higher than for any other comparable area in the country, and Massachusetts and Rhode Island were the two

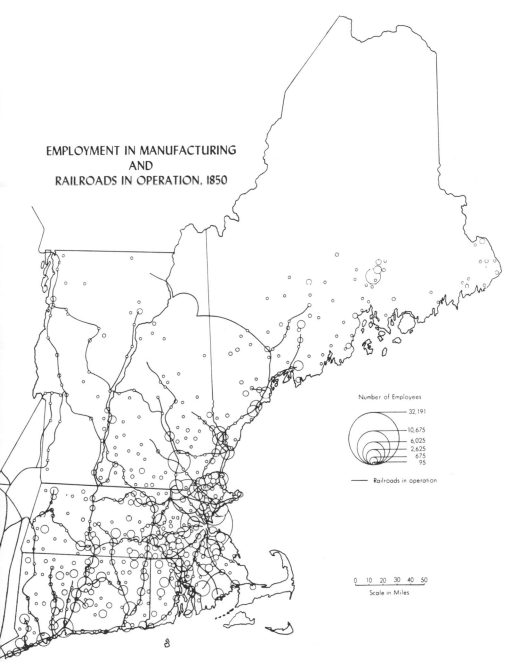

EMPLOYMENT IN MANUFACTURING
AND
RAILROADS IN OPERATION, 1850

Number of Employees

32,191
10,675
6,025
2,625
675
95

Railroads in operation

0 10 20 30 40 50
Scale in Miles

Map 4.3. Employment in manufacturing and railroads in operation: New England, 1850. Adapted from Robert G. Leblanc, *Location of Manufacturing in New England in the 19th Century,* Geography Publications at Dartmouth, no. 7 (Hanover, N.H., 1969), p. 88.

most urbanized states throughout the 1840–1860 period. The second reason was the unrivaled density and connectivity of the railroad network in Boston's hinterland, which was not approached elsewhere until near the end of the 1850s (maps 3.1–3.3). In addition, most of the towns and cities through which the network passed had some kind of manufacturing specialty that both required a wholesaling outlet and demanded nonlocal inputs (map 4.3). By 1860 the railroads in the Massachusetts portion of Boston's hinterland had reached a remarkably high annual level of business by the standards of the times. These lines, which distributed imported items in addition to moving domestic agricultural and industrial goods, received almost $10 million in revenues, freighted over 3.9 million tons, and carried almost 12.4 million passengers.[71] The third reason was that the unusually lengthy coastal component of Boston's hinterland not only provided the city with seafood to be consumed and traded but also facilitated the exchange of goods at low transportation costs.[72] Since employment multipliers were generated in Boston's wholesaling sector and related activities by the intense flow of hinterland goods to its railroad terminals and docks, and since hinterland demands led to similar multipliers in Boston and intense flows in the opposite direction, Boston's rich array of hinterland interdependencies involved the spread of "growth impulses" upward as well as downward through the urban hierarchy. Furthermore, the specialties of one hinterland center frequently moved to another hinterland center through an indirect route that involved Boston and its wholesaling houses, thus encouraging growth in that major center.

SELECTED ASPECTS OF PHILADELPHIA'S CITY-SYSTEM
INTERDEPENDENCIES

Many of the economic interdependencies characteristic of antebellum major centers are revealed by source materials relating to Philadelphia's trade in anthracite coal, manufacturing outputs, and manufacturing inputs.

The Anthracite Coal Trade. Philadelphia's anthracite coal trade of the 1840s and 1850s is the most important antebellum example of a set of U.S. city-system interdependencies based on a natural resource coming from the hinterland of a major center.

During the 1840–1860 period the U.S. demand for anthracite coal grew quickly. Demand was created by almost every manufacturing establishment employing a steam engine; by countless other production units in the iron, iron-working, glass, paper, and distilling industries that required fuel for heating or smelting purposes; by home usage in selected urban locations; by steamboats; and finally, to a lesser extent, by railroads. Consumption was stimulated by the increasing awareness of the long- and clean-burning attributes of anthracite, and by the fact that it was often "proving cheaper to use . . . than wood, charcoal, or Virginia and foreign bituminous."[73] Consequently, the production of anthracite mushroomed in Philadelphia's hinterland, increasing by a total of 873 percent between 1840 and 1860 (table A.14).[74] The shipment of anthracite from Philadelphia assumed such magnitude that from 1845 onward the tonnage capacity of the city's coal-carrying vessels exceeded that of vessels participating in New York's foreign trade. In 1851, for example, over 8,600 vessels—mostly schooners—were loaded at the city's Richmond coal port. Moreover, as a result of the anthracite trade, during the 1850s "Philadelphia possessed the nation's largest coastal commerce in terms of volume if not value."[75]

Most of the anthracite flowing to Philadelphia for wholesaling and forwarding as well as for local consumption came from the Schuylkill area, centered at Pottsville (1860 population, 9,444), and from a number of other smaller mining communities between 90 and 110 miles northwest of the Quaker City. Coal from the Schuylkill area, which reached Philadelphia by both the Reading Railroad and the Schuylkill Navigation Canal, consistently accounted for about 50 percent or more of all the hinterland anthracite coal sent to market during the 1840s and 1850s.[76] Shipments of coal from the Lehigh valley, the second major area of hinterland production, presented quite a different picture. Only a portion of its market shipments found their way to Philadelphia. In the late 1850s only about 5 percent of these shipments proceeded there by railroad. More important, anthracite shipments moving from Mauch Chunk (1860 population, 2,066) and other small mining towns in the Lehigh valley first went via the Lehigh Canal (or, after 1855, by the Lehigh Valley Railroad) to Easton, on the Delaware River. Some of these shipments then proceeded down the Delaware Division Canal to Philadelphia or to Bristol, where they turned upstream and into the Delaware and Raritan Canal, headed for New York. Other such shipments continued eastward across New Jersey via the Morris Canal to Jersey City, Newark, and New York City, as well as to intermediate canal locations of varying importance, such as Paterson (1860 population, 19,856) and Boonton (1860 population, less than 2,500). (The New Jersey Central Railroad also carried some of this traffic after 1852). In the early years the production of a third area, the coal fields around Scranton and Wilkes Barre (1860 populations 9,223 and 4,253 respectively), as well as of less populous mining centers somewhat farther down the Susquehanna River, was consumed "mainly" in nearby towns and cities, though some eventually arrived in Philadelphia, Baltimore, or New York via a string of canals. But after 1856 increasing quantities were sent toward New York from Scranton via the Delaware, Lackawanna and Western Railroad and either the Morris Canal or the New Jersey Central Railroad. Lastly, almost all the output of the most distant hinterland anthracite area, the Lackawanna field around Carbondale (1860 population, 5,090), went to New York via the Carbondale and Honesdale Railroad (and another feeder) and via the Delaware and Hudson Canal, which ran from Honesdale, near Carbondale, to the Hudson River at Rondout.[77]

If all of Philadelphia's hinterland anthracite areas except the most important, Schuylkill, are considered as a group, it can be argued that the city-system interdependencies of the variously sized mining centers in those areas were "complex" in the sense that each center had direct linkages with major (and minor) centers outside of Philadelphia's primary sphere of economic influence. They were also complex in the sense that coal flowed occasionally from small hinterland mining places to other hinterland urban places of comparable or larger size where it was needed for manufacturing. The second form of complexity also characterized Schuylkill production to a small degree; for some secondary anthracite shipments were made to Reading, whose 1860 population (23,162) far surpassed that of any of the Schuylkill mining places.[78] However, the existence of these complexities should not be taken to mean that employment- and income-multiplier effects did not occur in Philadelphia when anthracite was shipped from a hinterland mining center to its ultimate destination without passing through the Quaker City. Through their direct investment in anthracite mines, as well as their ownership of coal-carrying transportation facilities such as the Lehigh Canal, Philadelphia mercantile interests extracted profits that often were transferred to the local economy of that city. The profits to be made by Philadelphia entrepreneurs through direct sales and the provision of wholesaling and transportation services were often handsome, even if shipments were not physically handled in their city. In the mid-1850s, when the price of anthracite at the mine went as low as $2.00 per ton, the wholesaling price in Philadelphia ranged from $4.25 to $4.75 per ton, while the retail price elsewhere in the Northeast varied from $7.00 to $9.00 or more per ton, depending on the distance the coal had been transported.[79]

Of the numerous destinations to which the 50 percent or more of hinterland anthracite production actually was shipped from Philadelphia in any year, New York was clearly the most important. In 1845 the steam-boats departing from New York were alone generating a demand for from 160,000 to 180,000 tons of anthracite per year.[80] By 1849 the total demand in New York and those places to which it forwarded shipments stood at almost 670,000 tons. Nine years later this demand had more than tripled to nearly 2.25 million tons.[81] Despite the large quantities of anthracite arriving in New York via the Morris Canal, the Delaware and Hudson Canal, and the New Jersey Central Railroad, Philadelphia was the largest single supplier of the nation's most populous city. This supply was shipped mostly via the Delaware and Raritan Canal, and it accounted for almost 35 percent of all the Schuylkill coal that *arrived in* Philadelphia during 1850 and 1854 (table A.15). (In those years the Delaware and Raritan shipments to New York apparently accounted for a somewhat larger percentage of the total tonnage of anthracite *shipped from* Philadelphia; for, though the latter city received further, but unspecifiable, amounts of hinterland anthracite, its own homes and industries also consumed considerable quantities.)[82] Additional, indeter-minable quantities of anthracite moved from Philadelphia to New York by schooners, sloops, and other coastwise vessels by sailing around Cape May, New Jersey. This was especially so during the late 1840s, when coastwise vessels cut their freight rates sharply. Furthermore, during winter months some anthracite was transported from Philadel-phia to New York by way of the Camden and Amboy Railroad, which crossed New Jersey and provided through service with a steamboat connection.[83]

The significance of Boston as another recipient made intraregional large-city interdependencies as a group all the more prominent in Phila-delphia's anthracite coal trade. Boston wholesalers also acquired an-thracite and bituminous coals from such dissimilar places as Baltimore, Richmond, and the Rondout terminus of the Delaware and Hudson Canal, as well as from Great Britain, but their Philadelphia anthracite receipts normally accounted for 70 or more percent of the total coal tonnage purchased annually. Throughout the 1840s and early 1850s, Boston's anthracite imports from Philadelphia consistently corre-sponded to about 15 percent of all the Schuylkill coals that arrived in the Pennsylvania center (table A.16).[84]

Although Boston had become an "anthracite city" by the end of the 1830s, mainly by virtue of home usage and pioneering large-scale con-sumption in a glass works and in the rail-producing Bay State Iron Works, not all the Philadelphia coal that arrived there was used locally.[85] Boston coal dealers also supplied some inland hinterland centers, especially those with steam-powered textile mills. Lowell (whose factories consumed 12,500 tons in 1844 and 30,575 tons in 1852) and Worcester (whose production units used 4,000 tons in 1844) were the principal recipients of such shipments.[86] But a number of other New England locations with coal-consuming production units received anthracite directly from Philadelphia by coastwise or coastwise and riverine shipments. Among those places were centers as important as Providence, Hartford, and New Haven. Other recipients were Portland in Maine, Bridgeport in Connecticut, Newport in Rhode Island, Springfield, Fall River, Newburyport, and Salem in Massachusetts, and Portsmouth in New Hampshire, all intermediate-sized cities with 1860 populations of close to 10,000 or more. Even smaller urban places, such as Bristol, Rhode Island, and Middletown and Stonington, Connecticut (Stonington's 1860 population was below 2,500), obtained Philadelphia anthracite directly.[87] In short, the anthracite coal trade resulted in direct city-system interdependencies between Philadelphia and variously sized places that were unquestionably within the trading hinterlands of Boston and New York.[88]

Most of the remaining antebellum shipments of anthracite from Philadelphia resulted in large-city interdependencies both inside and beyond the Northeast. Baltimore acquired some anthracite directly from the Quaker City, although the quantities were apparently rather small compared to those arriving in Boston. (Not only could Baltimore dealers avoid Philadelphia and procure anthracite by the canals leading from the Susquehanna valley to Chesapeake Bay,[89] but with the aid of the Baltimore & Ohio Railroad they also could market the semibituminous coals that were available from the Cumberland field within Baltimore's own hinterland.)[90] During the 1850s a packet line between Philadelphia and Albany carried anthracite through to the latter city, and from there some shipments apparently continued onward to the gas works of Rochester. Even San Francisco, which had to be reached by way of Cape Horn, secured sizable quantities of anthracite, perhaps as much as 41,000 tons or more in 1860, although most or all of this went first from Philadelphia to New York before being borne by clippers to the Golden Gate.[91] However, little if any anthracite went to the major coastal centers of the South, largely because their climate did not promote high levels of household demand. Moreover, Richmond could more than satisfy its own industrial needs from the nearby bituminous coal seams that were worked twelve or more miles from the city. And whatever demand was engendered by the steam-powered sugar mills and steamboats of New Orleans apparently could be met by coals that had been floated down the Ohio and Mississippi rivers.[92] For several reasons the major river and lake centers of the Midwest also obtained little Philadelphia anthracite: western Pennsylvania coals were marketed from Pittsburgh; Mahoning valley coals were barged to Cleveland and from there forwarded to other Great Lakes centers; and a relatively small but growing output came from the central interior coalfields of Illinois and Indiana.

Manufacturing Outputs. As previously indicated, Philadelphia was one of the first major centers in the country whose economy began the transition from a situation in which income and employment were propagated principally by a complex of wholesaling-trading activities, to a situation in which local manufacturing was the leading source of jobs and capital accumulation. By the early 1840s Philadelphia was emerging as a production center of such capital goods as machine tools, steam engines, locomotives, and textile machinery. In contrast, the manufacturing of major centers dominated by a wholesaling-trading complex was almost entirely made up of "entrepôt," commerce-serving, and local-market-oriented activities.[93] When the census of 1850 was taken, Philadelphia's manufacturing was credited with employing close to 60,000 hands and turning out products with a total annual value above $64.1 million.[94] Ten years later, the percentage of Philadelphia's population employed in manufactuing (17.5) considerably exceeded that of all other U.S. major centers except Pittsburgh (18.0), Cincinnati (18.3), Richmond (19.0), Newark (26.2), and Lowell (35.9).[95] At that time, the Pennsylvania city had well over 98,000 people employed in manufacturing, which included forty-two branches of industry whose individual annual output surpassed $1.0 million (table A.17). Under these circumstances, it is evident that a substantial set of Philadelphia's city-system interdependencies involved the shipment of local manufacturing specialties.

Not surprisingly, urban places in Philadelphia's agricultural and mineral-rich hinterland were very important as destinations for its manufactures. At the beginning of the 1840–1860 period, perhaps as much as one-half of Philadelphia's industrial products were ultimately consumed by either the residents of hinterland urban places or the rural dwellers who journeyed to them in order to make purchases. Since the household sector generated most of the demand focused on hinterland towns and cities, manufacturing shipments from Philadelphia to such places, at least during the 1840s, were composed predominantly of clothing, textiles, processed foods, and beverages, shoes, hats, hardware, and earthenware. About 1840 such merchandise accounted for approximately 64 percent of the value of all the manufactured and nonmanufactured goods distributed by the various canals leading north and west from Philadelphia. Metals and metal products constituted only another 6.5 percent of such shipments. In keeping with central-place theory, hinterland-bound Philadelphia manufactures, unless consumed in its immediate vicinity, usually went to high-order places such as Columbia, Easton, Pottsville, York, and Reading (1860 populations ranging from 5,-007 to 23,162), where they were either sold to final-demand consumers or transshipped and forwarded to hinterland locations of lesser consequence. Although the relative (but not the absolute) significance of manufacturing-based linkages between Philadelphia and its hinterland apparently fell off to an increasing degree in the late 1840s and 1850s as Philadelphia's industries became more diversified and served more distant markets, the readily identifiable sources do not specify how far this decline had progressed by 1860.[96]

Despite the importance of hinterland destinations, a large share of the manufactured goods shipped from Philadelphia resulted in large-city interdependencies with the Northeast. Philadelphia's exports of manufactured and nonmanufactured goods to nonhinterland domestic locations and foreign locations grew from 25.1 to 47.3 million constant dollars between 1837 and 1851, and virtually all of that expansion can be attributed to increased shipments to major (and lesser) centers within the Northeast. More specifically, the share of all nonhinterland exports accounted for by northeastern destinations grew from 35 to 63 percent, with most shipments going to New York, Boston, or Baltimore "for their consumption or for reexport into their hinterlands" or to points beyond.[97]

Textiles and related products were, in terms of value, the most important Philadelphia manufactures marketed in New York and Boston. In 1860 it was reported that "carpets are largely consigned to New York [wholesalers], and jeans, checks, cottonades, and other standard descriptions of 'Philadelphia goods,' are now, as they have long been, sent in very large quantities both to New York and Boston." In that same year, goods worth about $2.0 million, or one-fourth of the value of "Philadelphia goods" production, went directly to commission houses in New York and Boston. In addition, Philadelphia wholesalers, who took roughly 6.0 million dollars' worth of such goods from local manufacturers, in turn reconsigned a goodly (but unspecified) share of their purchases to New York wholesaling merchants.[98]

Iron and iron products (such as rails, railroad car wheels and axles, machinery, and spikes), were probably the next most important group of Philadelphia manufactures sold in New York and Boston by specialized commission merchants.[99] In 1854, 37,000 tons of iron, with a pre-shipment value of at least $1,365,000 (and more likely about $2,000,000), were sent to New York through the Delaware and Raritan Canal. A few years later the Camden and Amboy Railroad was acting as a supplementary carrier of iron and iron goods toward New York, not only during those portions of the winter when the Delaware and Raritan Canal suspended its operations because of ice, but throughout the year.[100]

Among the more precisely defined Philadelphia industrial products that, by the late 1850s, appear to have gone to New York in larger quantities than to any other place were the following: chemicals of various sorts; watches and watch cases; cigars; millinery goods; scales and balances; wallpaper; starch; hand-powered fire engines; metal parts for umbrellas; bookbinders' tools and machinery; marbled paper; ornamental, or colored, printed items (labels, show bills, and so forth); silverware; saddle-trees; and whips. And even Philadelphia-produced bricks, which must have been costly to transport in relation to their value, seem to have been sold in significant quantities on the New York market.[101] Among the more specific Philadelphia manufactures for which Boston appears to have acted as the first or second largest nonlocal market were Morocco leather, railroad spark arresters, paper boxes, millinery goods, starch, bookbinders' tools and machinery, marbled paper, and wallpaper.[102]

Baltimore, too, had become established as a major destination for Philadelphia textiles before 1840. "By the late 1850s, Philadelphia's Board of Trade was lamenting the frequency with which the city's merchants exported their [textiles and other] goods destined for Southern consumption via [commission houses in] New York and Baltimore." Baltimore was also a very high-ranking destination for numerous Philadelphia industrial goods other than textiles, ranging in variety from watches and watch cases to safes.[103] Although Baltimore's dependence on the more populous Philadelphia for goods was consistent with Christallerian central-place models and related hierarchical diffusion models of city-system growth, the known movement of Baltimore manufactures in the opposite direction was not. Moreover, whereas the only other manufacturing interdependencies involving the four largest centers of the Northeast permitted by these models would have taken the form of flows from New York—the first-ranking city-system member—to Philadelphia, Boston, and Baltimore, in actuality there was a complex criss-crossing of both similar and highly specialized industrial shipments in both directions between every possible pair of these cities.[104]

Outside the Northeast, Pittsburgh was the leading antebellum recipient of Philadelphia's manufactured goods. The Philadelphia products arriving in Pittsburgh were consumed locally or sent onward by forwarding and commission agents either to the city's western Pennsylvania hinterland or to major centers along the Ohio and Mississippi rivers and around the Great Lakes, particularly in the 1850s when railroad connections were developed. Until through connections were provided between Philadelphia and Pittsburgh by the Pennsylvania Railroad in 1854, manufactures moved from the former to the latter city by the "mongrel" Pennsylvania Main Line of canals and railroads.[105] While the Main Line was carrying the Philadelphia-to-Pittsburgh traffic during the mid-1840s, the principal categories of shipment were "merchandise" (a catchall for textiles, shoes, hats, earthenware, glassware, hardware, and chinaware), bar and sheet iron, drugs and dyes, and leather (table A.18). (Significantly, in at least two of these categories westbound shipments arriving at Pittsburgh from Philadelphia were amplified by the direct receipt of output from places in Philadelphia's hinterland.)[106] When the Pennsylvania Railroad began to take over the Philadelphia-to-Pittsburgh trade, thus removing the en route transshipment costs of the Main Line, the tonnage of goods nearly doubled during a five-year span in the mid-1850s, rising to over 77,000 tons.[107] By the late 1850s, the variety of Philadelphia manufactures going to Pittsburgh in significant quantities was also somewhat greater, with machinery and castings being the most important newcomer category in terms of value. However, a single category, "dry goods," or textiles and clothing, stood out from the rest in terms of weight (table A.19). Just as was the case with the interdependencies between Philadelphia and New York, Boston, and Baltimore, a crisscrossing of manufacturing flows occurred. In 1858 Pittsburgh actually sent Philadelphia (in lesser quantities) twelve of the seventeen goods listed in table A.19, and in two other instances (glass and glassware, hemp and cordage) Pittsburgh's reverse-direction shipments were actually greater.[108]

It is difficult to ascertain the extent to which the sale of Philadelphia manufactures to other major centers in the West and South involved direct, as opposed to indirect, city-system interdependencies. It is known that Philadelphia manufacturers and their local wholesalers maintained or intermittently utilized commission agents in places such as New Orleans, Charleston, Mobile, St. Louis, and Cincinnati for the direct marketing of goods as diverse as drugs, iron wire, lamps and chandeliers, wagons, agricultural implements, and saddles and harnesses.[109] It is also known that during the 1850s, Philadelphia producers of items such as ornamental iron work, railroad equipment, carriages, safes, boxes, propeller engines for steamboats, and other kinds of steam engines filled orders directly placed from cities such as Richmond, New Orleans, Mobile, San Francisco, St. Louis, Buffalo, Chicago, and Cleveland. At the same time Philadelphia's coastwise vessels apparently delivered furniture, straw hats, and other local industrial outputs directly to the major ports of the South. In addition, retailers from major midwestern and southern centers made trips to Philadelphia to arrange for the direct purchase of textiles and other goods.[110] On the other hand, in the mid-1840s some Philadelphia manufactures reached major western centers via New Orleans middlemen, as well as through Pittsburgh forwarding agents. Furthermore, Fishlow has suggested that many of the Philadelphia industrial commodities reaching southern ports probably did so indirectly, first going through the hands of New York wholesalers and shippers. Indirect interdependence also characterized many of the sales made to Detroit; in 1857, for example, a newspaper of that city complained that local merchants purchased Philadelphia drugs, medicines, shoes, cotton fabrics, jewelry, leather, perfumes, "etc." in New York and Boston rather than buying such goods more cheaply at the source.[111]

On a presumably smaller but still widespread scale, the distribution of local manufactures led to direct city-system interdependencies between Philadelphia and nonhinterland intermediate- and smaller-sized urban places. This was true for some places in the Northeast as well as in the South and Midwest. Although many Philadelphia manufacturers allegedly were marketing "in every State in the Union" and others were supposedly shipping "to all parts of the West and South,"[112] it is clear that sales to nonhinterland cities and towns of medium or small size normally went indirectly by way of wholesalers in the major center that was most accessible to the ultimate point of consumption. Nevertheless, it is also evident that Philadelphia manufacturing flows, moving through local commission agents, coastwise shipping, and the direct fulfillment of special orders, resulted in direct nonhinterland interdependencies with many lesser places: some that had not attained a population of 2,500 by 1860 (for example, West Newton, Massachusetts, Salisbury, North Carolina, and Mankato, Minnesota); some small places that were in the 2,500–5,000 range by 1860 (for example, Monroe, Michigan, and Vicksburg, Mississippi); and some intermediate-sized cities that had 1860 populations in the vicinity of 20,000 (for example, Memphis, Tennessee, Columbus, Ohio, and New Bedford, Massachusetts).[113]

Manufacturing Inputs. Between 1850 and 1860 the consumption of raw materials by all Philadelphia industries burgeoned, even apparently doubled, to a total of over $72.3 million.[114] By 1860 there were twenty categories of manufacturing whose individual raw material costs exceeded $1.0 million and whose combined raw material costs accounted for 64 percent of all such costs incurred in the city (table A.20). The physical-input acquisition behavior of entrepreneurs associated with these twenty categories was on the whole rather simple. Many of these industrial branches confined their purchases of raw materials—aside from coal for fuel or power—largely to agricultural crops or animal products. This was true, for example, in the case of cotton goods, flour mills, sugar refineries, cured meats, and the various leather processing branches. Other branches (such as clothing, boots and shoes, and bread and crackers) acquired most of their raw materials in the form of a single processed good that had originated as an agricultural crop or animal product. Even the machinery industry, which needed many parts in order to assemble finished products, limited most of its input buying to rolled and unrolled pig iron and coal. This was the case because machine parts typically were produced by specialized laborers working in the same establishment where assembly was to take place. Such purchasing behavior was also characteristic of other segments of the iron products category. In short, this absence of extended "production systems" prevented the pattern of city-system interdependencies springing from raw material acquisition from being more complex.[115]

Some of the manufacturing branches listed in table A.20 were heavily dependent on local sources for their physical inputs. The boot and shoe branch, for instance, relied on local leather, the bread and cracker producers on local flour, and the clothing industry on local textiles. However, more typical of the Quaker City's manufacturing was a pronounced dependence upon hinterland input sources. After all, agricultural products, coal, and processed pig iron were the leading raw materials needed by all the other branches listed in the table, and Philadelphia's hinterland had a bountiful agricultural output (especially of grains), as well as rich anthracite resources and what was then the country's leading area of pig iron production. The procurement of rolled and unrolled pig iron illustrates the nature of these hinterland interdependencies.

Until the early 1840s, when there was a real spurt in hinterland production, wholesalers of foreign pig iron and iron goods had vied for the business of those Philadelphia manufacturers whose iron needs were not met by local output. But later, between 1846 and 1847, the volume of processed iron delivered to Philadelphia by canal and railroad from hinterland furnaces, rolling mills, and foundries jumped from just under 92,000 tons to almost 127,000 tons, whereas in the latter year less than 5,500 tons of imports arrived in Philadelphia. And by 1856, the Pennsylvania portion of Philadelphia's hinterland was producing over 360,000 tons, exclusive of rolled production, or 44.3 percent of the national total.[116]

As anthracite displaced charcoal in the manufacturing process, hinterland pig iron and rolling production became increasingly concentrated along canals and improved waterways at places such as Allentown, Easton, Wilkes Barre, Pottsville, Reading, Danville, Montour, Phoenixville, and Norristown (all in Pennsylvania), as well as in Trenton, New Jersey, and Wilmington, Delaware—places whose 1860 populations ranged from under 2,500 to over 23,000.[117] In most of these variously sized cities and towns, iron production was directly responsible for a significant share of the local job opportunities. Hence, a two-way growth relationship existed. As the economic health and population levels of these places depended in some measure upon the ability of Philadelphia's iron-consuming manufacturers to create demand, so also the employment scale and variety of Philadelphia's iron products and machinery industry were linked to the iron output capacity of these hinterland urban places. This should not suggest, however, that the iron production of hinterland centers went solely to Philadelphia. Secondary flows made matters somewhat more complex. The output of iron works in some hinterland places, if not locally consumed, went to industrial users in other hinterland places of similar or larger size. Some hinterland pig iron and iron products also went directly to manufacturers in Baltimore, Boston, and New York, as well as other places.[118]

Despite the natural wealth of Philadelphia's hinterland, the city's industrial branches that led in the purchase of raw materials had to secure some items from the middlemen of major centers both in the Northeast and in other parts of the country. Some of the domestic textiles and imported dry goods coming to Philadelphia from New York and Boston, and to a lesser extent from Baltimore, were dyed and printed after arrival, while others must have found their way into the Quaker City's clothing industry.[119] Copper, tin, and other secondary inputs were also obtained from New York, Boston, and Baltimore. Of the out-of-state coastwise and canal tonnage arriving in Philadelphia in 1851 with finished goods, industrial raw materials, and foodstuffs, something in the neighborhood of 68 percent came from New York, Boston, and Baltimore.[120] Through the agency of the Pennsylvania Railroad, which made the transmontane shipment of goods with a low value-per-unit weight more economical than had been the case with the Main Line, Pittsburgh wholesalers and forwarders in the late 1850s helped to provide Philadelphia manufacturers with inputs. Among these were cotton and wool for the city's textile plants, flour for its bread and cracker bakeries, grain for its flour mills, hides for its leather industries, livestock for its curing and packing establishments, and tallow for its soap and candle makers (table A.21).[121] Mobile, and especially Charleston and New Orleans, were key sources of cotton for Philadelphia's textile mills. New Orleans shipments of cotton to Philadelphia grew from about 6,200 bales in 1840 to 19,362 bales in 1853, and then fluctuated downward to below their 1840 level as the Civil War approached. Charleston's cotton exports to Philadelphia reached 19,118 bales in 1854–1855 and, though unstable, they were still close to that total in 1860.[122] New Orleans was also the only domestic sugar source of any significance for Philadelphia's sugar refiners. The quantities of raw sugar varied wildly with market conditions: for example, 21,804 hogsheads and 2,421 barrels in the year ending August 31,1846, but only 55 barrels during 1856–1857.[123] Among the other raw materials provided by major centers to Philadelphia were tobacco from Louisville for cigar production, and lead from St. Louis (usually via New Orleans) for paint manufacture.[124]

Although not nearly so significant, some direct interdependencies between Philadelphia and nonhinterland urban places of intermediate and small size did arise in connection with raw material procurement by its manufacturers. As many as 21,466 bales of cotton were obtained directly from Savannah in the shipping year 1855–1856, and lesser quantities of the same commodity were secured from the much smaller port of Apalachicola, Florida.[125] Also, Philadelphia wholesalers acquired sheet brass from Waterbury, Connecticut (1860 population, 10,004), and rivets from Plymouth, Massachusetts (1860 population less than 2,500), for the use of local locomotive and machinery producers as well as other manufacturers.[126] As a further example, Philadelphia shipbuilders secured naval stores (for caulking purposes) and some of their timber directly from places such as Wilmington, Washington, and New Bern, North Carolina, and Jacksonville and Pensacola, Florida (1860 populations from under 2,500 to 9,522).[127]

BUFFALO'S LAKE ARRIVALS IN 1851

As coastal, river, or lake ports, most antebellum major centers were involved in various types of city-system interdependencies associated with the break-in-bulk or transshipment of goods of hinterland, intraregional, interregional, or foreign origin. Several of Boston's and Philadelphia's interdependencies partly or totally fall into this more general category of interdependencies moored to wholesaling and forwarding activities. A snapshot of lake shipments arriving in Buffalo during 1851 provides an unusually broad panorama of such break-in-bulk and transshipment-related interdependencies. That snapshot covers no less than 134 different classes of commodities (worth $27 million) that were dispatched from thirty-three domestic ports around the Great Lakes.[128]

At least three facts should be kept in mind in interpreting the scope and complexity of the city-system interdependencies revealed by the 1851 Buffalo snapshot. First, not all the goods arriving at Buffalo on lake-going vessels from the Midwest were destined to be wholesaled and forwarded to points farther east. Some of the arriving foodstuffs and other items were eventually to be retailed to Buffalo's own population; and a portion of some goods was consumed by local manufacturing establishments, such as flour mills and distilleries, which bought grains in significant quantities, and shipyards, which bought timber and iron.[129] Second, the snapshot reflects nothing of the city-system interdependencies resulting either from the forwarding of goods to New York, Boston, Rochester, Albany plus Troy, and other northeastern urban places, or from the acquisition of manufactures and other goods from those places for wholesaling and forwarding in the opposite direction. Third and finally, there is no indication of the ultimate midwestern destinations of goods received by railroad and the Erie Canal from the Northeast. Yet in 1851 almost 205,000 tons of goods, valued at $44.2 million, were forwarded from Buffalo to U.S. and Canadian ports on the Great Lakes.[130]

By 1851, Buffalo's jobbers, commission merchants, and forwarding houses had used a number of means to compound that city's original advantage as the terminus of the Erie Canal. They had exploited their telegraphic connections so as to keep abreast of grain price changes in northeastern centers. They had begun using the as yet unintegrated railroads paralleling the Erie Canal, particularly during winter months.[131] They had usurped the marketing function of the Erie Canal's boat lines at a time when canal and rail feeders to Lake Erie and Lake Michigan were increasing in number. They had consolidated and perpetuated business affiliations with their counterparts farther to the west, especially through the provision of credit and financial arrangements with the Northeast.[132] As a result of all this, Buffalo had established itself as one of the country's leading wholesaling centers in general, and as "the most important produce market west of New York City" in particular, with "the principal part of the city's [almost 50,000] inhabitants being employed in occupations more or less closely connected with the commerce of the lakes and canals."[133] The commercial position secured for Buffalo by her merchants is mirrored by the fact that the value of lake shipments arriving there had increased by more than 73 percent between 1846 and 1851. In the next year, too, the value of such commerce apparently grew by roughly another 42 percent, and by the mid-1850s Buffalo's lake trade was being supplemented by all-rail shipments from the West.[134]

For twenty-five of the thirty principal commodity classes arriving in Buffalo by lake from domestic sources during 1851, more than half the value was accounted for by the major midwestern centers of Chicago, Cleveland, Detroit, and Milwaukee and by the quickly expanding city of Toledo (1850 population, 3,829).[135] Vessels from these same five cities delivered almost 65 percent of the total value of all domestic commodities reaching the western New York port by lake (table A.22).

As the writings of Clark and others indicate,[136] Buffalo's lake-originating interdependencies with intraregional major centers were dominated by flour, grains, and other farm products. However, sawed lumber worth almost $1.0 million was the single most important good arriving from Detroit, and smelted copper (almost entirely from Cleveland and Detroit) and iron products (mainly from Cleveland) also were unloaded in significant quantities. Moreover, a variety of manufactured goods, such as paper, carriages, furniture, glassware, pig lead, paints, machines, reapers, and hardware came to Buffalo either from other leading centers on the Great Lakes or from Toledo. These last-named manufactured goods are not itemized in table A.22 because in no instance did their value exceed $100,000.[137]

The prevalence of large-city interdependencies in Buffalo's lake trade was not peculiar to 1851, but characterized the entire 1840–1860 period. In 1840, before Chicago and Milwaukee had attained much stature, Cleveland clearly held the leading position in Buffalo's Great Lakes shipping pattern, with Detroit occupying second place. By 1841 one regular line of eight steamboats ran between Chicago and Buffalo, and by 1845 three lines were in operation.[138] In both relative and absolute terms, there was a strengthening of the already strong economic linkages between Buffalo and Chicago, whose agricultural hinterland had recently been widened by the Illinois and Michigan Canal and by railroad construction. In fact, during the years immediately succeeding 1851, "more than half of Chicago's exports of wheat and corn went to Buffalo, while more than 50 per cent of the wheat and 65 percent of the corn entering Buffalo's harbor came from Chicago."[139] As a result of railroad-based hinterland expansion, commodity flows from Milwaukee to Buffalo also grew considerably more intense after 1851, with the Wisconsin port rising to the position of Buffalo's second most important wheat supplier by the mid-1850s.[140] And by 1860, although dropping off in relative importance, the absolute volume of wheat shipments eastward from Detroit also increased noticeably. Only the tonnage of Cleveland's grain flows to Buffalo declined in the final antebellum years. This occurred partly because new railroads reduced Cleveland's agricultural hinterland (by allowing goods to move directly eastward from the central part of Ohio), and partly because these same railroads carried some of the Ohio city's receipts toward the Northeast instead of allowing them to move by boat to Buffalo. However, the reduced flow of grains toward Buffalo also reflected a shift within Cleveland's immediate hinterland (the Western Reserve) away from the cultivation of wheat, for which conditions were unsatisfactory, toward "dairying, the manufacture of cheese, and other types of farming."[141] This in turn presumably meant that, by 1860, cheese and other foodstuffs were shipped in greater volume from Cleveland to Buffalo. Finally, because of production increases, the movement of iron and copper products from Cleveland and Detroit to Buffalo also appears to have grown significantly after 1851.

The prominent contribution of Toledo to Buffalo's intraregional city-system interdependencies in 1851, despite that city's unimposing population, was in keeping both with its strategic location at the terminus of a crucial canal system and with its later rapid progress through the size ranks of the coalescing midwestern city-system. Toledo's population increase of nearly 10,000 between 1850 and 1860 allowed it to advance from thirty-second to fifteenth position among all urban places in the Midwest, and from ninth to sixth position among all ports located on the shores of Lakes Erie, Huron, and Michigan.[142] During the 1840s Toledo merchants and shippers had begun to act as large-scale forwarders to Buffalo of agricultural produce and other goods, first as a result of the completion of the Wabash and Erie Canal in 1842, and latter because of the completion of the Miami Extension Canal in 1845. The Wabash and Erie gave Toledo access to flour, wheat, corn, and pork, not only from western Ohio but, more important, from farms located along and near the upper reaches of Indiana's Wabash valley that had formerly dispatched their vast surplus output to New Orleans via flat-boat. The Miami Extension Canal, which linked up with the Wabash and Erie at Defiance, Ohio, and the older Miami Canal at Dayton, enabled Toledo to acquire grains from Dayton northward and beef and pork from Piqua northward, and thereby to tap areas that formerly had been solely within Cincinnati's hinterland.[143]

It is of more than passing interest that, to a secondary but significant degree, the 4.2 million dollars' worth of Toledo-to-Buffalo commodity flows summarized in table A.22 serve as a mask for indirect large-city interdependencies between Buffalo and Cincinnati. For example, all or most of the tobacco valued at over $128,000 that moved from Toledo to Buffalo in 1851 had been procured via canal from Cincinnati processors, wholesalers, and forwarders. Lard oil and other pork products, corn, whiskey, flour, flax, hemp, and sugar, as well as diverse manufactures and other items, are also known to have traveled from Cincinnati to Toledo to Buffalo about this time.[144]

Not surprisingly, port centers in Buffalo's own immediate hinterland along the shores of Lake Erie provided shipments that were either to be sent onward by jobbers, commission merchants, or forwarding houses, or to be consumed within Buffalo itself. Four such places, the relatively insignificant towns of Silver Creek and Barcelona, New York, the somewhat more substantial town of Dunkirk, New York (1850 population less than 2,500), and Erie, Pennsylvania (1850 population 5,858),[145] generated commodity flows from the hinterland to the dominant center. However, only the flows originating in Erie were of significant size. In terms of both physical quantity and value, sawed lumber was the most important element in the Erie-Buffalo trade, with close to ten million board feet worth roughly $1.07 million being shipped in 1851. (This was equivalent to about 23 percent of the value of all domestic sawed lumber arriving by lake in Buffalo that year.)[146] During the same year, other leading items dispatched from Erie and unloaded at Buffalo included wool ($149,040, or 4.05 percent of Buffalo's domestic wool arrivals by lake), cheese ($96,010, or about 27.73 percent of Buffalo's domestic cheese receipts by lake), and iron (about $44,600, or 42.18 percent of Buffalo's iron acquisitions by lake), as well as oats, butter, sheepskins, flour, and glassware.[147]

On the whole, however, smaller cities and towns within the immediate hinterlands of other major Great Lakes centers were much more important commodity sources for Buffalo's businessmen in 1851 than were the four ports within the city's own immediate hinterland. This is best illustrated by the flow of sawed lumber—the single most highly valued commodity received at Buffalo—from seventeen nonhinterland places, most of which had populations below 2,500. The combined value of the sawed lumber shipments from these places within the immediate hinterlands of Cleveland, Detroit, and Chicago was nearly $2.3 million (table A.23), or very close to half the value of all the domestic sawed lumber freighted to Buffalo by lake, and 8.5 percent of the value of all domestic commodities arriving at Buffalo by the same means. Many of these lesser ports, and additional centers within the immediate hinterlands of Milwaukee and Chicago, provided Buffalo with varying quantities of agricultural products whose aggregate value, though far less than that of similar shipments from Chicago, Cleveland, Detroit, Milwaukee, and Toledo, was still significant. Wheat, wool, flour, and corn were the most important of these items, which came either from within a small radius of the shipping points[148] or from areas reached by railroad, as in the cases of Sandusky, Ohio, and Monroe, Michigan (table A.24).[149]

It is worth noting that the full range of interdependencies arising from the 1851 shipment of sawed lumber, agricultural products, and other goods from nonhinterland smaller cities and towns to Buffalo would not be considered possible by the proponents of the hierarchical diffusion models of growth within city-systems. Such would be the case even if it were conceded that Buffalo (New York State's gateway to the West) was at the time larger than any major center on the Great Lakes (table 2.1) and was therefore hierarchically dominant over all medium- and small-sized urban places around those lakes. For if one adopts a conventional view of hierarchical dominance, one must deny the possibility of commodities moving from any lesser urban center to any large, or major, center that dominates it. Moreover, any conception of city-system interdependencies based upon such a hierarchical-dominance stance would have to deny the possibility of all the flows from Chicago, Detroit, Milwaukee, and Toledo to Buffalo that have just been described.

SOME GENERAL CHARACTERISTICS OF CINCINNATI'S CITY-SYSTEM INTERDEPENDENCIES

During the last two antebellum decades, Cincinnati's economy underwent vigorous growth and development, despite some downward swings that were for the most part reflective of national trends. The local manufacturing sector, which had been led by the packing and processing of pork and its by-products in 1840, continued to emphasize those activities over the next twenty years while simultaneously becoming specialized in the production of clothing, furniture, iron products, whiskey and other alcoholic beverages, and an assortment of other goods destined primarily for nonlocal markets. By taking advantage of the tremendous expansion of western markets, the increasing availability of iron and coal, and the city's improved canal and railroad connections (especially with western Ohio, Indiana, Illinois, Wisconsin, and Missouri, as delineated in maps 3.1–3.3), the industrial capitalists of Cincinnati and its Kentucky suburbs of Covington and Newport reputedly were able to propel the aggregate value of their output from $17.8 million in 1841, to $54.6 million in 1851, and to $112.3 million in 1859.[150] The mounting contribution of industrial activities to the growth of Cincinnati is also captured by the 1860 employment statistics, which put the manufacturing work force at 18.3 percent of the city's population, or at a higher level than that of any other major center in the Midwest.[151] As for the Queen City's wholesaling-trading sector, over the 1840–1860 period businessmen also multiplied the scale at which they turned over goods of nonlocal and local origin. The sales of dry goods to country merchants soared from $4.0 million in 1840, to $10.0 million in 1850, and to $25.0 million in 1859. After falling off from an 1848 high, the value of all goods sold beyond the city by Cincinnati wholesalers and forwarders fluctuated upward from over $30.0 million in 1850 to, at the very least, an estimated $77.0 million in 1860. At the same time Cincinnati middlemen increasingly attracted out-of-town retailers who previously had made their annual or semiannual purchasing trips to New York or other major northeastern centers. Furthermore, Cincinnati established itself as the fifth largest primary grain-receiving point in the country; and the value of all commodities shipped into the city climbed, with intermittent descents, from $9.1 million in 1840, to $41.3 million in 1852, and to $96.2 million by 1859.[152]

Because of the diversity and changing composition of Cincinnati's growing economy, most of the functional types of city-system interdependencies already depicted in the snapshots of Boston, Philadelphia, and Buffalo were clearly discernible for all or much of the 1840s and 1850s. More precisely, Cincinnati was involved in separate sets of city-system interdependencies associated with the wholesaling and shipping of hinterland agricultural products, the marketing of hinterland manufacturing specialties, the distribution of hinterland natural resources, the sale of local manufacturing specialties, the acquisition of physical inputs for local manufacturing, the securement of investment capital and financial services, the nonhinterland procurement of foodstuffs for local consumption and forwarding, and more generally, the break-in-bulk and transshipment of goods (including industrial products) of intraregional, interregional, and foreign origin.

Interdependencies with Other Major Centers. Taken as a whole, intraregional and interregional linkages with other major centers were the most prominent characteristics of Cincinnati's antebellum city-system interdependencies. As long as railroads did not effectively compete with steamboats for long-distance commodity traffic, Cincinnati's most important interdependencies within the Midwest apparently were with Pittsburgh, St. Louis, and Louisville; and her most important interregional city-system ties were with New Orleans. The validity of such an assertion may not be immediately apparent from the statistics showing that New Orleans, Pittsburgh, and St. Louis together only accounted for roughly 35 to 40 percent of all the steamboats arriving at, and departing from, Cincinnati during the late 1840s, and for about 25 to 35 percent of those totals during the mid-1850s after railroad competition had set in (table A.25). However, those statistics fail to separate out a sizable number of Louisville shipments from other nonhinterland and hinterland shipments. Moreover, the statistics are deceptive inasmuch as they equate all steamboat arrivals and departures with one another, whereas in reality the boats employed on the longer interurban runs to and from Cincinnati were generally much larger than those used on shorter hauls to and from points along the upper Ohio and its tributaries.[153] A more convincing suggestion of the preeminence of Cincinnati's large-city interdependencies is provided by 1850–1851 data, which reveal that, for most major commodities other than iron, well over half the quantity shipped from the Queen City by all means of transportation was destined initially for New Orleans (table A.26).[154]

As can be surmised from the observations usually made on the reorientation of agricultural flows from the West to the Northeast following the opening of trans-Allegheny rail routes, the significance of New Orleans in Cincinnati's overall pattern of city-system interdependencies was much diminished by 1860 (see table A.2). As late as 1854, "considerable quantities of farm produce from Cincinnati continued to seek New Orleans. In 1855 this traffic almost vanished. In the early 1850s Cincinnati furnished New Orleans with some 30 to 35 percent of her flour . . . In 1854 this had dropped to 17 percent, and the annual average for 1855–61 was 4 percent, while in 1857 less than 20 percent" of New Orleans's pork and lard receipts originated in the Queen City.[155] Nevertheless, until close to the outbreak of the Civil War, New Orleans retained a not unimportant position within the matrix of Cincinnati's economic relationships. Cincinnati, which had emerged as one of the country's major centers of "grocery" distribution during the 1840s, was able to maintain that role due to its persistently large imports of high-value sugar and molasses, obtained virtually entirely from New Orleans, and foreign coffee, acquired at least partly from New Orleans middle-men (table A.27).[156] In 1859, New Orleans was still one of the main out-lets for manufactures produced or sold in Cincinnati. Furniture and whiskey shipments to New Orleans from Cincinnati for the year ending August 31, 1859, were alone worth approximately $708,000 and $1,301,000 respectively.[157] Iron foundry products and doors and other building materials also moved over the same river route. And "so far as lard oil and star candles are concerned, it seems that Cincinnati pos-sessed such a monopoly in their manufacture that it shipped practically all the New Orleans receipts."[158] Moreover, although the absolute vol-ume of Cincinnati–to–New Orleans pork shipments had dropped sub-stantially, it still had a value of roughly $1,879,000 during the shipping year 1858–1859.[159]

As the antebellum era neared its end, the absolute magnitude of Cin-cinnati's intraregional interdependencies with St. Louis and Pittsburgh grew rather than declined, despite the establishment of important eco-nomic links between the Queen City and other major midwestern cen-ters following the transportation developments of the early 1850s. (The percentage falloff in Pittsburgh-Cincinnati steamboat traffic shown in table A.25 does not reflect diminished commodity flows between the two places but a partial shift to rail shipments.) The two-way trade be-tween St. Louis and Cincinnati was somewhat further facilitated by the opening of the Ohio and Mississippi Rail Road in 1856. That trade was dominated by the west-to-east movement of lead (about 208,000 dollars' worth in 1850–1851) and various agricultural surpluses, and the east-to-west carriage of iron, stoves and other foundry products, whiskey, furni-ture, and locally produced clothing.[160] Among the leading goods moving from Pittsburgh to Cincinnati by regularly scheduled packets, by other steamboat arrangements, or by rail were coal, lumber, glass, pig iron, nails, and northeastern manufactures. The flows in the opposite di-rection (much of which were forwarded to Philadelphia and beyond) consisted mainly of pork and pork products, grains, and whiskey.[161]

Although Cincinnati's trade with Louisville also continued to be im-portant through the 1850s, its relative significance gradually slumped far below what it had been in 1840. Pork products, men's wear, other local industrial goods, and northeastern manufactures were among the principal items sent to the Kentucky center, while forwarded cotton and tobacco and locally processed tobacco and hemp topped the list of received items.[162]

Once long-distance commodity traffic by railroad became possible over several lines during the 1850s, Cleveland and Chicago joined the roster of major centers having notable intraregional economic linkages with Cincinnati. After the inauguration of through rail service between Cincinnati and Cleveland in 1851, large quantities of processed pork and bacon moved from the former to the latter place, as did less impressive amounts of flour, wheat, groceries, and Cincinnati manufactures.[163] (Much of the freight arriving thus in Cleveland was sent onward by its forwarders and wholesalers all the way to New York—either by lake and then canal or railroad, or, after 1857, by an all-rail route—while a smaller number of forwarded shipments were unloaded at the major centers of Buffalo, Rochester, and Albany plus Troy.) The rail connection with Cleveland also provided Cincinnati's middlemen with a new source for the acquisition of butter, cheese, and industrial products from the Northeast and abroad. The shipment of manufactures from Cleveland to Cincinnati usually meant increased indirect intraregional interdependencies with Buffalo, just as had been the case earlier with interregional industrial imports from Toledo via the Miami Extension Canal.[164] The completion of various rail routes to Chicago during the final antebellum years enabled Cincinnati's clothing-producing entrepreneurs and wholesalers of northeastern and foreign manufactures to carry on a brisk business with the Illinois city. By 1860 a combination of lines also made rail shipment from Cincinnati to Detroit at least theoretically feasible, but there is no readily apparent evidence that this alternative had an immediate impact on the relatively low level of intraregional interdependence already existing between those two major centers via Lake Erie and the Miami Extension Canal.[165]

As has already been suggested with respect to the Cincinnati-Pittsburgh and Cincinnati-Cleveland flows of goods, sizable interdependencies existed between the Queen City on the one hand and New York, Philadelphia, Baltimore, and Boston on the other. Also, as can be concluded both from the conventional literature on the antebellum reorientation of foodstuff flows from the West to the Northeast[166] and from the description of altered Cincinnati–New Orleans interdependencies, the interregional transport of pork products, flour, beef, and whiskey from Cincinnati to the four largest major centers of the Northeast went largely via New Orleans until 1853. Then, with the opening of the Pennsylvania Railroad to Pittsburgh and the Baltimore and Ohio to Wheeling, flows were set in motion that were to be subsequently encouraged by the integration of those trunk lines with Ohio railroads and by rate competition.[167] Although no precise figures are available on foodstuff shipments made separately from Cincinnati to New York, Philadelphia, Baltimore, and Boston, there is abundant indirect evidence to support such a conclusion.

As long as Cincinnati was clearly New Orleans's main supplier of pork products and other major processed and unprocessed agricultural goods, the Louisiana center shipped large amounts of such goods to New York, Philadelphia, Baltimore, and Boston. However, when the Cincinnati-to-New Orleans traffic in foodstuffs dwindled, so did the corresponding traffic totals from New Orleans to the leading northeastern cities (table A.28).[168] Furthermore, the percentage of Cincinnati's agriculturally based exports moving to unspecified northeastern and midwestern destinations by railroad and canal expanded very quickly just as Cincinnati-to-New Orleans flows were shrinking. In 1851, a mere 1 percent of the flour shipped by Cincinnati dealers went via railroad and canal to northeastern and intraregional points (table A.26). By 1854, that figure had risen to 27 percent, with canal movements "a minor factor," and one year later the same figure shot up to 62 percent. In a similar manner, by "1857 some 55 to 65 per cent of pork and lard exports were shipped by railroad from Cincinnati," as compared to roughly 5 to 10 percent some six years earlier.[169] (Neither for flour nor for pork products do the increasing percentages include any shipments that proceeded by steamboat to Wheeling or Pittsburgh before making their way to New York, Philadelphia, Baltimore, and Boston by rail.) Furthermore, "during 1850–52, only 8 per cent of Cincinnati beer and 15 per cent of her whiskey went directly to eastern ports; by 1860 the proportions were 30 and 33 per cent, respectively." It should also be noted that with increasing railroad usage, the quantity of raw cotton and wool assembled in Cincinnati for transshipment to major northeastern centers "grew rapidly."[170]

The commodities reaching Cincinnati by various routes from the Northeast's four largest cities were characteristically of high value per unit of weight. In aggregate terms dry goods were far and away the most valuable of such commodities. Cincinnati's receipts of packaged merchandise, the "great bulk" of which consisted of dry goods, mushroomed from $13.0 million in 1852 to $40.0 million in 1860, chiefly as a result of purchases from wholesaling houses in New York, Philadelphia, and Baltimore. Among other items of significance were boots and shoes from Boston (table A.7), imported metals and foreign and domestic industrial goods from New York, miscellaneous manufactures from Philadelphia, coffee from Boston, Baltimore, and Philadelphia, and oysters from Baltimore.[171] In addition, banks and investors in Boston, New York, and Philadelphia not only shifted capital to Cincinnati for pork-processing establishments, transportation facilities, and other investment projects, but also provided exchange and other financial services on a large scale for the Ohio city's commercial community.[172]

Other Nonhinterland and Hinterland Interdependencies. Although there is little doubt about the primacy of Cincinnati's two-way economic relationships both with other major centers within the Midwest and with more populous major centers outside that region, interdependencies with towns and cities within the Queen City's own hinterland were also of considerable importance. A great deal of the export business conducted with other major centers by the representatives of Cincinnati's manufacturing and wholesaling-trading sectors rested upon their acquisition of goods from small and medium-sized urban places within the city's immediate sphere of economic influence. Chief among these acquisitions were hogs, grains, other farm products, and the output of food-processing plants and other manufacturing units. Likewise, the merchants of towns and cities in Cincinnati's hinterland also purchased a good portion of the major-center imports and local manufactures wholesaled from that place. (Cincinnati's hinterland is generally considered to have encompassed a trading area with a radius of between about 100 and 150 miles, including much of southwestern Ohio, southeastern Indiana, and northern Kentucky.)[173]

Economic interaction between Cincinnati and its hinterland urban units was facilitated by short canals and railroads, many of which eventually connected with lengthier transportation works such as the Miami Extension Canal and the Cleveland, Columbus & Cincinnati Railroad. The Miami Canal, which at first operated only sixty-six miles north to Dayton, provided a highly significant share of Cincinnati's agricultural imports (for example, almost 66 percent of total flour receipts in the peak year of 1851), until railroad competition reduced its role to a secondary one (sending ony 73,000 barrels, or 12.4 percent of total flour receipts, in 1859).[174] The Little Miami Railroad, which opened over a tiny stretch in 1841 and attained its full length of eighty-four miles to Springfield in 1846, was the most important of the short railroads penetrating northward into Cincinnati's hinterland. Shortly after its completion this line alone was able to supply Cincinnati with 23 percent of its flour receipts, 17 percent of its whiskey imports, and 15 percent of its grain acquisitions.[175] Later the Little Miami's traffic was further amplified when it was linked with the Mad River & Lake Erie Railroad to Sandusky.

By 1860, Springfield, Hamilton, and Xenia, Ohio, Madison, Indiana, and a number of other places within Cincinnati's hinterland had close to 5,000 or more inhabitants. Two other hinterland centers, Dayton and Columbus, had reached population levels of 20,081 and 18,554 respectively, which placed them among the nation's largest intermediate-sized cities. The size levels acquired by each of these places depended in considerable measure upon the volume of commercial services each place was able to provide to its changing subhinterland, and upon the degree of nodality each had secured within the area's rapidly ramifying railroad network. Size levels also depended upon the presence or absence of interregional trunk routes, and the scale and mix of agricultural processing industries and other manufacturing activities that had been developed by local capital.[176] However, as was the case with Boston's and Philadelphia's hinterland urban places, the employment opportunities and population levels of these places also were dependent upon the effectiveness of Cincinnati's wholesaling and forwarding establishments in both exporting agricultural and industrial surpluses and importing goods for eventual distribution by hinterland merchants.

Cincinnati's economic interactions with small and medium-sized urban places were not confined to its own hinterland; they also included origins and destinations that were plainly within the hinterlands of St. Louis, Chicago, New Orleans, Louisville, and other major centers. For example, by the late 1850s if not earlier, iron products, furniture, building materials, and clothing from Cincinnati were being shipped directly to cities such as Memphis and Nashville, Tennessee, Keokuk, Iowa, Evansville, Indiana, and numerous other places that were not major centers and that were situated either on a river—the upper or lower Mississippi, the lower Ohio, the Missouri, the Illinois, the Tennessee, or the Cumberland—or along the newly constructed midwestern railroads.[177] Likewise, flour, pork products, and whiskey moved directly to lesser ports in Mississippi and Arkansas as well as to smaller and medium-sized places in other states throughout the Midwest and South.[178] At the same time, Cincinnati wholesalers acquired cotton, iron, and other goods directly from Memphis, Nashville, and a variety of other locations, including some as far away as northwestern Georgia.[179]

The pattern of city-system interdependence associated with Cincinnati and its hinterland became even more complex during the 1850s, when canal connections and railroad trunk lines enabled some foodstuffs to be transported from Dayton, Columbus, and other hinterland cities and towns directly to Cleveland and to the principal major north-eastern centers without ever passing through the Queen City. (Prior to that period, too, several Ohio River ports within Cincinnati's hinterland had made some foodstuff shipments to New Orleans and Pittsburgh that did not involve the services of Cincinnati's wholesalers and for-warders.) Moreover, the railroad trunk lines permitted some manufac-tures to be shipped and marketed directly from New York, Philadel-phia, Baltimore, Boston, and other northeastern centers to hinterland urban places without ever going through the hands of Cincinnati mid-dlemen. Finally, some manufacturing specialties were sent from one hinterland urban place to another; and Dayton and Springfield, and perhaps other hinterland centers, shipped local industrial products to various nonhinterland locations in the Midwest.[180]

CHARLESTON'S IMPORT AND EXPORT OF STAPLES

In comparison with the economy of Cincinnati or of other major cen-ters in the Midwest and Northeast, Charleston's economy during the 1840s and 1850s was characterized by a rather limited range of activities and a relative failure to diversify. The wholesaling-trading complex of the South Carolina city, though very much involved in the overseas ex-port of staples, was comparatively inactive in the import of foreign goods. This situation apparently arose for at least three reasons. First, the local jobbers and importers had difficulty in providing their poten-tial customers with long-term credits similar to those offered by com-petitors from New York and elsewhere in the Northeast. A second con-tributing factor was the unhealthy and uncomfortable summer heat, which encouraged local and hinterland retailers and planters to com-bine business with pleasure by journeying to New York to replenish their stocks. Third, local importing activities were discouraged by the wide fluctuations in cotton prices, which led to great year-to-year varia-tions in the ability of planters to make purchases.[181] (Between 1843 and 1845 the value of Charleston's direct foreign imports averaged only 13.6 percent of the value of international shipments from that port. Twelve years later the values had roughly doubled, but direct foreign imports were still only 12.8 percent of overseas exports.[182] Moreover, almost all of Charleston's foreign and domestic trade was carried in nonlocally owned vessels.)[183] In addition, Charleston was the least industrial of the country's major centers, with only 2.1 percent of its population em-ployed in manufacturing activities in 1860.[184]

Except for a very modest railroad-car industry and five comparatively small machinery-producing establishments, in 1860 Charleston's diminutive manufacturing sector was apparently still composed mainly of very small-scale staple-processing facilities and of locally oriented production units in branches such as brickmaking and the custom-made output of boots and shoes.[185] A long list of reasons has been put forth by nineteenth-century observers and twentieth-century scholars in the attempt to explain this extremely low level of industrial commitment. The following factors, among others, have been proposed: (1) conservative attitudes toward joint undertakings and new enterprises in general; (2) a more specific view, held by much of the planter aristocracy, that manufacturing was ungentlemanly, "incompatible with liberty, freedom, culture, and virtue," a threat to the existing social order—especially if practiced in cities—and thereby unworthy of investment; (3) a related deficiency of capital (Charleston's merchants and bankers even appeared to prefer out-of-state investments to local manufacturing); (4) a limited potential market owing to the low level of urbanization in Charleston's hinterland, and the inadequate purchasing power of the hinterland rural majority—slaves, subsistence farmers, and poor whites; (5) opposition to the use of slave labor for manufacturing purposes when it was more profitable to employ such labor in plantation agriculture (it is estimated that 10,000 Charleston slaves were sold during the 1850s when cotton prices returned to high levels); (6) the often poor quality of local goods; (7) a widespread preference for "Yankee goods," especially among fashion-sensitive women; (8) local ordinances restricting the use of steam engines to certain locations and circumstances; (9) a shortage of white labor, stemming largely from the extremely low status ascribed to industrial workers and the failure of the city to attract many skilled immigrants; (10) production units that were often poorly constructed and inadequately equipped and therefore could not survive very long; (11) the absence of local water power; and (12) "internal [intraregional] transportation difficulties."[186] Whatever the relative merits of these various reasons, some combination of them severely curtailed the volume of manufacturing not only in Charleston but also in its hinterland. In fact, "except for the state of Florida [in 1860], South Carolina ranked lowest in the annual value of industrial products among the commonwealths to the east of the Appalachian Mountains."[187]

Because very few of Charleston's city-system interdependencies were generated either by the movement of local and hinterland manufacturing specialties or by the acquisition of raw-material inputs for local and hinterland industrial establishments, and because its wholesale-trading

sector was very much oriented toward foreign exports, Charleston's antebellum interdependencies within the U.S. system of cities were dominated by two sets of relationships. One was the wholesaling and shipment of hinterland and nonhinterland agricultural specialties and
natural resources. The other was the import and distribution of both
domestic manufactures and foreign goods procured from northeastern
points. Not enough concrete data exist on the second set of interdependencies, which mainly involved New York, to make further discussion
worthwhile, but ample evidence is available on the first set of relationships.

*The Shipment of Cotton and Other Hinterland and Nonhinterland
Staples.* Although economic-historical accounts and interpretations of
the antebellum period in general emphasize the significance of cotton
shipments from the South's "cotton ports" to the Northeast as a whole,
they rarely present any breakdown indicating the absolute and relative
volumes dispatched to specific destinations. However, available records
make it possible to determine the amounts of cotton shipped annually
between 1849 and 1860 from Charleston to specific destinations. New
York took anywhere from 53.5 to almost 80.0 percent of Charleston's
annual cotton shipments to domestic ports during the 1850s, and its
merchants reshipped a major share of those receipts to England and the
Continent (table A.29). These figures, however, fail to do full justice to
the cotton-based interdependencies existing between Charleston and
New York since middlemen, insurance agents, and shippers from the
country's largest city were often involved in cotton shipments that went
directly from Charleston to Liverpool and other European points.[188]
Boston, whose merchants were importing for hinterland mills (see table
A.10), and Philadelphia, whose wholesalers sold both to local and hinterland textile factories, were the next two ranking domestic destinations—the two together acquiring anywhere from about 15 to 35 percent
of all the cotton moved from Charleston to U.S. ports. Although lesser
quantities of cotton apparently were also carried to secondary New England ports in some years,[189] the bulk of the remainder of Charleston's
internal cotton shipments went to Baltimore and Providence. In short,
the interdependencies derived from Charleston's domestic cotton trade
were confined almost entirely to major centers. And, in keeping with
the Callender-Schmidt-North view and other depictions of Northeast-
South relationships, those major-center independencies were interregional rather than intraregional.

Rice had been grown on a plantation basis on reclaimed swamplands
in the vicinity of Charleston before 1690, and for a long time it was the

most important commodity shipped from the South Carolina port.[190] By the mid-nineteenth century, although cotton had displaced rice as the leading export, the annual quantities of the foodstuff leaving the docks of Charleston for domestic points were as great as they had ever been.[191] Between 1849 and 1860 New York consistently received about half or more of the milled and "rough" rice exported from Charleston to U.S. ports (table A.30). Boston, Philadelphia, and Baltimore in combination consistently took between roughly 24 and 31 percent of the domestic rice shipments from Charleston, with Providence receiving additional minor quantities in most years. Thus, to an overwhelming extent, the interdependencies spawned by Charleston's rice trade involved major centers in another region. However, unlike the case of cotton, there was also one intraregional component to the major-center interdependencies associated with the activities of Charleston's rice merchants: wholesalers in New Orleans obtained 18.6 percent or more of Charleston's shipments in each of the eleven years between 1849 and 1860. Indirect interdependencies also existed with Cincinnati and other upriver major centers as a result of the forwarding that occurred in New Orleans. (The average annual volume of rice arriving in Cincinnati during the late 1850s—just under 1,300 tons[192]—corresponded to about 24 percent of New Orleans's receipts from Charleston.) In addition, during the final pre-Civil War years businessmen in smaller nonhinterland ports answered for 2.4 to 3.4 percent of Charleston's domestic rice sales.[193]

The pine barrens of South Carolina, sandwiched between the cotton-supplying hilly Piedmont uplands and the rice-growing swampy lowlands and tidewater areas of that state, were the source of Charleston's third major staple export—lumber. Charleston's domestic lumber shipments reached a peak total of 16.5 million feet in 1854–1855, or nearly twice the total of ten years earlier.[194] The detailed pattern of domestic destinations for the 1850s is somewhat unexpected, for Providence was the largest recipient in four separate years, and the wholesalers of either Philadelphia or Baltimore were the largest single group of purchasers in each of the remaining years (table A.31). Nevertheless, the aggregate pattern was similar to that for cotton. Because of the demand level created by the construction, shipbuilding, and other wood-consuming activities of major centers in the Northeast, in any given year the interdependencies associated with Charleston's internal lumber trade mainly involved those centers. Thus, in comparison to many of the specific commodity interdependencies previously observed for Boston, Philadelphia, Buffalo, and Cincinnati, the striking fact about the sales of Charleston's lumber middlemen and forwarders is the absence of linkages with intraregional major centers. This absence is attributable partly to the fact that one such center, Mobile, had a lumber trade of its own, using New Orleans as a major outlet, and partly to the meager scale of the South's shipbuilding industry, which was hampered by a shortage of skilled workers and by high labor costs.[195] The lumber-trade interdependencies of Charleston are also arresting because of the degree to which they seem to have involved nonhinterland ports of intermediate and small size (over 24 percent in 1849–1850).[196]

The 1851 completion of the Western and Atlantic Railroad, from Atlanta to Chattanooga, and the opening of the Nashville and Chattanooga Railroad a couple of years later, enabled Charleston to become a major outlet for the surplus grain of Tennessee and Georgia, even if only for a relatively brief time. During what was apparently their peak antebellum year (1855–1856), Charleston grain wholesalers and forwarders sent onward to domestic ports almost 600,000 bushels of wheat, most of which had originated in areas of the South well beyond what normally would be considered the city's trading hinterland (table A.32).[197] (By comparison, domestic wheat shipments from Charleston in that year exceeded those from Chicago to Buffalo five years earlier, and were nearly as great as those from Cleveland to Buffalo at that same earlier date.)[198] Here, too, the interdependencies resulting from the movement of wheat (and flour) from Charleston were confined almost completely to major centers in the Northeast, with New York receiving the lion's share of total domestic shipments. These short-lived but significant interregional large-city interdependencies fly in the face of the Callender-Schmidt-North thesis, which makes no provision for grain flows from the South to the Northeast. The wheat-and-flour-shipping activities of Charleston resembled the city's cotton and lumber trades inasmuch as they did not generate any notable intraregional interdependencies with major centers. However, interdependencies involving nonhinterland ports with varying populations below the major-center level almost certainly existed, as is indicated by the three instances in table A.32 in which "other U.S. ports" received approximately 12 percent of all domestic shipments.[199]

The Receipt of Staples and Other Goods from Southern Major Centers. Charleston in the 1850s was "in many respects the most progressive city in the South," and during that decade it continued "to serve as the spearhead of political resistance against national power."[200] All the same, its business community, by refusing to place greater emphasis on manufacturing or to diversify its trading practices, failed to provide the leadership necessary to make the South Carolina major center part of a highly integrated regional economy. Despite the variety and quantity of staples leaving Charleston's harbor, the only intraregional linkage of significance with another major center stemming from the city's domestic exports involved the carrying of rice to New Orleans. And even in that instance, the degree of interdependence was slight in comparison with the aggregate rice-based relationships with major northeastern centers. Moreover, the interdependencies traceable to the importing undertaken by members of Charleston's wholesaling-trading sector show comparatively few of the intraregional large-city relationships that were so prominent and plentiful in both the Northeast and the Midwest.

Although New Orleans was far and away the most populous city and the most active port in the South between 1840 and 1860, not many commodity exports from that city either terminated in or passed through Charleston in very significant quantities. As of 1850 the tonnage capacity of packets bearing freight and passengers between New Orleans and Charleston was dwarfed by that of similar vessels moving between major northeastern ports and Charleston.[201] And, ten years later, only the most roundabout of rail connections existed between New Orleans and Charleston (map 3.3). Between 1842 and 1860, sugar and molasses were brought to Charleston from New Orleans in amounts that were not insignificant, but in percentage terms they were not nearly as important as the shipments destined for the major centers of the Northeast (table A.33). Charleston's foodstuff dealers also imported flour, pork, bacon, lard, beef, and corn from New Orleans, but the quantities involved, with the occasional exception of bacon, were either secondary or minor until 1850–1851 (table A.34). After that date, when the impact of rail connections beyond Atlanta began to be felt, New Orleans-to-Charleston grain shipments "practically ceased," and the volume of meat products moving from New Orleans to Charleston declined to a level where they no longer merited separate mention in the annual tables of the *New Orleans Prices Current.*[202]

Richmond was the South's leading manufacturing city. Before the Civil War Richmond and Charleston were the South's second- and third-ranked cities, and they were much closer to each other geographically than New Orleans and Charleston. In spite of these two circumstances, however, evidence is scarce regarding goods flows from the major Virginia center to the city on the banks of the Ashley. The paucity of economic interaction between the two places is reflected by the absence of any regularly scheduled shipping vessels operating between them in either 1850 or 1859.[203] Some flour, wheat, and corn are known to have been shipped from Richmond to Charleston during the 1840s, but those flows apparently either stopped totally or became insignificant in the 1850s when rail-transported grain supplies from North Carolina, Tennessee, Georgia, and Alabama (as well as coastwise shipments from Baltimore) achieved primary importance.[204] Richmond wholesalers sent their tobacco products to New York, Philadelphia, and Baltimore, but not to Charleston; and Richmond's famed Tredegar Iron Works made only occasional shipments of railroad axles and spikes to South Carolina's major center.[205]

Mobile was the least populous of the South's major centers. Since its manufacturing sector also was very poorly developed and its domestic exports were composed largely of cotton, lumber, and ship's timber, there was little basis for the shipment of its commodities to Charleston.[206] Although between 1849 and 1860 cotton wholesalers and forwarders in Mobile normally sent 35 to 50 percent of their annual domestic shipments to New Orleans for foreign or domestic reexport, and although a smaller but still important share of their business had gone to New Orleans during the early and mid-1840s, it is quite unlikely that the Alabama city's merchants made any similar use of Charleston's cotton-exchange market. Throughout the 1840–1860 period, the share of Mobile's domestic exports going to all ports other than New Orleans, New York, Boston, Providence, Philadelphia, and Baltimore was usually well under 2.0 percent.[207] And, predictably, in those instances where the domestic destinations of Mobile's antebellum lumber shipments are specified in full, not a single foot is indicated for Charleston.[208]

Savannah, though not classified here as a major center, was the South's fifth largest city for most of the final antebellum period,[209] and it was only about a hundred miles southwest of Charleston. Despite those trade-promoting conditions, Savannah had very little to offer Charleston. Its manufacturing operated at an extremely low level,[210] and its businessmen exported little but cotton, lumber, and rice. Thus, the traffic in goods from Savannah to Charleston was restricted to cotton, in significant secondary quantities (table A.35), and to rice, in usually rather minor amounts,[211] both of which were reexported from the more active South Carolina market place. (As tables A.29–A.32 demonstrate, trade in the opposite direction—from Charleston to Savannah—was too small to be specified.)

Taken together, the data on Charleston's domestic staple exports and southern receipts verify the earlier contention that, as late as 1860, the South as a whole lacked a very well articulated regional system of

cities.[212] Rather than having economic linkages of primary importance
with New Orleans, Richmond, and Mobile (or Savannah), Charleston's
interdependencies (including those based on her manufacturing imports) were such as to make the city more a "colonial" outlier of the
northeastern regional city-system than a member of a southern regional
city-system. The overall antebellum interdependencies of New Orleans,
Richmond, and Mobile, as well as Savannah, were also such as to make
each of them, in varying degrees, more of a colonial outlier of the northeastern regional city-system than a participant in a southern regional
city-system.[213] Although railroad construction had permitted each of
these places to further its trade in hinterland staples, the railroads had
either failed totally to tie them together, or had done so in a quite indirect manner (map 3.3).[214] In short, New Orleans and Mobile were the
only pair of southern major centers to have a high level of economic interaction, and even that was limited almost entirely to staples.

*Interdependencies Involving Hinterland and Nonhinterland Urban
Places of Small and Medium Size.* Comparatively few hinterland
places of a pronounced urban character were economically interdependent with Charleston, simply because of the low level of urbanization
associated with South Carolina's economy, which was dominated by en-
clavelike plantations whose owners generally purchased their goods and
services directly from the seaboard rather than from nearby.[215] (Only
1.3 percent of the state's 1860 population outside Charleston was officially recognized as urban by census sources, although additional settlements with fewer than 2,500 residents were certainly urban in form and
function.)[216] As of 1860, Charleston's hinterland interdependencies were
confined to the coastal ports of Georgetown and Beaufort; the Fall Line
river towns of Hamburg, Cheraw, Camden, and Columbia (the sole un-
shared hinterland place with more than 2,500 inhabitants); a few rather
small places, such as Greenville, Spartanburg, Newberry, Manchester,
and Florence, which were situated either at the termini of various
prongs of the South Carolina Railroad or at intersections between that
carrier and its feeder lines; and the cities strung out along the Georgia
Railroad between Augusta (1860 population 12,493) and Atlanta (1860
population 9,554), all of which also fell within Savannah's economic
sphere of influence.[217]

Presumably, with only this relatively limited array of urban places
fully or partly within its hinterland, Charleston's growth possibilities
were curtailed. This was so only partly because the places in question
offered a limited market for the city's wholesalers and provided little or
no manufacturing specialties to be sold and forwarded beyond the Ash-

ley River port. It was also the case partly because the agriculturally based interdependencies existing between Charleston and these towns and cities were for the most part confined to the months between September and January, with little in the way of coastward flows—other than lumber—occurring in spring or summer.[218]

The complexities associated with the antebellum interdependencies of Charleston and its hinterland urban places did not arise solely from the forwarding of cotton, rice, lumber, and grains directly to small and medium-sized ports within the hinterlands of major northeastern centers. It is clear that the shipment of wheat and flour from Charleston in the mid-1850s was made possible largely by the direct acquisition of those foodstuffs from points well beyond the city's trading hinterland. Those collection and forwarding points included cities and towns within the hinterlands of New Orleans, Mobile, St. Louis, and Louisville: for example, Memphis, Chattanooga, Nashville, Knoxville, and Murfreesboro, Tennessee (1860 populations ranging from below 2,500 to 22,623), and Columbus, Kentucky (1860 population below 2,500).[219] Occasionally, some of the cotton brought to Charleston for marketing had originated in Memphis, or in some lesser towns of northern Alabama and eastern Mississippi that belonged to the hinterlands of Mobile and New Orleans. Retail merchants from hinterland urban settlements frequently created direct interdependencies with New York by securing from the jobbers of that city goods that could have been purchased from Charleston jobbers or commission merchants. Railroad wheels and other iron castings are known to have arrived in small quantities from the Philadelphia hinterland center of Wilmington, Delaware (1860 population 21,258). Finally, on an ironic note, the cotton textile products of Graniteville—one of Charleston's very few hinterland towns with any factory-scale manufacturing—supposedly sold better in New York and Philadelphia than in South Carolina's major center.[220]

THE TOTAL PATTERN OF CITY-SYSTEM INTERDEPENDENCE: SOME SUMMARY OBSERVATIONS

In some senses it may be true that it was not until "between 1880 and 1910 [that] the American urban network, as an integrated system, came of age."[221] Nevertheless, the fragmentary but presumably representative evidence presented in this chapter for Boston, Philadelphia, Buffalo, Cincinnati, and Charleston indicates that the total pattern of interurban economic relationships continuing or emerging between 1840 and 1860 included numerous elements suggestive of a more than primitive integration among the expanding membership of the nation's city-system. Further voluminous details, which are contained in additional fragmentary materials for New York, Baltimore, Chicago, San Francisco, New Orleans, Mobile, and other major centers but have not been presented here, reinforce the impression that many antebellum interdependencies were reflective of maturing system integration. Most important, the total pattern of interdependencies was not confined to simple relationships of hierarchical dominance between major centers and lesser cities and towns in their respective trading hinterlands. It is true that there was an absence of the extremely complex pattern of interdependencies engendered today both by the job-control, capital-allocation, and decision-making behavior of large multi-locational organizations and by the input-output relationships associated with extended production and distribution systems. However, the mix of commodity flows and other urban economic interactions prevailing in the final decades before 1860 showed unmistakable signs of the complexity that over the next 120 years was to become more entrenched and ramified with each successive round of increase in the average scale of production, capital investment, and capital organization.

5

Growth and Development within the
U.S. City-System, 1840–1860: A Model

The foundation for interpretation has been laid. The various snapshots of interdependence presented in chapter 4 permit a direct consideration of the questions that have been raised regarding the consequences for urban growth and city-system development that followed from antebellum interurban economic relationships.

To begin with, it is essential to recognize that regardless of historical or geographical setting, every sizable interurban interrelationship plays an important role in the process of city-system growth and development by, among other things, preserving or creating nonlocal job opportunities, or by directly generating nonlocal employment multipliers.[1] Consequently, a type-by-type review of the various interdependence dyads directly or indirectly revealed in the previous chapter, coupled with their employment-multiplier consequences, is fundamental to the modeling of the growth and development of the U.S. system of cities and its regional components during the urban economic transformation of the 1840s and 1850s (see figure 5.1).

ANTEBELLUM URBAN INTERDEPENDENCE DYADS: TYPES AND
MULTIPLIER GROWTH CONSEQUENCES

Individually, the most important antebellum city-system interdependencies were the linkages between pairs (dyads) of major centers (figure 5.1, case *a*). Both well-established and newly emerging major centers (which held most of the country's pre-Civil War urban population and captured most of the absolute urban population growth of the 1840–1860 period) were more likely to be heavily interdependent with other major centers than with smaller cities or towns. Major centers in the regional city-system of the Northeast had their most voluminous and valuable individual interdependencies with their intraregional counterparts or with one or more major centers in other parts of the country. Similarly, the major centers of the Midwest formed their most significant interdependence dyads with other major centers inside and outside the Midwest. However, in the South, with the exception of the New Orleans-Mobile dyad, the largest and most valuable economic link-

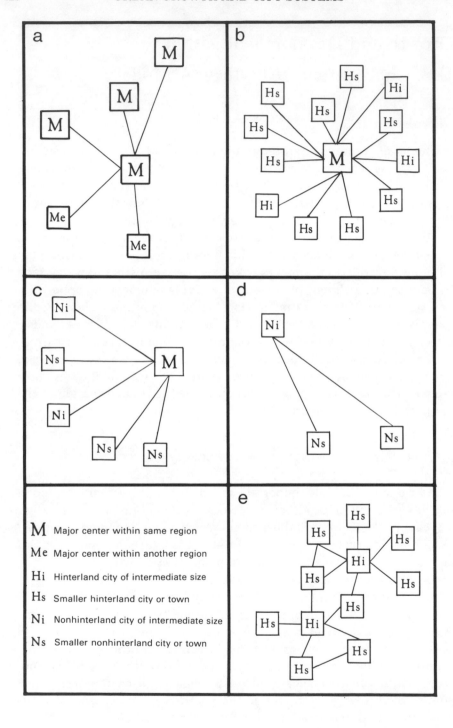

M   Major center within same region

Me Major center within another region

Hi Hinterland city of intermediate size

Hs Smaller hinterland city or town

Ni Nonhinterland city of intermediate size

Ns Smaller nonhinterland city or town

ages were interregional, either involving major centers in both the Midwest and the Northeast (as in the case of New Orleans),[2] or being confined to major centers in the Northeast (as in the cases of Charleston, Richmond, and Mobile).

To put it otherwise, as a result of the functional specialization evolving both among the major centers themselves and within and between their hinterlands, each major center simultaneously had key lateral linkages of an intraregional or an interregional character with several other major centers.[3] And, regardless of its regional location, each major center was involved in one or more important sets of interdependencies in which New York City was a very prominent element. This was in no small part attributable to the credit-extension practices of members of New York's wholesaling-trading complex and the related hegemony of the city with respect to the nation's importing activity and foreign trade in general (table A.36).

Under this set of circumstances, any meaningful expansion of either the manufacturing or the wholesaling activities of a major center usually had a considerably greater probability of triggering a nonlocal employment multiplier in New York or some other specific major center than in a specific small- or intermediate-sized urban place located inside or outside the major center's hinterland. In like manner, any significant expansion of manufacturing or of wholesaling activities in a major center usually was much more likely to be the effect of a nonlocal employment multiplier from New York or from some other specific major center than to be the effect of such a multiplier from a specific small- or intermediate-sized urban place situated within or beyond that major center's hinterland. Moreover, due to the magnitude and variety of major center interdependencies, the expansion of manufacturing or of wholesaling-trading activities in one such center was apt eventually to cause an increase of manufacturing or of wholesaling-trading job oppor-

Figure 5.1. Types of antebellum interdependence dyads as illustrated by hypothetical and idealized examples. In case *a*, only the most important interdependence dyads involving the major center (M) in the middle of the diagram and other major centers are shown. (The full array of principal major-center interdependence dyads is not shown for the other five places.) One of the intraregional or interregional dyads in case *a* is almost certain to include New York. The distance scales in the five diagrams are not necessarily the same. The variety of hinterland and nonhinterland place-types, in terms of population, is grossly simplified in cases *b* through *e*. Whether goods are moving in one or both directions in any of the illustrated dyads, employment multiplier effects can move in either direction. See text for further explanation.

tunities in another major center, even when expansion in the first city did not require either direct procurement of industrial inputs from the second city or direct import or export transactions with the wholesalers and forwarders of the second city. This was the case because employment multipliers could also flow from one major center to another at times when local population increases, stemming from another type of interdependence, magnified the local demand for agricultural and industrial goods normally purchased from or via another major center.[4]

Second, an individually less important but more common type of interdependence dyad involved a major center and a less populous town or city within its sphere of dominant economic influence, or trading hinterland (figure 5.1, case *b*). Although this was the case for the city-system as a whole, the data on Boston, Philadelphia, Buffalo, Cincinnati, and Charleston have shown that the relative importance of this type of interdependence dyad varied considerably from one major center to another. Some variations depended upon the relative location and primary functions of the major center in question or upon the degree of urbanization reached in its hinterland. Other variations stemmed from the presence or absence of manufacturing specialties in hinterland towns and cities, or from the nature and physical extent of hinterland agriculture and natural resources. In specific instances the relative significance and character of interdependence dyads involving major centers and hinterland urban places were also affected by the level of transportation and settlement development (including overall population density) within the hinterland area.[5]

The procurement by major-center middlemen of manufacturing specialties, agricultural surpluses, or natural resources from a hinterland production or collection point, either for local consumption or for forwarding to domestic or foreign destinations, could result in the transmission of employment multipliers in either direction between the two places. On the one hand, either the nonlocal (intraregional and interregional) demand captured by a major center's wholesaling and forwarding establishments, the input demand mounted by a major center's manufacturing facilities, or the demand accumulating from its population growth could be translated into additional jobs in one or more of the hinterland urban places acting as suppliers. On the other hand, the expansion of production or of collecting and forwarding activities in a hinterland urban place could either require the filling of more jobs directly or indirectly related to the wholesaling-trading complex of the receiving major center, or could facilitate the enlargement (or additional birth) of manufacturing enterprises in that same receiving center.

When flows from a major center to a hinterland urban place consisted of the movement of local manufactures, local financial and insurance services, or nonlocally originating commodities, employment multipliers could again be transmitted either from the smaller to the larger of the two interacting urban units or from the larger unit to the smaller. Increased demand originating for whatever reason in a hinterland urban community could stimulate the further expanse (or additional birth) of producing, wholesaling, or shipping activities in the supplying major center. In some instances the increased provision of goods from a major center could generate employment growth in a hinterland urban place either by pushing manufacturers to increase their scale of input purchase and thereby their scale of production, or by encouraging merchants to attempt to secure a larger volume of business, possibly at the expense of retailers operating from other hinterland urban locations with less transport nodality.

Although it was generally only of minor importance, a third type of interdependence dyad, involving a major center and a less populous town or city outside its hinterland, was not uncommon during the 1840–1860 period (figure 5.1, case c).[6] This occurred especially where new transportation facilities had freed interior areas from their almost complete commercial dependence on the nearest major entrepôt. The intraregional and interregional flows to or from any major center and nonhinterland places of small and intermediate size were usually in aggregate quite small in comparison with the sum of economic flows involving that same major center and either other major centers or hinterland urban places. (Buffalo and Providence, with their highly attenuated hinterlands, appear to be the only major centers of note where the total pattern of economic interactions did not adhere to the hinterland portion of this generalization.)[7] In contrast, the complexity of interdependencies in the present-day U.S. city-system is such that the volume of economic relationships between a major center, or metropolitan complex, and all the nonhinterland urban places of intermediate and small size with which it interacts is usually greater than that between the same major center and all the urban places within its traditionally defined hinterland.[8]

It did not matter whether agricultural, industrial, or other flows passed from a major center to a nonhinterland urban place of medium or small population, or from the smaller nonhinterland place to the major center: employment multipliers could be transmitted in either direction. The shipment of an agricultural or industrial good from a nonhinterland lesser town or city to a major center could have come about because demand conditions had precipitated it. In such an instance major center importers might have caused an increase in the employment opportunities directly or indirectly associated with the sending place's wholesaling, forwarding, or production activities. Or the same type of shipment could have come about because the supply situation had provoked it; and in that instance nonhinterland exporters could have stimulated an increase in the number of jobs directly or indirectly affiliated either with the receiving major center's wholesaling-trading complex or with its manufacturing sector. Likewise, depending on whether demand or supply factors were at the root of interaction, the movement of a good, service, or capital from one major center to an urban place in the hinterland or another major center could have entailed the transmission of an employment multiplier either to or from the sending major center.

Occasionally a fourth type of interdependence occurred, one formed directly between two urban places of small or intermediate size located in the hinterlands of two different major centers (figure 5.1, case *d*). But mainly because of the antebellum organization of manufacturing sales in particular and of wholesaling distribution in general, such interdependence dyads were relatively infrequent until 1860, even though the railroad construction of the 1850s increased their feasibility. Here, too, for supply and demand reasons that do not require repeating, commodity flows could involve the propagation of employment multiplier effects either at the urban place of origin or at the town or city of destination.

Fifth, but by no means least important, various economic flows capable of generating employment multipliers in either direction also brought pairs of cities or towns within the hinterland of the same major center into interdependence with each other (figure 5.1, case *e*). (Such intrahinterland interdependence dyads were not given their full due in chapter 4 because of the character of the source materials used.) These dyads assumed many forms, including the nearby sale of local manufacturing specialties and the forwarding of agricultural goods or natural resources from a lower-order collection point to a higher-order collection point. Dyads of this type also arose when the wholesalers or forwarders in a place of high hinterland nodality delivered goods to retail merchants located elsewhere—goods obtained either from the major center that economically dominated both places or from a more distant major center. Finally, in keeping with central-place theory, intrahinterland interdependence came about through the journeys of urban residents to a more populous urban place where higher marketing "thresholds," or entry conditions, had been fulfilled and a greater variety of services and retail goods were thus available.[9]

A SUBMODEL OF MAJOR-CENTER LOCAL GROWTH

In antebellum U.S. cities, job-opportunity expansion and population growth via the capture of migrants and holding of residents was the consequence not only of interdependence patterns and their muliplier effects but also of locally occurring self-perpetuated feedbacks. Because major centers acquired most of the country's absolute urban population growth between 1840 and 1860 and because in so doing they usually solidified or maintained their national or regional rank stability, it is appropriate to glance briefly at the operation of local-growth feedbacks within such centers (and, by extension, within cities in general) before proceeding to model the antebellum growth and development of the U.S. system of cities and its regional components. (The locally based urban growth processes of the 1840–1860 period actually deserve a treatise of their own, rather than the highly synoptic treatment given here.)

Feedback Structure of the Submodel. If the economy of any antebellum major center could be seen in isolation from its specific nonlocal relationships, its internal workings probably could best be summarized by many or all of the elements of the circular and cumulative feedback process shown in figure 5.2.

Whether locally or nonlocally induced, each significant expansion of activity within the center's wholesaling-trading complex and each birth or enlargement of manufacturing establishments gave rise to initial local multiplier effects.[10] First, multipliers arising from the wholesaling-trading complex could bring into being additional job opportunities for some of the following types of workers: (1) bank and insurance company employees, draymen, stevedores, and people in other nonindustrial occupations directly serving the local complex itself; (2) manufacturing workers either in entrepôt branches (which processed wheat, sugar, leather, and other raw materials of domestic or foreign origin) or in branches that directly supplied the local wholesaling-trading complex (for example, shipbuilding and repairing, commercial printing, and coopering); and (3) individuals with occupations at least partly dependent upon the income expenditures or tax payments of those employed in the initially expanding activity (such as construction laborers, workers associated with retailing, household services, or the provision of local transportation, and local government employees). Second, local manu-

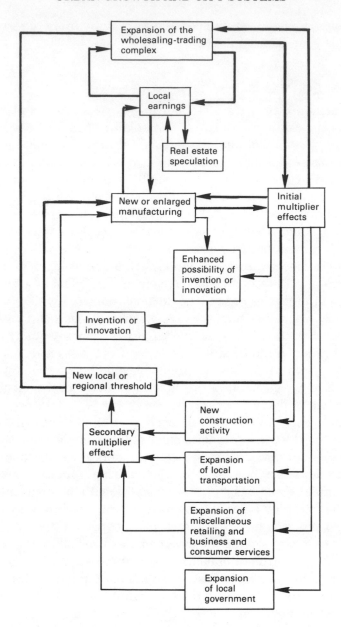

Figure 5.2. A submodel of locally generated urban size-growth for a single major center, 1840–1860.

facturing multipliers could bring forth an increased number of job opportunities for some of the following kinds of employees: (1) workers involved in the construction or fitting out of the new or expanded facilities in question; (2) industrial laborers in backward- or forward-linked branches, or in branches either providing inputs to, or consuming outputs from, the new or expanded manufacturing activity itself; (3) wholesaling-trading complex employees connected with the acquisition of nonlocal inputs or the nonlocal marketing of finished products;[11] and (4) persons who could fill occupations supported by the income expenditures or tax payments of those employed in the newly born or enlarged manufacturing units.

Eventually, any local growth set in motion by the expansion of either wholesaling-trading or manufacturing activities could be further propelled by the spinoff of secondary multiplier effects from the initial employment multipliers. In other words, the new construction activity, the expanded operation of local transportation and local government, and the increased volume of retailing activity and service provision stemming from the initial multiplier effects in turn could create multipliers of their own.

The combined impact of the new mercantile or manufacturing employment opportunities, the initial and secondary multipliers, and the consequent population growth resulting from the attraction and retention of migrants was likely to be the attainment of new local or regional thresholds for either some market-oriented manufactures or some importing activities within the wholesaling-trading complex that emphasized local and short-distance distribution. (A threshold may be defined as the minimum population or minimum volume of sales required either to support a new market-oriented establishment or to justify economically an addition to such facilities.)[12] Once manufacturing facilities or wholesaling-trading establishments were founded or enlarged in response to the fulfillment of these higher threshold levels, a new round of growth could be triggered. This round would have its own initial and secondary multiplier effects and would thereby contribute to the achievement of yet higher thresholds. As soon as action was taken on these later thresholds, the same sequence of feedback events (locally based activity expansion, multipliers, and threshold fulfillment) could be reiterated repeatedly, at an irregular pace, and in a circular and cumulative manner, unless it was interrupted or impeded by either local diseconomies or unfavorable changes in the economic or political environment.[13]

The locally based growth of major centers was reinforced and compounded under normal circumstances by the reinvestment of local earnings. Over-accumulated capital either from the wholesaling-trading complex or from manufacturing activities could be plowed back into the home sector (even if the receiving activities were not local-market oriented or threshold-sensitive), thus touching off an initial multiplier and subsequent growth round of its own. Similar consequences could follow from the infusion of mercantile profits into both threshold and nonthreshold industries. (It is clear that wholesaling merchants "controlled most of the [country's] available capital" throughout the pre-Civil War period and held a "virtual monopoly" on the outside financing of manufacturing, especially since banks usually were not very active in that respect and since, after 1844, the use of the telegraph sharply reduced the need for major-center merchants to tie up their dollars in inventory.[14] And capital invested in manufacturing could retain earlier migrants [or surplus labor], as opposed to attracting new migrants, especially when local or neighborhood manufacturing previously had been skewed heavily toward industries that employed mostly members of the same sex.)[15] Additionally, insofar as wholesaling-trading interests placed excess capital in manufacturing, they could convert any profits so obtained into an expansion of their own activities. Moreover, local earnings from both of the major center's leading growth sectors were often diverted into real-estate speculation and a considerable amount of related construction. Real-estate speculation could yield enormous capital gains that could be reinjected into the expansion of mercantile or manufacturing activities, thereby sparking additional rounds of growth feedbacks. Construction could spur an expansion of the local building-products industry, promote more lumber importing and wholesaling, and create other initial multiplier effects.

In many instances the growth of major centers was also perpetuated by the increased local generation and circulation of specialized information that occurred because of local manufacturing births and enlargements (in particular) and local multiplier effects and population increases (in general). The greater volume of specialized information flowing through the ever more complex network of interpersonal communications enhanced the possibility of industrial inventions and innovations by increasing the likelihood of problem awareness, demand perception, and the interindustry transfer of solutions to problems. Once inventions were implemented (or became innovations through the appearance or expansion of manufacturing establishments), multipliers and population increases normally followed, the web of specialized local information circulation was extended and intensified again, and the chances for local invention, innovation, and subsequent feedbacks of a similar nature were enhanced.[16]

Variations in the Operation of the Submodel. Quite clearly, the submodel of local growth did not function in exactly the same way or at exactly the same tempo for all major centers, and these differing circumstances contributed to some of the population-ratio adjustments and minor regional rank shiftings that occurred among those places between 1840 and 1860. Although there were numerous reasons for differential functioning of the submodel, it is sufficient to mention briefly only those that are most readily identified.

The relative composition of the wholesaling-trading complex varied from major center to major center, with foreign exports or any one of the complex's other three components being more prominent in some centers than in others.[17] To the extent that each of the four components of any wholesaling-trading complex had a different propensity to generate local multiplier effects, dissimilarly composed complexes were associated with growth feedbacks of different magnitudes.

Although scholars are in general agreement that the 1840–1860 period was one in which manufacturing began to surpass mercantile activities as the principal engine of large-city growth, it is evident from the substance of chapter 4 that even if such a changeover was true for northeastern and midwestern centers such as Boston, Philadelphia, Cincinnati, Cleveland, and Detroit, it was not true for any major southern center except Richmond.[18] Moreover, even where such changes did take place, they did not do so at precisely the same time or to precisely the same extent. Not only did the share of the work force in industrial occupations vary among those major centers in which manufacturing had become the main growth stimulus, but there also were pronounced variations from one major center to another in the mix and size of manufacturing branches. Different manufacturing specialties—whether of the finished consumer-good type (which was becoming increasingly important) or of some other type—obviously had different growth impacts because of the different characteristics of their local multipliers and their differing sensitivities to market and price conditions.

Moreover, the local earnings feedbacks of the local-growth submodel must have operated at a variety of paces partly because the availability of capital differed from one major center to another. Such differences were attributable to prevailing attitudes toward risk taking and the investment of surplus mercantile capital, the prevailing local interest rates set by banks, and, to a lesser degree, the extent to which the local capital market was organized through banks (table A.37).[19]

Some circular and cumulative local-growth feedbacks almost certainly functioned more slowly in southern centers for reasons other than a low level of commitment to manufacturing. Among these reasons were the above-normal leakage of wholesaling-trading complex multipliers to New York and other major northeastern centers (due either to the direct control of mercantile activities from those places or to credit-extension practices) and the reduction of income-expenditure employment multipliers through the use of slave labor. (Slaves made up between approximately 26.0 and 34.3 percent of the 1860 populations of Richmond, Charleston, and Mobile.)[20]

Variations in the nature of real estate, construction, local transportation, and local-government feedbacks also contributed to the dissimilar functioning of the local-growth submodel from one major center to another. Differences in the character of the local housing stock and other related local market conditions, along with varying speculative proclivities on the part of resident capitalists, led to different absolute and relative rates at which large real-estate speculation earnings could be accumulated and steered into other sectors. For example, within a period of only seven years there was a considerable range in real-estate value increases in three midwestern centers: Cleveland, Chicago, and Cincinnati (table A.38). For similar reasons, major centers did not always experience comparably proportioned construction spurts, or booms, as a consequence of the economic-activity expansion and population growth associated with recent feedback rounds. For instance, during 1856 "more than 2,500 buildings were erected" in St. Louis "at a cost of more than seven millions of dollars," while in the same year the cost of all of the construction occurring in Chicago—including the laying of sewers and gas and water pipes, as well as the preparation and improvement of streets and plank walks—amounted to $5.7 million. This discrepancy occurred despite the fact that both cities were witnessing similar absolute population increases at the time (table 2.1).[21]

Omnibuses (horse-drawn vehicles normally seating twelve persons), steam-driven commuter trains, and horse-powered street railways, each of which had different capital requirments per mile of operation and different capacities to generate local multipliers, were introduced at different dates (if at all) in each of the U.S. major centers. For example, omnibus lines did not appear in Baltimore, St. Louis, and Pittsburgh before the mid-1840s, in Chicago and San Francisco until the early 1850s, and in Richmond and Cleveland until 1857. Likewise, commuter trains were employed prior to the Civil War only in Boston, New York, and Philadelphia. And although horse-drawn street railways began functioning before 1840 in New York and New Orleans, they did not spread to fourteen of the other major centers until between 1854 and 1860. (Cleveland, Buffalo, San Francisco, Milwaukee, and Mobile were among the large cities whose permanent operations did not commence until 1860.)[22] Furthermore, the absolute and relative extent to which each of these modes of public transportation was invested in, speculated upon,[23] and utilized[24] varied widely once they had gained local acceptance, as the data for horse-drawn street railways provided in table A.39 illustrate.

Finally, the existence of different local taxing policies and political pressures contributed to differences in the extent to which local major-center governments could commit revenues and expand employment opportunities for police, firemen, teachers, lamplighters, street repairers and cleaners, librarians, poor-relief workers, Board of Health members, sundry additional city-hall officials and administrators, and other individuals whose aggregate income expenditures would generate multiplier effects of their own. Two examples will clarify this point. In Richmond between 1839 and 1858 the expenditures of city government grew 485 percent, from $85,000 to $480,000, or to roughly $12.61 per capita at the latter date. In Philadelphia, during the shorter interval separating 1843 and 1857, expendable tax income increased 691 percent from $514,652 to $4,072,267, or to about $8.18 per capita in the latter year.[25]

In conjunction with these observations on the differential functioning of the local-growth submodel in major centers, a further conclusion can be drawn about all cities and towns. In those cities that had reached only small or intermediate size by 1860, growth via the attraction of migrants and retention of residents also must have occurred, to varying degrees, through the partial or full functioning of the same feedbacks contained in the submodel. In other words, some low-metabolic version of the local-growth submodel presumably was in operation in all other antebellum urban places. Outside of the major centers, however, it often happened that only wholesaling-trading feedbacks or only manufacturing feedbacks were of real significance. In addition, under those circumstances real-estate speculation and local transportation expansion were not likely to make such an important contribution to local growth except in some rapidly growing intermediate-sized cities.

A GROWTH AND DEVELOPMENT MODEL FOR THE ENTIRE ANTEBELLUM CITY-SYSTEM AND ITS REGIONAL COMPONENTS

Two preliminary steps that are essential to this exercise in model building have been completed. The types of interdependence dyads and associated nonlocal multiplier effects characterizing the U.S. city-system between 1840 and 1860 have been identified, and the manner in which locally centered feedbacks presumably contributed to urban growth has been outlined. Now it is possible to turn to a heuristic and probabilistic model of the process of city-system growth and development that is applicable both to the United States as a whole and to those regions of the country that had a well-articulated system of their own. Since previously existing and newly emerging major centers were the most successful attractors and retainers of migrants, the contents of such a model can be best appreciated by first elaborating upon the factors that enabled major centers to reinforce one another's growth and, in so doing, to solidify or continue their national and regional dominance and rank stability.

   Circular and Cumulative Growth Feedbacks among Major Centers. It has already been established that the individually most important interdependence dyads, or interurban trade and multiplier channels, of antebellum times were those connecting pairs of major centers, and that because of local and hinterland specialization each major center was simultaneously interdependent to a significant degree with several other major centers located either within the same region or in one or more other regions. Whatever the exact content of these economic relationships, their growth consequences were not confined to the direct transmission of nonlocal employment multipliers between the involved centers and to the immediate fueling of the local-growth submodel in each place. In addition to these feedback loops, two other types of growth-reinforcing feedback loops could be put in motion by each increment in interdependence that transpired between any pair of places belonging to the national or regional set of major centers, $M_1, M_2, M_3 \ldots M_n$ (figure 5.3). The operation of these feedback loops originated from the exchange and accumulation of specialized information, which is always necessary for the initiation and carrying out of interurban commodity transactions—whether or not pairs of major centers are involved. During the 1840–1860 period, for example, almost all of the specialized information flows that both preceded and paralleled each interurban commodity and capital flow took one (or more) of four different forms. These included face-to-face contacts in conjunction with business trips; newspaper items such as advertisements, reports of prices, accounts of market and crop conditions, and shipping and railroad-operating intelligence; letters; and, increasingly after 1844, telegraphic messages.[26]

   At the heart of the first pair of feedback loops was specialized information about market changes, prices, and business opportunities, and

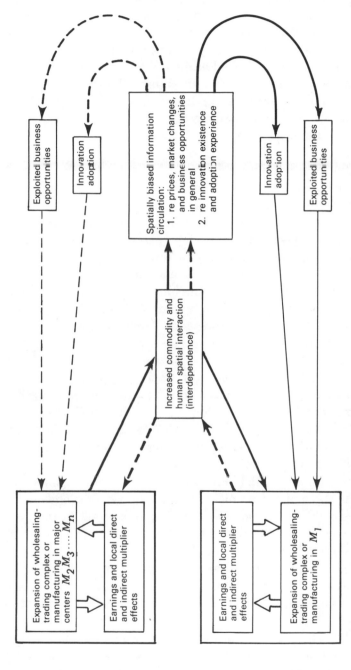

Figure 5.3. The circular and cumulative growth feedbacks occurring among the major centers of both the U.S. city-system as a whole and the regional city-systems of the Northeast and Midwest, 1840–1860. Solid lines indicate feedback sequences terminating at M_1; dashed lines indicate feedback sequences originating at M_1.

this information was unevenly distributed geographically, or spatially biased. Because of the overall pattern of information-steering interdependence dyads, new specialized information either originating in or entering the national (or regional) city-system at one major center had a greater probability of being acquired early and acted upon by the entrepreneurs of another major center than by those of lesser cities within the system. Once a major business opportunity, or implicit locational decision,[27] was exploited at one major center, for example at M_1, it led to further stimulation of the local-growth submodel. For one of two reasons this led, in turn, to increased interdependence with one or more large centers and a consequent strengthening of spatial biases in the circulation of specialized information. One reason was that the previously unexploited opportunities directly involved the manufacturing or wholesaling-trading activities of another major center belonging to the same national or regional city-system. The other reason stemmed from the fact that the previously unexploited opportunity strengthened or created an interdependence dyad with either a smaller city or another national (or regional) city-system; for the local-activity expansion and population growth resulting from such action often fostered a greater demand for locally consumed agricultural and industrial goods normally acquired from or through one or more other major centers.

The second pair of feedback loops was based upon specialized information concerning either the existence of, or the demand for innovations (commercial, industrial, or financial), as well as information regarding the experience of previous adopters of such growth-inducing innovations. Because of the spatial biases in information availability created by the total array of interdependencies, any innovation originating in or entering the city-system at one major center had a much greater probability of early (and multiple) adoption at other major centers than at less populous urban places within the system. The chances of adoption in smaller cities and towns, in fact, must have been especially low when the characteristics of the diffusing innovation were such that its successful application depended either on the fulfillment of large-market, labor-supply, or capital requirements, or on the local availability of external economies. For one of two reasons, adoption at one major center (such as M_1 in figure 5.3) resulted in increased interdependence with one or more other major centers and further fortification of spatial biases in the circulation of information. The first reason was that single or multiple adoption of the innovation precipitated previously nonexistent forms of interdependence with other dominant units of the national or regional city-system (through the purchase of manufacturing inputs, for example). The second and probably more common reason was that innovation adoption brought local employment multipliers and population growth to the major center, which in turn bred a greater local demand for agricultural and industrial products customarily imported from or via at least one other major center.[28]

Both the business-opportunity and the innovation-diffusion feedback loops binding major centers can be cast in a somewhat more formal light through recourse to two simple equations. The first of these (5.1) merely states that, over a given period of time, the total volume of specialized economic information, or messages $(m_{i \to j})$, flowing from one city i to another city j—regardless of whether or not either of the cities is a major center—is some function of the total volume of trade moving in both directions between the two places $(T_{i \to j}$ and $T_{j \to i})$.

$$m_{i \to j} = f\left(T_{i \to j}, T_{j \to i}\right) \tag{5.1}$$

Since the businessmen of city i are simultaneously participating in interurban trade with several places, the probability $(I_{i \to j})$ that city j will be the first place either to acquire business-opportunity information from city i or to have a person or firm influenced toward innovation adoption will depend on city j's share of city i's total imports and exports. Hence, $I_{i \to j}$ may be expressed as follows:[29]

$$I_{i \to j} = f\left(T_{i \to j}, T_{j \to i}\right) \bigg/ \sum_{j=1}^{n} f\left(T_{i \to j}, T_{j \to i}\right) \tag{5.2}$$

Even if the business-opportunity or innovation-relevant information were to come from a small city i, the operation of equation (5.2) would most probably make it jump quickly to a major center due to the major-center dominance of most small-city trade patterns.

It is clear that the combined essence of figure 5.3 and equation (5.2) is consistent with antebellum comments on the difficulty of diverting "commerce from long established channels." The contents of figure 5.3 and equation (5.2) are also consistent with James Vance's more recent observations on the stability of nineteenth-century interurban wholesaling linkages (despite the appearance of new trade commodities) and on the role of "information exchange" and "intelligence flows" in establishing and concentrating wholesaling activities at major centers.[30] The equation is also consistent with modern evidence on the role of limited-search and uncertainty-reduction behavior in decision-making by entrepreneurs and by firms. Limited-search decisions are likely to be based

upon the most readily accessible infomation, or that which is intentionally or unintentionally acquired through established economic contacts.
Uncertainty is often coped with, once enough redundant and reassuring
information has been accumulated, by imitating the action of another
firm or individual whom one has business contacts with or has learned
of through such contacts. This is apparently true whether uncertainty is
due to (1) awareness of an individual's or firm's own ignorance, (2) the
risks associated with supply and demand factors, new technology, and
capital availability, or (3) other factors, including the timing of decision
implementation.

*Circular and Cumulative Feedbacks among All City-System Mem-
bers.* It is impossible for a single model to capture the totality of factors
that influenced growth and development within the U.S. system of
cities and its various regional city-systems between 1840 and 1860.
Here, no explicit account has been taken of social institutions, international economic influences, the political environment in general, or the
accumulation of North-South tensions in particular. Yet each of these
phenomena undoubtedly influenced the ways in which particular local
and nonlocal multipliers operated, specialized economic information circulated, accumulated capital was invested, business opportunities were
exploited, and economic innovations diffused. There is, all the same,
some justification for focusing heuristically on the handful of feedbacks
that were most persistent and that consistently interacted at various
levels. Such focusing provides insights that otherwise could not be attained. Furthermore, the questions and vantage points of human geography, or any other single branch of social science or the humanities,
cannot be expected to explain fully the urban transformation of
1840–1860 or any other period.[31]

All reservations aside, it is possible to imagine the full mix of documented types of interdependence dyads (figure 5.1) and their nonlocal
employment-multiplier consequences in simultaneous operation, and to
permit the feedback relationships diagramed in figure 5.3 to function for
urban places of all sizes and not merely for major centers. If this is
done, the 1840–1860 process of growth and development for both the
U.S. system of cities as a whole and the clearly existing regional city-
systems of the Northeast and Midwest can be summarized in somewhat
oversimplified form by the circular and cumulative model depicted in
figure 5.4. In that model the full interurban matrix of wholesaling-trading and industrial (and capital) flows, or interdependence dyads and attendant multipliers, existing at one point in time (T_1) possesses a corresponding interurban matrix of specialized economic information flows.

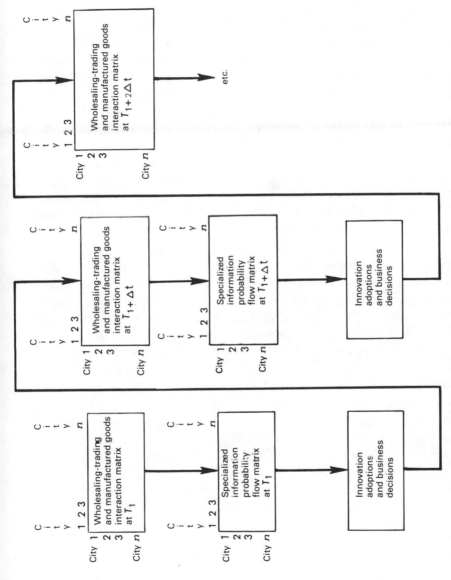

Figure 5.4. A simplified model of the growth and development process of both the entire U.S. system of cities and the regional city-systems of the Northeast and Midwest, 1840–1860.

The corresponding matrix is based on the fact that each good and capital flow, or business transaction, has an information dual, or parallel.[32] The information matrix is envisaged as a probability matrix, which, in accord with the functioning of equation (5.2) for all city-system members, influences both the places at which business opportunities are exploited and the places to which growth-inducing innovations diffuse. After a period of time $(T_1 + \Delta t)$ during which numerous business decisions and innovation adoptions have occurred, and when, consequently, some existing interdependencies have been fortified and other new interdependencies have been established, a new slightly modified interurban matrix of wholesaling-trading and manufacturing goods emerges. This matrix, in turn, has a slightly changed counterpart matrix of specialized economic information flows, which exercise a slightly altered probabilistic influence on the location of subsequent business decisions and innovation adoptions. Therefore, at a later date $(T_1 + 2\Delta t)$, yet another interurban matrix of goods flows develops and yet another round of feedbacks begins to unfold.[33]

Several amplifying and clarifying observations can be made concerning the model diagramed in figure 5.4. To begin with, the national city-system and its component regional city-systems were open—not only in the sense that existing member units were interdependent with foreign (or extraregional) shipping and production cities, and otherwise subject to outside forces, but also in the sense that continuous settlement spread and infilling resulted in the admission of new system members. As a consequence, each successive round of model feedbacks starts with a somewhat larger matrix of interurban goods (and capital) flows. This means that with time the overall structural organization of city-system interdependence becomes increasingly more complex because of simple expansion in the number of places at which mercantile and industrial decisions are reached and because of the ramification of economic interactions originating and terminating at previously existing members (or the round-by-round accumulation of refinements and additions to the geographic division of labor). It also means that Edward Muller's "pioneer periphery," "specialized periphery," and "transitional periphery" periods of development concurrently unfold in different areas. By extension, therefore, the changing assortment of interdependencies between major centers, intermediate-level cities, and smaller towns and cities associated with each of those periods could exist simultaneously in different parts of the country or in the same large-scale region.[34] In other words, the indication of an increasingly larger matrix of interurban economic relationships is one way of emphasizing that the relative

importance of different types of interdependence dyads could, at a given
date, vary from subregion to subregion, as well as from region to region.
In a related connection, it is apparent that, for any antebellum sub-
period the model under discussion can accommodate the full range of
urban interdependencies contained implicitly or explicitly in the Callender-Schmidt-North thesis and in Lindstrom's "Eastern demand
model,"[35] as well as in Muller's framework. The expanded matrix at the
beginning of each round also can be taken to mean that as settlement
spread and infilling allowed the total array of hinterland and nonhinterland interdependence dyads radiating outward from any single major
center to grow in number, the relative significance of particular older
hinterland dyads was diminished, or their weight in equation (5.2) was
reduced, even if the absolute volume of trade associated with those
dyads did not fall off.[36]

The probabilistic qualities of the systemwide model suggest that the
size characteristics attained by all U.S. cities by 1860 represented but
one of a myriad of possible process outcomes. Those qualities also provide two insights into the selective urban growth of the 1840s and 1850s
that would otherwise not be apparent. In the first place, the probabilistic operation of the model's feedbacks should have contributed to the
population-ratio adjustments and minor regional rank shiftings that occurred among major centers by enabling any particular business opportunity to be exploited and any particular innovation to be adopted in
some rather than all such urban places, with the consequence that specific local multipliers unfolded in some rather than in all of those cities.
(As a result, there also would not have been a uniform passing of nonlocal employment multipliers from one major center to another; hence
the distribution of probabilities among major centers for future business
opportunity exploitation and innovation adoption would have under-
gone some minor adjustment.) In the second place, the probabilistic
functioning of the model's feedbacks should have greatly influenced the
wide discrepancy in 1840–1860 growth rates among medium-sized and
especially small-sized cities. More precisely, such feedbacks should have
influenced the exceptional emergence of leading intermediate-sized
cities—such as Dayton and Memphis—and the comparatively rapid
progress that a few other medium- and small-sized cities made through
the size ranks of either the national city-system or the regional city-systems of the Northeast and Midwest.[37] In particular, such accelerated
growth and size-rank progress, whether persistent or uneven, should
have been helped along by three factors: the temporal concentration of
local multipliers following local business-opportunity exploitation or in-

novation adoption; increased interdependence with other cities; and a higher probability of business opportunity or innovation adoption at later dates.[38] (In addition, graduation into the official urban ranks by exceeding a population level of 2,500 was normally synonymous with a pulling away from competing smaller towns and villages that did not acquire or develop growth-inducing activities.)

The feedbacks of the city-system growth and development process outlined in this chapter were reinforced and modified by the route developments and other transportation improvements referred to in the interdependence snapshots for Boston, Philadelphia, Buffalo, Cincinnati, and Charleston. In fact, the implementation of transportation improvements at or between major centers and other urban places can be viewed as an intergral part of the model of city-system growth and development. Such improvements either represented the adoption of an innovation, or they were included in—or necessary to—efforts to exploit nonlocal business opportunities. By the mid-1840s it was being acknowledged that the "effect of railroads, and of transportation by steam generally, is to stimulate growth of towns, and especially of large towns" by augmenting their business and thereby their ability to attract migrants and retain inhabitants.[39] New rail routes, as well as faster and more frequently running trains and similar steamboat service improvements, were generally instigated, promoted, and backed in one way or another by the business interests of large cities. Transportation advances of this nature served both to strengthen existing channels of interdependence between major centers and to create new growth-transmission linkages between major centers and less populous urban places in a multitude of interrelated ways, only a few of which can be mentioned here.[40]

Transportation improvements often increased the variety and intensity of interdependencies associated with major centers, and therefore they magnified the probabilities that those places would be the scene for business-opportunity exploitation and innovation adoption. More precisely, transportation improvements permitted major-center goods to be marketed over an ever wider area for a given investment in shipping costs, thereby encouraging the concentration of specific manufacturing and wholesaling activities. Similarly, transportation improvements occasionally fostered activity concentration and the consequent compounding of local agglomeration economies by enabling staples and industrial raw materials to be procured at lower costs or from more distant locations. Transportation improvements also indirectly caused some smaller-center competitors to move to a major center with their capital and skills. Such improvements, by reducing the delivery prices of indus-

trial goods and raising the returns to farmers on goods sold, consequently stimulated nonlocal rural and urban consumption of locally
manufactured items. They also led frequently to the establishment of
preferential freight rates for long-haul shipments (or shipments from
one major-center terminus to another) as opposed to short-haul or trib-
utary-route shipments. In addition, transportation improvements sometimes meant the provision of "through-service" for the passenger traffic
between major centers, or an easing of the flow of business travelers
and specialized economic information between nationally and regionally
dominant cities. Furthermore, transportation improvements often markedly reduced shipping times and thus frequently facilitated a more
rapid accumulation of profits and additional investment capital.[41] The
intensification and multiplication of major-center goods flows and interdependencies before the Civil War commonly led to three results: further local demands for more rapid and more frequent transport services,
especially to other major centers; the actual apperance of additional
transportation improvements focused on major centers; and more goods
flows, multiplier effects, and feedbacks of the types shown in figures 5.3
and 5.4.[42]

Finally, transportation improvements, and especially route developments, affected the operation of feedbacks within the city-system
growth and development process by, as Muller has suggested, unevenly
altering the nodality of medium- and small-sized cities and towns.
Every time the nodality of such a city or town was enhanced by either
a new rail, steamboat, or canal route, or by the acquisition of more frequent service on a previously existing route, this improvement was
likely to be translated into new or more intense interdependence dyads.
Alternatively, enhanced nodality was translated into the growth-pro-
moting probabilistic feedbacks normally associated with commodity
flows and related spatial biases in the circulation of specialized economic information.[43] Conversely, every time a medium- or small-sized
city or town was bypassed by either a new transportation route or by a
newly scheduled service on a route already passing through that place,
its relative importance in the overall pattern of interdependence was
decreased and there was less probability that it would benefit from nonlocal employment multipliers and the population-building feedbacks
connected with equation (5.2).[44]

6

Spatial Biases in the Antebellum Circulation of Specialized Economic Information

Much of the reasoning concerning the models of the previous chapter rests on the influence supposedly exerted by spatial biases, or geographical inequalities, in the availability and circulation of specialized economic information. Admittedly, the spatially biased information aspects of figures 5.3 and 5.4 cannot be either formally or literally verified. For one thing, it is extremely difficult and impractical to assemble detailed evidence concerning the manner in which specific interurban information flows paralleled specific interurban commodity (or capital) movements. It also is no easy matter to ascertain the subsequent influence of information on the adoption of economic innovations and the exploitation of business opportunities. However, less formal and partial substantiation of the probabilistic model of antebellum city-system growth and development can be obtained through briefly considering some elements of the wide range of general evidence pertaining to spatial biases in the availability and circulation of specialized economic information. Such piecemeal evidence points strongly toward the existence in major centers of considerable growth-inducing informational advantages.

INFORMATIONAL SPATIAL BIASES AT THE OUTSET OF THE 1840–1860 PERIOD

Despite the advances in transportation technology that had occurred in the preceding decades, during the early 1840s the nonlocal flow of specialized economic information via the mails, newspapers (themselves moved by the posts), and business travel was extremely slow by present-day standards. Except in those very rare instances where carrier pigeons or semaphores were employed for message conveyance, all long-distance movement of news and other information (unless carried on horseback) required the use of humanly guided vehicles or vessels whose operating speeds on the most efficient routes ranged from eighteen to twenty-four miles per hour.[1] With much slower movement characterizing other routes, the time required for specialized information to pass over distances greater than one or two hundred miles usually could be measured in days.

Foreign information on prices, markets, and other economic matters normally was disseminated in published form first from the New York press to the press of Boston, Philadelphia, and Baltimore, and then to the newspapers in the immediate hinterlands of those major centers. This was the case because New York dominated the country's foreign trade, because foreign news was acquired from publications and accounts carried by ship, and because New York had the greatest number of regularly scheduled vessels sailing back and forth to England and the Continent. Specialized economic information of foreign origin normally moved into the Midwest when papers in the major centers along Lake Erie and the banks of the Ohio and the upper Mississippi openly plagiarized the pages of a New York, Boston, Philadelphia, or Baltimore paper. Published economic information from Europe ordinarily entered the South when the papers of that region's major centers reprinted items from the New York press. This form of outward spread was generally possible because daily newspaper publication—as opposed to triweekly, semiweekly, and weekly publication—was largely confined to major centers and because of the well-entrenched system of mutual journalistic plagiarism of foreign and domestic news. (The latter was facilitated by long-standing legislation that enabled editors to exchange copies with one another on a postage-free basis.)

During the early 1840s, the volume and variety of domestic specialized economic information available in print were usually greatest in major centers because of the frequency of newspaper publication in those places and the superiority of the postal and transportation services between them. Within the Northeast, New York increasingly became the entry point and dissemination node for specialized information originating elsewhere in the country. Economic information in newspaper form generally moved more rapidly and more often among New York, Philadelphia, Boston, and Baltimore than between any one of those centers and most, if not all, subservient places in its hinterland. In a clear-cut, but somewhat less dramatic fashion, Pittsburgh, Cincinnati, Louisville, and St. Louis, on the one hand, and Buffalo, Cleveland, and Detroit, on the other hand, enjoyed the same kind of regional published-information advantages as the four most populous cities of the Northeast. However, while the major southern ports easily exchanged economic press reports with New York, thanks to that city's fleet of regularly scheduled packets, New Orleans, Richmond, Charleston, and Mobile remained for the most part relatively distant from one another in terms of the movement of printed economic news.[2]

Not only were the governmental postal services linking major centers, especially in the Northeast, generally superior to those elsewhere in both speed and frequency, but, as of 1840, the receipt and dispatch of mails was disproportionately concentrated in the major centers. At that date—when the high cost of distance-graduated postage charges restricted private correspondence mostly to wholesalers, forwarders, and other businessmen—New York, Philadelphia, Boston, and Baltimore together accounted for over 23 percent of all U.S. Post Office receipts, although they held less than 5 percent of the country's population. In like fashion, New Orleans, Richmond, Charleston, and Mobile generated 6.3 percent of the country's postal receipts, although they answered for just under 1 percent of the nation's inhabitants. And the seven dominant centers of the Midwest were jointly responsible for over 4.6 percent of all U.S. postal receipts even though their combined population corresponded to approximately 0.9 percent of the national total.[3]

The cost of interurban travel was still very high about 1840, except under the special, highly crowded, one-way conditions sometimes provided for migrants on canal boats and steamboats. This meant that interurban round trips by common carrier were still pretty much confined to businessmen and the economic elite in general. In terms of absolute passenger volume, the most heavily traveled (and efficiently served) interurban routes in the United States at that time were those between the following cities: New York and Philadelphia; New York and Boston; New York and Albany (and on to Rochester and Buffalo); Philadelphia and Baltimore; Cincinnati and Louisville; Pittsburgh and Cincinnati; Buffalo, Cleveland, and Detroit; and New York and the major "Cotton Ports." Hence, New York was directly involved in four of the eight cases. In two other instances (Philadelphia-Baltimore and Buffalo-Cleveland-Detroit) a considerable number of travelers had New York as their ultimate origin or destination. Even in the remaining two cases (Cincinnati-Louisville and Pittsburgh-Cincinnati) many journeyers were either coming from or going to New York. Thus, to the extent that absolute passenger numbers best reflect the quantity of travel-generated specialized information entering and leaving a city, and to the extent that higher service frequency and en-route speed mean reduced time lags in the long-distance receipt of travel-borne news, New York plainly dominated the long-distance circulation of economic information via travel at the national level, while other major centers did so at the regional and subregional levels. In the South, however, because of comparatively infrequent departures, travel-based specialized information flows among the major centers were slow even by the standards of the period.[4]

In keeping with the character of spatial biases in the availability and circulation of specialized economic information at the outset of the 1840–1860 period, the diffusion processes associated with economic innovations in the years immediately preceding 1840 accorded with what one might expect from equation (5.2) and figures 5.3 and 5.4. Among the typical attributes of these pre-1840 processes were the very early receipt or adoption of innovations in the major centers of the national city-system and its component regional city-systems; the large-scale or multiple adoption of innovations in major centers when adoptions were either nonexistent or limited in smaller urban places; the spread of adoption-relevant information and influence from one major center to another; and other elements of nonhierarchical as well as hierarchical information and influence spread. Among these other elements were the occasional diffusion of an innovation from a small- or intermediate-sized city to a major center and the occurrence sometimes of pronounced "neighborhood effects," or concentrated adoption patterns, especially in the vicinity of major centers.[5]

DEVELOPMENTS DURING THE 1840–1860 PERIOD

Important developments in the availability and circulation of specialized information occurred between 1840 and 1860 as a result of changes associated with newspapers, postal services, business travel, and the telegraph.

Newspapers. The importance of the specialized information contained in newspapers to the successful conduct of wholesaling and other economic activities was an antebellum fact of business life. As one writer put it: "The idea that a man generally can succeed in mercantile pursuits without knowing [via the press] what is going on in the [nonlocal] commercial world is absurd—this knowledge he must have in some way or other, or he will most assuredly have to foot up serious losses."[6] Seen in this context, the growth in the number of dailies and of newspapers in general that occurred between 1840 and 1860 (table A.40) can easily lead to the conclusion that just before the Civil War, businessmen outside of major centers were at less of a disadvantage with respect to the availability of published specialized information than they were at the outset of the 1840s. Such a conclusion is very likely to be mistaken, and for a number of reasons.

Between 1840 and 1860, although daily newspapers became more common in medium-sized cities and some smaller urban places, they actually piled up in major centers, where their numbers alone must have ensured that the available volume and variety of nonlocal economic information continued to be greater than elsewhere. (By 1857 there were twelve dailies being published in Philadelphia. Cincinnati had eight to ten daily papers throughout the 1850s. In 1860 St. Louis had ten dailies, or one less than Chicago and four less than San Francisco.)[7] Furthermore, the adoption of Hoe's rotary "lightning press" by the *Philadelphia Public Ledger* in 1847, and by one or more papers in numerous other major centers by 1850, allowed newspapers to be printed at a rate of between 5,000 and 10,000 four-page copies per hour. This, in turn, permitted major-center newspaper circulation to expand at a pace that usually was not matched in less populous cities where the use of Hoe's costly and large-scale machinery was not justified.[8] Consequently, by 1850 a highly disproportionate share of the country's annual newspaper (and news-bearing periodical) circulation was associated with the dailies and other publications of major centers. In fact, twelve of the twenty-nine major centers considered in this work were together responsible for about 60 percent of the total 1850 circulation, or eight times more than would be expected in view of their combined share of the nation's population (table A.41). However, the circulation of these publications was far from being local within the twelve major centers, for many of the large dailies, such as the *New York Tribune* and the *Boston Evening Transcript,* issued special weekly or fortnightly editions designed for smaller city and rural audiences.[9] Nevertheless, businessmen who received such special editions unavoidably acquired any included price or market information later than major-center readers, and the purchasing actions of small-town and country merchants were frequently influenced by the major-center advertisements appearing in these editions.[10]

The availability of specialized economic information through the press often was also greater in major centers because the assortment of business intelligence and reports on the "Mechanic Arts" printed in the regular dailies[11] was augmented by highly specialized commercial newspapers—such as the *New York Shipping and Commercial List, New York Journal of Commerce, New Orleans Price Current, Cincinnati Price Current, Commercial List and Philadelphia Price Current,* and *San Francisco Mercantile Gazette and Prices Current*—whose threshold (or minimum market) conditions for publication could not be met elsewhere. Furthermore, "mercantile libraries" and retail "literary

depots," or newspaper agencies, where numerous nonlocal papers relevant to business activities could be perused or purchased, were restricted to places such as New York, Boston, Philadelphia, Baltimore,
Cincinnati, New Orleans, Pittsburgh, St. Louis, Louisville, San Francisco, and Charleston, again because of threshold requirements.[12]

Since antebellum daily newspaper circulation was so heavily concentrated in major centers, businessmen in those large cities stood to gain
most from the informational benefits generally bestowed upon dailies by
the spread of the telegraph after 1844. In particular, the use of the telegraph to forward information greatly reduced the time lags between the
nonlocal generation of economic news and the local publication of such
news—to a degree that was not generally possible in the less populous
urban places that lacked a daily newspaper. For example, time lags in
economic news between New York and New Orleans were cut down
from an average of 10.6 days in 1841 to an average of about one day,
not long after the first telegraph connections between the two places
were completed in 1849. Likewise, between 1846 and 1847, when New
York and Buffalo became telegraphically linked, the average delay in
the publishing of New York market reports in Buffalo tumbled from 4.1
days to less than a day (0.9). And, whereas the market and other economic accounts from Philadelphia, New York, and Boston carried in
Pittsburgh's dailies were commonly five or more days old in 1841, they
were typically less than one day old in 1847.[13] As telegraphic operations
became more dependable, the late afternoon dailies of major centers
carried same-day market reports from other major centers.[14] The telegraph also enabled the same-day transmission of incoming European
economic news from Boston or New York to the dailies of other major
centers, especially after the formation of the New York Associated
Press in 1848. (Subsequent to 1850, Halifax, Nova Scotia, became the
principal point used by the Associated Press from which to forward European information to major-center dailies.)[15]

Postal Services. In 1845, costly distance-graduated postage rates,
which ran as high as twenty-five cents per sheet for any distance over
400 miles, were reduced considerably. Rates fell to five cents per sheet
for any distance under 300 miles and ten cents per sheet for any distance beyond that. In 1851, the prepaid postage rate was further cut to
three cents per sheet for any distance up to 3,000 miles.[16] Yet despite
three factors—these rate reforms, which presumably put the frequent
use of governmental postal services within the reach of a larger segment
of the nonbusiness population,[17] the expanded operations of the U.S.
Post Office as a whole (table A.42), and the importance assumed by the

telegraph as a means for moving specialized economic information
directly from one person to another—businessmen, and especially those
based in major centers, apparently remained the leading (but not the
completely dominant) users of the official mails throughout the antebellum period. As late as 1857, the mails were still recognized as a vital
"means of extending commerce," and it was asserted that "it is clear . . .
the adult male business population have occasion to write from a hundred to a thousand letters each, per annum."[18] The continued high-vol-
ume use of the mails by wholesalers, forwarders, industrial entrepreneurs, and other men of commerce probably resulted from their need to
dispatch bills, detailed orders, and routine business documents in writ-
ten form at a time when the cost of sending lengthy inquiries, instructions, and reports by telegraph was still high.

That the absolute and relative volumes of specialized economic information locally circulating as a result of the mails continued to be quite
a bit larger in major centers than elsewhere is suggested strongly by the
1852 data contained in table A.43. There it can be seen that the letters
arriving in and departing from New York alone corresponded to over 22
percent of the total carried by the U.S. Post Office, and that approximately 28 percent of all letters *originated* in the country's five largest
cities and San Francisco. The superior availability of mail-acquired and
mail-dispatched economic information in major centers is further supported by less precise data for 1856, which show reported major centers
generating four to eight times the volume of mail that might be expected from their population levels (table A.44), and also by statistics
for 1854 indicating the quantities of letters and newspapers conveyed
between major centers and foreign origins and destinations (table A.45).
Admittedly, the 1854 figures were influenced by contractual agreements
between the Post Office and shipping companies operating out of the
listed ports; that is, some of the mails conveyed to and from the centers
in question must have had their ultimate origin or destination elsewhere in the United States. However, under these arrangements foreign
economic news carried by post must normally have circulated in a given
major center before it was available in other places receiving forwarded
mail from the same center.

Major centers did not only continue to dominate the volume of specialized economic information conveyed by the mails throughout the
1840s and 1850s, but businessmen in major centers also continued to be
favored during those decades by interurban public postal services that
were generally faster and more frequent between such centers than between other places. (Nevertheless, in the South, postal connections in-

volving the major centers remained decidedly inferior to those between major centers in the Northeast or Midwest.) Where existing railroads made it possible, special attention was devoted to through rail deliveries between major terminal centers.[19] Moreover, medium- and long-distance mails that were *not* bound for a major center usually were carried to the major center nearest to the ultimate destination and redistributed from there. This often put the smaller-city recipient of exploitable information at a disadvantage of at least one day, especially after intraurban delivery services developed during the mid- and late 1850s in New York, Philadelphia, Boston, Baltimore, New Orleans, Washington, St. Louis, San Francisco, Providence, Lowell, and Syracuse.[20]

The 1840s in particular saw the mushrooming of so-called "express" firms, or privately operated mail services specializing in the conveyance of newspapers and packages as well as drafts, banknotes, specie, and bills between major centers.[21] Express firms flourished because of the speculative profits that often could be reaped from the early receipt of specialized information, because of the high premium placed on the quick completion of business transactions, and because of the occasionally unreliable operations of the U.S. Post Office along its principal routes. The first of these private services, dating back to 1839, had linked New York and Boston. Philadelphia and Albany joined the private express network in 1841. Baltimore, Richmond, and Charleston were added two years later. In 1845 the Wells Fargo Company provided an express line between Buffalo and Detroit; and by 1850–1851 the businessmen of every major center in the country, including San Francisco, could take advantage of the services offered by one or more express firms. (Expresses from New York and New Orleans reached San Francisco by a combination of steamship travel to Panama or Nicaragua, then movement overland, and finally steamship up the Pacific Coast.)[22] Even though the telegraph somewhat reduced the urgency of acquiring out-of-town newspapers as quickly as possible, the express firms were still known in 1860 for their ability to supply such newspapers to major-center consumers in advance of the mails.[23]

Business Travel. The interurban travel via common carrier of wholesalers, retailers, and other businessmen—who often transferred or acquired detailed information on supply and demand factors, innovations, and economic conditions in general while pursuing their purchase or sales errands—was promoted in several ways during the 1840–1860 period. Not only did the country's total railroad mileage grow more than tenfold during that span of years (table A.1), but major river and lake steamboat lines augmented their service frequencies, steamships increasingly replaced sailing vessels on lengthy coastal routes, and rail-roads stepped up their operating speeds through the use of improved tracks and rolling stock. In 1860, the most efficient rail routes were characterized by average operating speeds of thirty to thirty-five miles per hour. And on more typical routes, the average operating speed of twenty miles per hour was about double what it had been twenty years earlier.[24] At the same time, railroad passenger fares declined somewhat, although they remained appreciably higher than prevailing water rates and thus were costly for those with a normal income. For example, an 1854 round-trip New York–Boston fare of ten dollars would have cost an average nonfarm laborer the equivalent of ten or eleven days' hard-earned wages.[25] "In 1848 [railroad passenger] rates a mile averaged 3 cents or less in New England, 2.5 to 3.5 cents in New York, less than 4.5 in the West, and 4 to 5 cents in the South. By the middle fifties they appear to have been slightly lower."[26]

In spite of the general inducements to increased business travel, the overall pattern of movement established by the early 1840s appears to have been preserved and reinforced during the pre-Civil War period, not least by the accumulation of railroad nodality (and service fre-quency) at major centers, especially in the Northeast and Midwest (maps 3.1–3.3). Clearly, the building up of such nodality and service fre-quency accords with the previously outlined manner in which transpor-tation improvements between major centers spawned feedbacks that eventually led to additional transportation improvements focused on those same major centers.[27]

New York retained its unique position as the national city-system's hub of long-distance economic information circulation via business travel. Competition encouraged faster and more frequent trains (and connecting steamboats) on the lines linking New York with Boston, Philadelphia, Baltimore, and Buffalo.[28] Better service to the last three cities also meant improved access to and from Pittsburgh, Cincinnati, St. Louis, Chicago, and the other major centers of the Midwest. In addi-tion, competition led to increased use of speedier steamships instead of sailing packets between New York and New Orleans and the other major southern ports.[29] By the early 1850s several million one-way busi-ness trips originated or terminated in New York, and the advantages accruing to the city's merchants from "the multitude of people" with whom they came in contact were often acknowledged by observers.[30] During the year ending in July 1851, about 840,000 passengers were car-ried on the New York-Philadelphia railroad and steamship route. In the same year nearly one million passengers journeyed up and down the

Hudson between New York and numerous places, the most important of which was Albany with its connections to western major centers.[31]

The clear dominance of regional-level business travel by traffic to and between major centers—except in the South—is illustrated by a few selected pieces of evidence pertaining to conditions in the crystallizing midwestern regional city-system.[32] In a twelve months' period of 1850–1851, Cincinnati-Pittsburgh steamboats transported almost 90,000 passengers, the equivalent of 476 one-way trips per thousand persons for the combined population of the two cities. This constituted a higher level of relative interaction than had existed on the prime route between New York and Philadelphia in 1840.[33] Based on a nine months' nagivation season and what is known of the number of cabin, or first-class nonmigrant, passengers carried on a single trip, it is quite likely that the absolute and relative volume of one-way trips between Cincinnati and Louisville was even greater in 1854.[34] Immediately upon completion of the Michigan Central Railroad in 1852, two daily through trains were offered in each direction between Detroit and Chicago, with direct steamer connections to Cleveland and Buffalo (and on to New York and Boston via an additional "Express train" connection).[35] By 1857 the number of passenger trains daily entering and leaving Chicago via all of its railroads had reached 120. And one year later, the Milwaukee and Chicago Railroad alone carried 90,475 through passengers (or 575 one-way trips per thousand persons for the combined 1860 population of Milwaukee and Chicago), while the Pittsburgh, Fort Wayne and Chicago Railroad moved 44,275 through passengers over its 465-mile length.[36] Not least impressive, as early as 1850–1851 the total number of business and migrant passengers arriving at and departing from midwestern major centers was in each case several times greater than the local population (table A.46).[37]

The Telegraph. In an era when time was "the great item with commercial men,"[38] the electromagnetic telegraph was bound to have profound impacts on the acquisition, exchange, and circulation of specialized economic information by major-center businessmen—impacts other than those already mentioned in conjunction with the use of telegraphic services by daily newspapers. This fact should be self-evident inasmuch as a great deal of the capital invested in telegraph-line construction between 1844 and 1860 came from major-center entrepreneurs intent upon exploiting the informational advantages of telegraphic services.[39]

Except under life-and-death circumstances, the cost of antebellum telegraphic services, and thereby the cost of avoiding lengthy informational time lags, must have appeared prohibitive to the vast majority of people who were not connected with business ventures or the press. More precisely, message rates in the late 1840s and thereafter typically ran to twenty-five cents for the first ten words or less sent up to one hundred miles, with widely ranging higher charges assessed for longer distances, and further payments exacted (for all distances) for each additional word. For example, a 10-word message sent from Washington, D.C., to New Orleans, or a 21-word message wired from Chicago to New York would have cost over two dollars, or about two days' wages for an average nonfarm laborer.[40] In the face of rates that greatly discouraged the general public, the total volume of telegraphic messages for the country as a whole during the 1840–1860 period never surpassed more than four or five million per year, a figure equal to only a small percentage of the total number of letters carried in 1860 alone (see table A.42).[41] High costs so limited the use of the telegraph that even on the relatively inexpensive lines between New York and Boston approximately 74 percent of the 20,400 messages sent during November 1856 were business-related, with the press presumably accounting for the largest share of the remainder.[42]

There were many purposes to which businessmen put the electromagnetic telegraph with its capacity for transmitting information over long distances with unprecedented speed. (Even the rapidity with which a few Boston, New York, Philadelphia, and Baltimore businessmen had moved shipping and Stock Exchange intelligence by means of semaphores and carrier pigeons was minimal in comparison with the revolutionary speed of the telegraph.) Bankers, wholesalers, manufacturers, and other business people employed telegraphic services to negotiate back and forth several times in the course of a day and to finalize buying or selling arrangements, often on short notice, thereby presumably reducing the need to tie up capital in inventory. They also used the telegraph to give payment instructions, forward as yet unpublished stock prices and market reports, provide other forms of information relating to supply and demand conditions, indicate freighting or shipping desires, coordinate railroad operations so as to make them swifter and safer, extend credit or confirm the financial dependability of prospective customers, and make business appointments and travel bookings.[43] All of these specialized information transactions not only affected when and where business opportunities were exploited, but, since they were performed in minutes and hours rather than days and weeks, they affected the pace at which capital could circulate, turn over, and accumulate.[44] Thus, such transactions often made it more feasible for businessmen to reinvest the capital profits of both wholesaling-trading activities and

manufacturing activities either in their home sectors or in new industrial undertakings that were likely to involve the construction of local
or nearby facilities.[45]

From the very outset, both mercantile and manufacturing businessmen in major centers were in a position to benefit more from the
specialized information advantages and capital accumulation possibilities of the telegraph than were most of their less fortunately situated
colleagues. The course of the very first lines of telegraph wire strung
across the landscape for commercial purposes was much influenced by
the appointment in 1845 of Amos Kendall, a former Postmaster General, as the first agent for three-fourths of Samuel F. B. Morse's patent
interest. Based on his familiarity with what were already the principal
postal and business-travel routes of the country, Kendall sought to interest private capital in the construction of trunk lines that would
parallel those routes. One trunk line was to bring New York and Philadelphia into connection with Baltimore and Washington, which had
been linked by the country's first experimental line in May 1844. Another was to join New York and Boston. A third was to proceed from
New York to the major centers of the Great Lakes and the Ohio and
Mississippi valleys via Albany and Buffalo. A fourth was to continue
the New York–Washington linkage onward to New Orleans.[46] By the
early 1850s the construction organized both by the entrepreneurs who
were operating under contracts acquired from Kendall and by their
competitors (who either had gone off on their own or were using other
telegraph patents) had resulted in a telegraph network that included all
four of the trunk lines proposed by Kendall. The network of the early
1850s also included other lines connecting Philadelphia, Baltimore, and
New Orleans with the major centers of the Midwest, as well as lines
passing through or leading to intermediate-sized centers that were expanding quickly, such as Memphis, Indianapolis, and Dayton, though
this network contained relatively little in the way of side and feeder
lines.[47] As a comparison of map 6.1 with maps 3.2 and 3.3 reveals, the
telegraph had linked all the U.S. major centers (except San Francisco)
into a single network long before the railroads accomplished that feat.

It is even more striking that, by 1852, when the total mileage of telegraph lines was approaching 17,000, the provision of multiple wire services by one or more companies was confined almost entirely to situations in which both termini were major centers (table A.47). Along
these routes, but not elsewhere, fierce competition often resulted in the
assessment of preferentially low rates between the major termini, especially before the formation of the American Telegraph Company and

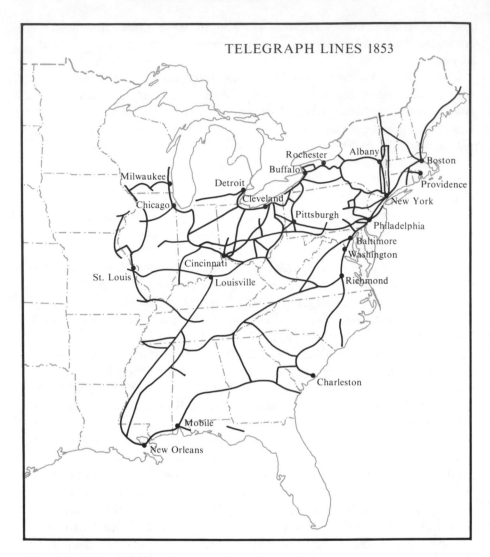

Map 6.1. Telegraph lines in operation, 1853. Adapted from an 1853 map, as reproduced in Robert Luther Thompson, *Wiring a Continent: The History of the Telegraph Industry in the United States, 1832–1866* (Princeton: Princeton University Press, 1947), facing p. 240, and modified by Clifford L. Lord and Elizabeth H. Lord, *Historical Atlas of the United States* (New York: Henry Holt and Co., 1953), p. 78.

the Western Union Telegraph Company in the late 1850s. The most pronounced of these rate reductions, which were sometimes regarded as suicidal, occurred between New York—"the grand focus" of the national telegraph system—and Boston, Philadelphia, and Buffalo.[48] In addition, business users of the telegraph were not so subject to undependable service and postponed messages if more than one wire connected two places. Because of the primitive technology and the cheap and careless construction techniques employed by profit-greedy contractors, the functioning of almost all the early telegraph lines was frequently unreliable and ephemeral. Wires were often grounded by heavy winds or sleet, poles often collapsed after rotting if they had not already been blown down or washed away, poorly jointed wires interrupted transmission, and faulty insulators were constantly troublesome.[49]

During their early years of operation, when the development and application of many important transmission improvements were still in the offing, telegraph companies further reinforced the high-priority information-flow linkages binding together nationally and regionally dominant urban centers by allowing "through business" between major cities to be given wire-access preference over "way business" involving places with less population and economic importance. To give one example, the conditions obtaining on the New York–Buffalo line in 1848 were described as follows: "In the morning, two or three of the most important stations, such as New York, Albany, and Buffalo, have exclusive possession of the wires till their business is completed. If that takes half the day or all day, well and good, so far as they are concerned. The moment the favored points have been served, there is a general scramble among the operators [at other locations] for the wires . . ."[50] After 1858 it became feasible to erect "special wires for direct communication between the great commercial centers."[51] This resulted from the introduction of the Hicks Automatic Repeater, which removed the necessity of retapping messages at intermediate points when they were to be transmitted over very great distances.

As the number of places in the United States served by the telegraph quickly expanded from about 450 in 1852 to over 800 in 1857,[52] major-center businessmen were able to keep any "hot" price changes or other sensitive economic information of local or distant origin secret from curious operators and listeners at smaller urban locations (where such information was less readily available) by employing agreed-upon code words, or ciphers. The usefulness of this procedure, which had the added advantage of reducing message costs when one cipher could stand for several words or an entire sentence, is reflected by the fact

that about 5 percent of the business-related Boston–New York telegraph traffic of November 1856 took this form. Sometimes unscrupulous
men exploited the general informational advantages of major centers by
using the telegraph to spread deliberately misleading or false reports in
order to manipulate markets for their own profit.[53]

Although the precise extent to which the businessmen of major centers dominated antebellum telegraph usage cannot be pinned down, a
few scattered fragments of data are highly suggestive. If the November
1856 volume and breakdown of message flows between New York and
Boston were representative of year-round conditions, then the annual
total of business-related telegraphic dispatches between those two
places alone must have amounted to about 180,000, or at least 5 percent
of all the business and nonbusiness messages wired throughout the
country in 1856.[54] (Not until 1858 were any claims made that the current number of messages annually passing over all U.S. telegraph lines
had reached 4 million.)[55] Moreover, if the ratios of previous years still
prevailed, the through traffic between New York and Boston was at
least two or three times greater than the combined intervening way
traffic associated with these two centers.[56] On the basis of the daily
message-volume figures for 1852, it would appear that the business traffic between New York and Albany and Buffalo exceeded the share of
the nation's total telegraphic traffic accounted for by New York–Boston
business dispatches.[57] The 1850 traffic over the 450-mile telegraph line
connecting Pittsburgh, Cincinnati, Louisville, and numerous intermediately situated urban places is known to have been overwhelmingly concentrated at the line's three major centers (table A.48). Two years earlier, the highest percentage of messages carried over this line consisted
of through dispatches between Cincinnati and Pittsburgh.[58] Finally, during the early 1850s the message flows between Philadelphia and Pittsburgh yielded some of the highest telegraph company dividends in the
country.[59]

NONLOCAL PLACE MENTIONS MADE BY MAJOR-CENTER NEWSPAPERS
IN AN ECONOMIC CONTEXT

The consideration of information circulation developments during the
1840–1860 period has left little doubt that major centers either strengthened their previously existing advantages and spatial biases with respect to the procurement and exchange of specialized economic information, or that they acquired new advantages and biases. However,
nothing has been said regarding the full array of locations with which

the businessmen of given cities, over a specific period of time, exchanged specialized economic information. Quite clearly, it is not possible to obtain a complete picture of the places from which the wholesalers, industrialists, and bankers of a particular center might have learned
of business opportunities or received innovation-relevant information.
Nevertheless, some insights can be obtained by performing limited content analyses of the nonlocal place mentions made by major-center
newspapers in conjunction with the presentation of economic news and
information.

Content Analysis Background. A single copy of any antebellum daily
published in a major center carried hundreds of pieces of nonlocal information with economic connotations, most of which were locationally
specific. To begin with, there were locationally specific news accounts of
market conditions, railroad construction and traffic, technological innovations, and the impact of the weather on agriculture, inland and
coastal shipping, and post-office and telegraph operations. Then there
were the more commonly occurring lists of many kinds: for example,
lists of shipping arrivals and departures, of nonlocal market prices, of
nonlocal bank-note exchange rates, of railroad stock prices, of post-office sending and receiving schedules, and of hotel guests and their
places of origin. Finally, there were the widely ranging advertisements:
advertisements and "business cards" placed by nonlocal jobbers, commission merchants, manufacturing agents, and insurance companies; advertisements submitted by local agents for nonlocal wholesalers and
manufacturers; advertisements placed by local retailers and wholesalers
indicating, among other things, the place of origin of their goods; advertisements describing railroad, steamboat, stagecoach, and telegraph services and rates; and advertisements for the sale of nonlocal real estate.

Because of the wealth of locationally specific economic matter carried
by the dailies of antebellum major centers, and also because of the time
and effort required to perform a content analysis of even a very small
sample of newspapers, it has been necessary to focus on one or two
years and also to limit analysis to nine major centers.[60] The year 1851
was chosen for closest scrutiny, partly because it was near the midpoint
of the 1840–1860 period, and partly because it was the first year in
which the telegraph was used commonly by the dailies of every major
center except San Francisco. Some attention also was given to newspapers published in 1860, so as to determine what significant changes, if
any, had occurred by the end of the period. For seven of the nine major
centers, a random, seasonally stratified sample of between three and
five newspaper issues was used in executing the 1851 content analyses,

and a similar sample was employed in the 1860 survey performed for a few of those same large cities.[61] Since well over a thousand place mentions were generated in any specific case, a larger sample was not called for, especially because of the highly repetitious character of many daily published lists and advertisements. Since the marketing of most agricultural goods was highly seasonal, and shipping on interior waterways normally was suspended for part of the year, it was necessary to stratify each sample seasonally by keeping the analyzed issues roughly two to four months apart from one another.

The content analyses resulting from the tallying of every nonlocal place name mentioned in an economic context suffer from several shortcomings.[62] Each newspaper mention of a place was given equal weight, even though, at one extreme, the place mention might be buried in a lengthy list of some kind, while at the other extreme the place mention might occur in an economic news story running several paragraphs and pertaining wholly or largely to the specific place. Inasmuch as editorial policies varied from daily to daily in the same major center—some, for example, might carry more commercially relevant lists than others—it is quite possible that the analysis of different papers might have yielded different results. In addition, newspapers other than those analyzed might have been more influential in the decision-making of local businessmen and therefore might have made better subjects of inquiry. Moreover, although the informational spatial biases identified from a particular content analysis may be assumed to be similar in array and significance to the patterns associated with business travel and the use of postal and telegraphic services at the same major center, it cannot be demonstrated that this was actually the case. Such an assumption is particularly questionable because privately conveyed information normally makes more of an impact upon individuals than information obtained from public sources (such as newspapers), unless public information is initially received or duplicated in verbal form from other respected individuals, or "influentials."[63]

Content Analysis Results. The summary data derived from the content analysis of selected dailies published in 1851 in New York, Philadelphia, Boston, New Orleans, Cincinnati, St. Louis, Chicago, Cleveland, and San Francisco speak for themselves in at least one very important respect (tables A.49 and A.50). As might be expected from both the summary of urban interdependence dyads and the probabilistic framework presented in chapter 5, mentions of other major centers were the most prominent feature of each content analysis. In fact, in all but one case other major centers accounted for reasonably close to 50 percent, or more, of the total number of nonlocal place mentions. And even in that case (Philadelphia), other major centers still captured over 41 percent of the total number of nonlocal place mentions.

In several other respects the data are consistent with previous empirical observations and conceptual arguments. New York, the leading unit of the national system of cities as well as of the Northeast's regional city-system, was the most frequently mentioned place in every content analysis except those for itself and St. Louis (table A.50). (New York finished second to New Orleans in the St. Louis analysis.) Although the surveyed dailies of New York, Philadelphia, and Boston contained numerous references to other northeastern major centers and to major centers in other parts of the country, their mentions of each other were far more numerous. In addition to their New York references, the most significant mentions found in midwestern major-center dailies were those referring to other midwestern major centers and to two or more of the following cities: Philadelphia, Boston, Baltimore, Albany plus Troy, and New Orleans. (The importance of Buffalo and Cleveland mentions in Cincinnati, of St. Louis mentions in Chicago, and of Cincinnati and Pittsburgh mentions in Cleveland presumably reflects the ongoing merger and expansion of the previously separate Lake Erie regional city-system and the Ohio and upper Mississippi valley regional city-system.) The content analysis for New Orleans supports the contention that the South as a whole lacked a well-articulated regional city-system prior to the Civil War. Mobile was the only southern major center to answer for more than 2 percent of the economic place mentions in the New Orleans sample. Moreover, the combined mentions in New Orleans of Charleston, Richmond, and Mobile amounted to little more than one-fourth of the combined mentions of New York, Philadelphia, and Boston, and to less than three-fourths of the combined mentions of St. Louis, Louisville, and Cincinnati.

A closer diagnosis of the 1851 and 1860 content analyses for both Boston and Cincinnati permits three additional observations of consequence (table A.51 and maps 6.2–6.5). First, even the use of very liberally defined hinterlands does not enable the number of hinterland economic place mentions to surpass the number of major-center economic place mentions.[64] (This holds true despite the fact that, throughout the 1840–1860 period, Boston's immediate sphere of economic influence was the most densely populated and urbanized hinterland in the country.)[65] To put it otherwise, a great many hinterland places were mentioned in an economic context in the dailies of antebellum major centers, but very few of those places were mentioned relatively often.

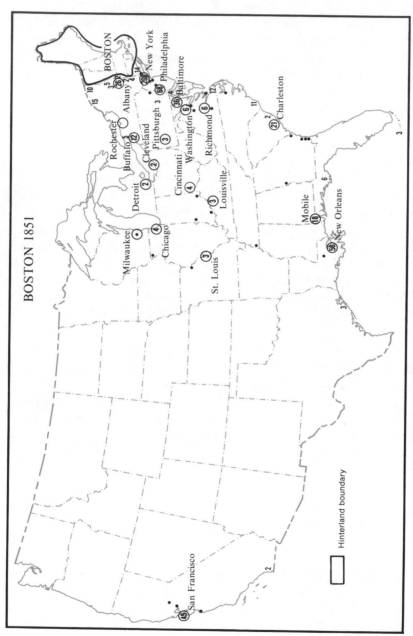

Map 6.2. Nonhinterland place mentions made in an economic context: Boston, 1851. Source: *Boston Evening Transcript*, Jan. 8, May 9, Aug. 29, 1851. Here, and in maps 6.3–6.5, dots indicate single mentions, and numbers specify higher mention frequencies. See note 64 to this chapter for a comment on the liberally defined hinterland boundaries employed here and in maps 6.3–6.5.

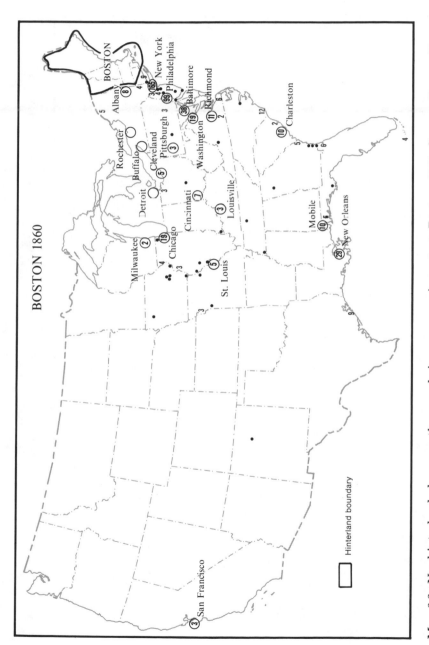

Map 6.3. Nonhinterland place mentions made in an economic context: Boston, 1860. Source: *Boston Evening Transcript*, Feb. 1, June 5, Sept. 8, Nov. 24, 1860.

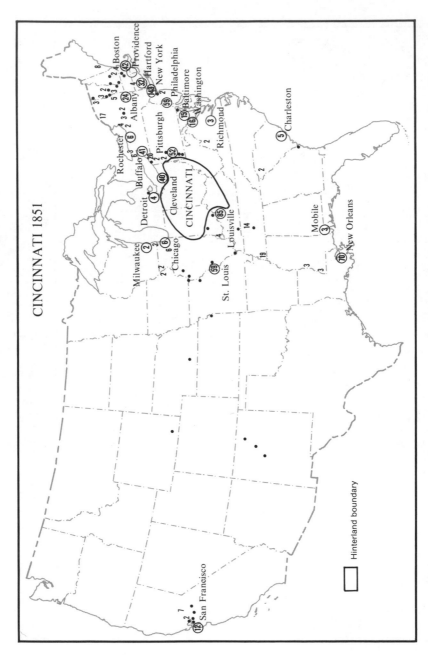

Map 6.4. Nonhinterland place mentions made in an economic context: Cincinnati, 1851. Source: *Cincinnati Enquirer*, Jan. 29, June 12, Aug. 12, 1851.

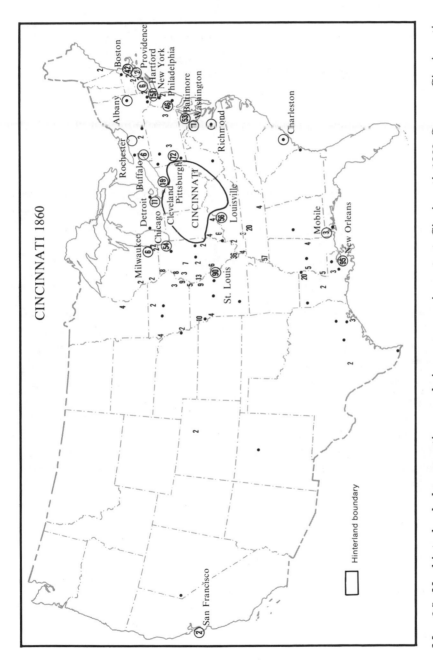

Map 6.5. Nonhinterland place mentions made in an economic context: *Cincinnati*, 1860. Source: *Cincinnati Enquirer*, Jan. 31, June 12, Oct. 3, 1850.

The most frequently mentioned hinterland place in the 1851 Boston content analysis was Worcester, whose number of mentions (thirty-six) was much lower than the number for New York, Philadelphia, New Orleans, and San Francisco, though equal to that for Baltimore. Columbus was the most commonly referenced hinterland place in the 1860 Cincinnati content analysis, but its mentions (nineteen) were exceeded, in that order, by those for New York, New Orleans, St. Louis, Pittsburgh, Memphis (fifty-seven), Louisville, Chicago, and Baltimore.[66]

Second, a closer review of the Boston and Cincinnati content analyses also reveals that as a group the mentions of nonhinterland lesser cities, towns, and settlements in an economic context were least important, but they were significant all the same.[67] Although the share of mentions garnered by nonhinterland places other than major centers is a little higher than might be expected, that should not seem surprising. Those mentions are consistent with the earlier evidence on the secondary importance of economic interdependencies between major centers and less populous nonhinterland places. (It may be speculated that because of the uncertainties involved in conducting new business with small distant places, newspaper mentions of such places did not reflect actual economic interaction to the same extent as mentions of other major centers did.)[68]

Third, between 1851 and 1860 there was some increase in the mention-frequency of nonhinterland lesser cities, towns, and settlements. The greater concentration of place mentions in the upper Mississippi and Missouri valleys in maps 6.3 and 6.5, as opposed to maps 6.2 and 6.4, suggests that this shift in importance was related to both the westward spread of settlement and to the possibilities for more distant economic linkages and more complex city-system interdependencies that the railroad construction of the final antebellum years was beginning to produce.[69] The shift, in short, may have been a harbinger of the even more intricate set of interrelationships that was to evolve in the economy and national city-system of the United States subsequent to the Civil War.

CONCLUDING OBSERVATIONS

It is clear from the discussion of newspaper, postal-service, business-travel, and telegraph developments during the 1840s and 1850s that major centers compounded their information availability and circulation advantages during that period. The content analyses of 1851 and 1860 major-center dailies, though not completely reliable, point to broad

parallels between some of the prevalent forms of urban economic interdependence (described in chapter 5) and the interurban flows of specialized economic information. The individually most important antebellum
city-system interdependencies were those between major centers, while
the most prominent economic place mentions made in large-city newspapers were those referring to other major centers. The most varied,
but not the most intense, interdependence dyads were those between
major centers and less populous urban units within their respective hinterlands, while the most varied, but not the most frequent, place mentions appearing in major-center dailies were those referring to hinterland locations. Dyads of economic interdependence between major
centers and less populous nonhinterland towns and cities were not uncommon, and by the same token small and intermediate-sized nonhinterland places took a secondary but quite visible share of the place
mentions made in an economic context in the daily press of the major
centers.

None of this evidence should be construed as verification of the specialized information component of either the simplified probabilistic
model of the process of antebellum city-system growth and development (figure 5.4), or of the somewhat more particular model of the
means by which major centers reinforced one another's growth, or propensity to attract and retain migrants (figure 5.3). But the evidence
does give plausibility to the specialized information components of both
figures 5.3 and 5.4.

7

Some Closing Words

A book such as this is very likely to cause some controversy. Controversy is likely because the process of urban growth is so complex as to defy total unraveling, regardless of the temporal or geographical setting, and because geographers and other scholars consequently are apt to select different analytical foci and to come up with a variety of interpretations. Controversy is also highly probable because of the period of U.S. history being considered. As a result of the social, economic, and political changes it encompassed, the 1840–1860 period has been the subject of a tremendous volume of scholarship. Much of that scholarship has engendered controversy on issues such as the economics of slavery, the role of the railroads in economic growth, and other matters directly or indirectly related to urban growth.[1] Inasmuch as an aura of controversy surrounds those issues, it is almost inevitable that any treatment of antebellum urban growth will be subject to contention.

Whether or not they awaken controversy, the following important conclusions can be drawn from the findings and arguments of this book.

First, because of the perverse manner in which census sources treat the population growth of newcomers to the urban category, a misleading impression is created as to the 1840–1860 growth performance of so-called major centers, or the twenty-nine cities with about 27,000 or more inhabitants before the outbreak of the Civil War. On the surface it would appear that the population growth of those nationally and regionally important urban units was slower than that of the urban population as a whole. In reality, the absolute population increases associated with U.S. urban growth during the 1840s and 1850s were concentrated highly in certain major centers and their surrounding spillover growth satellites. In particular, such growth concentration (which was largely synonymous with the attraction of in-migrants and the retention of potential out-migrants) was most notable in and around the long-established dominant cities of the Northeast. Growth concentration also characterized both the already identified and the emerging dominant urban units of the Midwest and California.

Second, during the 1840–1860 period the total pattern of interurban economic relationships, or interdependencies, that either continued or appeared for the first time was complex to a degree that suggests a more than rudimentary integration among the expanding membership

of the nation's city-system. Although this was a period in which the
economy of most major centers began (but did not complete) the transition toward a situation in which income and employment were generated primarily by local manufacturing rather than by a mix of wholesaling-trading activities, it was the specialization of manufacturing
functions rather than the nature of industrial technology that contributed to the early complexity of city-system interdependencies. (Unlike
the situation today, few manufacturing-based city-system interdependencies could be traced to extended production systems, or lengthy
input-output chains.) More important, the developing complexity of
city-system interdependencies was closely associated with the fact that
agricultural commodities, natural resources, and industrial goods moving beyond local or nearby markets were quite likely to become involved in a variety of middleman and forwarding transactions. On the
whole, the city-system interdependencies of the 1840s and 1850s were
more intricate than those of the 1790–1840 period in that intraregional
and interregional economic flows between major centers had become
more varied, numerous, and far-flung. For example, not a few major-
center interdependencies in the newly combining midwestern regional
city-system[2] had been either initially facilitated or reoriented by railroad construction and other transportation improvements, improvements that were not autonomous but part and parcel of the accumulating investment decisions associated with the city-system growth and
development process. As a forerunner of an ever more widespread phenomenon after the Civil War, there were complex interdependencies—
usually of secondary importance—that repeatedly took the form of economic flows between a major center and a less populous town or city located beyond the center's normally defined trading hinterland.

Third, the only reservation that need be made concerning the comparative complexity of antebellum city-system interdependencies in-
volves the major centers of the South. Just as had been the case prior
to 1840, those four places (New Orleans, Charleston, Richmond, and
Mobile) evidenced very few of the intraregional major-center relationships that were becoming increasingly prominent and plentiful both in
the Northeast and the Midwest. In fact, New Orleans and Mobile were
the only pair of major centers in the South linked together by a relatively high volume of economic flows, and even their shipments were
limited almost entirely to staples. Instead, each of the cities in question
remained more a "colonial" outlier of the northeastern regional city-system than a member of a well-articulated southern regional city-system.

Fourth, the process by which major centers reinforced one another's growth, and thereby solidified or continued their national or regional dominance and rank stability, can be portrayed in probabilistic terms. And those same terms are applicable to the 1840–1860 process of growth and development occurring both within the U.S. system of cities as a whole and within the regional city-systems of the Northeast and Midwest. The probabilistic model interpretation developed here initially rests on the local and nonlocal multiplier effects associated with each significant expansion of either local wholesaling-trading activity or local manufacturing. From there it builds upon the way in which the interurban economic flows deriving from both newly expanded and earlier established activities contributed to geographic inequalities, or spatial biases, in the circulation and availability of specialized information pertaining either to business opportunities in general or to commercial, industrial, financial, and other growth-inducing innovations. The model interpretation comes full circle when spatial biases in the availability of specialized economic information influence the urban places where business opportunities are exploited and growth-inducing innovations are implemented. (Such exploitation and implementation, by definition, affect where wholesaling-trading and manufacturing activities are expanded locally, and thereby contribute to interurban multiplier effects and flows and to the operation of subsequent growth-feedback rounds.) Furthermore, because of the probabilistic manner in which the system-wide model allows accumulating investment decisions to have a differential effect upon the growth of cities, it can be argued that the size characteristics attained by all U.S. cities as of 1860 represented but one of a tremendous number of possible process outcomes.

Fifth and finally, the little that is known of newspaper, postal-service, business-travel, and telegraph developments between 1840 and 1860 is entirely consistent with the model interpretation of antebellum city-system growth and development inasmuch as that knowledge strongly suggests that major centers reinforced their advantages over other urban places in regard to information circulation and availability. Perhaps more important, the content analyses conducted for selected major center dailies published in 1851 and 1860 indicate—as the model would require—that there were parallels between the general pattern of urban economic interdependence and the general pattern of interurban flows of specialized economic information.

Some readers may reasonably contend that the model interpretation of city-system growth and development presented here—and especially the probabilistic connections it draws between information circulation

and investment decisions—only deals with the surface events associated
with the process in question and thereby lacks a driving engine. It is acknowledged that such a contention is valid insofar as antebellum decisions concerning business opportunity exploitation and the implementation of growth-inducing innovations cannot be separated from the
capital accumulation context within which they occurred.

It certainly would be difficult to deny that decisions affecting the
scale and location of wholesaling-trading and manufacturing activities
were motivated in particular by the desire of businessmen and investors
to increase their excess accumulated capital, and were affected in general by the stage of development that capitalism had reached. It is in-
dicative of the times that wholesalers, industrial entrepreneurs, and investors of various types were often referred to proudly as "capitalists"
on the pages of the leading business periodicals of the 1840s and 1850s,
such as *Hunt's Merchants' Magazine* and *The Bankers' Magazine*; for
this was a period in which entrepreneurs "interpreted their role in production as the accumulators and manipulators of capital as equally important to, if not more important than that of manual labor." In a related vein it also is clear that the functional transformation beginning
to occur within the economy of most major centers between 1840 and
1860 was synonymous with the ongoing transition from commercially
based capital accumulation to industrially based accumulation.[3] (In
passing, it has been speculated here that the spread of the telegraph
network was instrumental in freeing major-center mercantile capital for
manufacturing investment or industrial accumulation, since it greatly
reduced the need for keeping dollars tied up in inventory by reducing
business transaction times, and later by affecting the average operating
speeds of railroads.)[4] It would further appear that there may well have
been a relationship among the following three factors: changes in the
scale at which capital accumulated; market-area and supply-area expansion; and the more widespread and complex interurban economic linkages that emerged in the twenty years preceding the Civil War. Yet it
should be remembered that despite a general shift toward larger-scale
and more capital-intensive means of production, truly large-scale urban
manufacturing facilities were still exceptional in 1860.

In spite of all these admissions, it is probable that a more detailed
consideration and consequently a deeper understanding of the undeni-
ably important capital accumulation context in itself would not have
permitted the feedbacks involved in antebellum city-system growth and
development to have been modeled very differently. To have focused on

the driving engine of capital accumulation, rather than on its decision-making expressions and consequences, would have required the posing of different questions and the writing of a different book.

It may be that this book raises more questions than it answers, partly because of its inherently controversial character and partly because some of its parts are less well documented than others. For instance, the suggested role of the telegraph network in converting major-center mercantile capital into manufacturing capital demands further inquiry insofar as such capital conversion contributed to the industrial and population growth of major centers. (Significantly, contemporaries viewed the telegraph network as a force helping "to consolidate business as to locations.")[5] Also, many questions remain to be answered concerning the ways in which urban growth and city-system development were affected both by specific international linkages between cities and by broader international economic influences.

More generally, much remains to be done in order to bestow greater plausibility upon the informational aspects of this book's model framework. Considerably more fine-grained documentation and analysis are necessary regarding the influences exerted on antebellum urban growth by the information-circulation attributes of newspapers, postal services, business travel, and, above all, the telegraph. The interurban diffusion of specific economic innovations between 1840 and 1860 was of such significance that it merits a tome of its own dealing both with information and influence channels and with growth impacts. (In this connection, there is also a need for a detailed locational analysis of 1840–1860 patent data, which are a good but less than perfect indicator of innovation-diffusion origins.)[6] Moreover, it would be useful to explore the role that spatial biases in the availability and circulation of specialized economic information might have played in place-to-place variations in risk-taking behavior and investment attitudes in general. After all, it can be argued, at least speculatively, that such behavior and attitudinal differences affected the dissimilar rates at which local-growth feedbacks accumulated at major centers.[7] Since differential urban population growth in the 1840s and 1850s has been depicted in terms of the differential ability of places to attract and hold migrants, it also would seem in order to go beyond the explicit specialized information components of the model framework presented in chapter 5. What is necessary, in particular, is a careful investigation of the influences that spatially biased information circulation brought to bear on interurban migration, and, more important, on cityward migration from domestic and foreign rural areas.[8]

In some very general respects, the process of city-system growth and development occurring between 1840 and 1860 was not unique. It is my contention that—regardless of the prevailing institutional, technological, and overall contextual framework—the process of city-system growth and development in all economically advanced countries since the early nineteenth century has involved (at least in part) feedbacks that in a very broad sense are quite similar.[9] In other words, for almost two hundred years the process has subsumed existing economic interdependencies, consequent local and nonlocal employment multipliers, and the impact of specialized information circulation on the investment of accumulated capital in new business opportunities and economic innovations. (This is not to say, of course, that the feedbacks have not become increasingly complex and given themselves new expression, nor is it to say that other outside factors have not exerted a wide range of influences at different times and places.) If this position is accepted, then some of the more general research suggestions just made need not be confined either to the United States or to the 1840–1860 period. It is hoped that other scholars will take up some of these suggestions or will challenge them either with frameworks emphasizing other factors or with differently oriented research undertakings. The state of knowledge concerning such an important question as urban growth (and decline) is still much too rudimentary for scholars to accept unquestioningly either my model formulations or those of anyone else.

Abbreviations

ARJ   *American Railroad Journal and General Advertiser*
BM   *The Bankers' Magazine*
DBR   *DeBow's Review*
HMM *Hunt's Merchants' Magazine*
NWR *Niles' Weekly Register*
NYSL *New York Shipping and Commercial List*
WJ   *The Western Journal*

Table A.1. U.S. population growth and economic change and development, 1840-1860.

Category	(A) 1840	(B) 1850	(C) 1860	(C/A) 1860/1840
Total population	17,069,453	23,191,876	31,443,321	1.84
Urban population as defined by census[a]	1,845,055	3,543,716	6,216,518	3.37
Urban population as a percentage of total population	10.8%	15.3%	19.8	—
Share of manufacturing in value of total commodity output (percent)[b]	17%	30%	32%	—
Value added by manufacturing (millions of dollars in 1879 prices)[b]	$190	$488	$859	4.52
Value added by manufacturing per capita (in 1879 prices)[c]	$11.13	$21.04	$27.32	2.45
Value added by manufacturing per gainful worker (in 1879 prices)[b]	$399	$542	605	1.52
Value of household manufactures production (millions of current dollars)	$29.0	$24.5	$23.2	0.80
Value of household manufactures production per capita (current dollars)	$1.70	$1.18	$0.78	.46
Pig iron shipments (thousands of short tons)	321	631	920	2.87
Anthracite coal production (thousands of short tons)	1,129	4,327	10,984	9.73
Bituminous coal production (thousands of short tons)	1,345	4,029	9,057	6.73
Share of agriculture in value of total commodity output (percent)[b]	72%	60%	56%	—
Value added by agriculture (millions of dollars in 1879 prices)[b]	$787	$989	$1,492	1.90

Table A.1 (continued)

Category	(A) 1840	(B) 1850	(C) 1860	(C/A) 1860/1840
Value added by agriculture per capita (in 1879 prices)[c]	$46.11	$42.60	$47.45	1.03
Value added by agriculture per gainful worker (in 1879 prices)[b]	$212	$202	$240	1.13
Wheat production (thousands of bushels)	84,823	100,486	173,105	2.04
Corn production (for grain purposes only, thousands of bushels)	377,532	592,071	838,793	2.22
Cotton production (thousands of bales)	1,348	2,136	3,841	2.85
Miles of railroad in operation	2,818	9,021	30,626	10.87
Miles of telegraph line in operation	0	12,100	50,000	—
Tonnage of steam and sailing vessels				
on Western Rivers	117,952	302,829	369,004	3.13
in Great Lakes trade	48,262	200,507	450,726	9.34
in coasting trade	1,010,144	1,313,761	2,014,005	1.99

Sources: U.S. Bureau of the Census, *Census of Population: 1970, Number of Inhabitants—United States Summary* (Washington, D.C., 1971), p. 42; idem, *Historical Statistics of the United States: Colonial Times to 1957* (Washington, D.C., 1960), pp. 297, 302, 357, 360, 366, 427; Robert E. Gallman, "Commodity Output, 1839–1899," in *Trends in the American Economy in the Nineteenth Century* (Princeton: Princeton University Press, 1960), pp. 26, 31, 43; Douglas C. North, *The Economic Growth of the United States, 1790–1860* (New York: W. W. Norton, 1966), pp. 252, 254; George Rogers Taylor, *The Transportation Revolution, 1815–1860* (New York: Holt, Rinehart and Winston, 1951), p. 152; Robert Luther Thompson, *Wiring a Continent: The History of the Telegraph Industry in the United States, 1832–1866* (Princeton: Princeton University Press, 1947), p. 241; Rolla M. Tryon, *Household Manufactures in the United States, 1640–1860* (Chicago: University of Chicago Press, 1917), pp. 308–309.

a. For comments concerning some misleading aspects of urban population totals as defined by the census, see chap. 2, second section.

b. Data for 1839, 1849, and 1859.

c. Value-added totals for 1839, 1849, and 1859 divided respectively by population totals for 1840, 1850, and 1860.

Table A.2. Antebellum western agricultural exports via New Orleans.

Commodity	Percentage of western exports shipped via New Orleans			Percentage of western exports reexported to the Northeast and abroad via New Orleans		
	1839	1849	1860	1842	1849	1860
Flour	53	31	22	31	22	3
Meat products	51	50	24	30	33	1
Corn	98	39	19	53	31	2
Whiskey	96	67	40	19	7	1
Total foodstuffs[a]	49	40	17	31	28	3

Sources: Albert Fishlow, "Antebellum Interregional Trade Reconsidered," *American Economic Review,* 54 (May 1964), 356; and idem, *American Railroads and the Trans-formation of the Ante-Bellum Economy* (Cambridge: Harvard University Press, 1965), p. 284.

a. Including wheat, which is not listed separately. Throughout the 1840–1860 period western wheat exports via New Orleans were relatively insignificant, reaching a high of about 9 percent in 1857 and falling off to virtually nothing by 1860. See A. L. Kohl-meier, *The Old Northwest as the Keystone of the Arch of American Federal Union* (Bloomington, Ind.: Principia Press, 1938), pp. 33, 83, 116, 146, 191.

Table A.3. Value of U.S. boot and shoe production in Boston's hinterland, 1850-1860 (in current dollars and percentages).

Value	1850	1860
Dollar value produced in United States	$53,967,408	$91,891,498
Percentage produced in Boston hinterland		
Massachusetts	44.7%	50.4%
New Hampshire	4.8	4.2
Maine	1.8	2.1
Total	51.3	56.7

Sources: *Eighth Census, Manufactures of the United States in 1860* (Washington, D.C., 1865), p. lxxiii; and Edgar M. Hoover, Jr., *Location Theory and the Shoe and Leather Industries* (Cambridge: Harvard University Press, 1937), p. 180.

Table A.4. Output and labor productivity in the boot and shoe industry of Lynn, 1845-1860.

Year	Total pairs of boots and shoes produced	Total workers employed[a]	Productivity (pairs per worker)[b]
1845	2,406,722	5,928	406.0
1848	3,190,000	8,458	377.2
1850	4,571,400	10,486	437.0
1852	4,952,300	11,623	426.1
1855	9,275,593	15,566	595.9
1860	6,000,000	8,629	695.3

Sources: "New York Industrial Exhibition, Special Report of Mr. George Wallis, Presented to the House of Commons by Command of Her Majesty in Persuance of Their Address of February 6, 1854," in Nathan Rosenberg, ed., *The American System of Manufactures* (Edinburgh: Edinburgh University Press, 1969), pp. 255–257; *DBR,* 7 (1850), 368; *ARJ,* 24 (1851), 294; *HMM,* 24 (July–December 1851), 132; Massachusetts, Secretary of the Commonwealth, *Statistical Information Relating to Certain Branches of Industry in Massachusetts* (Boston, 1856), p. 140; J. Leander Bishop, *A History of American Manufactures from 1608 to 1860* (Philadelphia, 1868), III, 318.

a. Includes local residents and rural outworkers.

b. The productivity ratios must be regarded as crude inasmuch as they make no allowance for year-to-year variations in the proportion of seasonal workers included in the total employment figures.

Table A.5. Production (1855) and population (1860) of urban places in Massachusetts acting as major suppliers to Boston's boot and shoe wholesalers.

Urban place	Production 1855		Population 1860[b]
	Total pairs of boots and shoes	Value[a]	
Lynn	9,275,593	$4,165,529	19,083
Haverhill	4,332,015	2,782,930	9,995
Marblehead	2,835,724	1,020,373	7,646
Marlborough	2,075,000	1,156,975	5,911
Abington	1,817,624	2,167,356	< 2,500
Stoneham	1,392,000	729,160	3,206
Danvers	1,330,000	1,000,000	5,110
Natick	1,281,865	1,163,808	5,515
Milford	1,047,992	1,787,315	< 2,500
Weymouth	987,332	1,593,080	7,742
North Bridgewater	761,356	724,847	< 2,500
Worcester	735,212	1,160,970	24,960
Randolph	708,400	1,269,400	5,760
Grafton	691,144	580,856	< 2,500
North Brookfield	625,500	655,450	< 2,500
Hopkinton	600,474	1,058,820	< 2,500
Westborough	597,000	421,000	< 2,500
East Bridgewater	445,320	399,200	< 2,500
Oxford	427,200	263,800	< 2,500
Stoughton	371,012	938,935	4,830
Woburn	354,684	279,287	6,287

Table A.5 (continued)

| Urban place | Production 1855 | | Population 1860[b] |
	Total pairs of boots and shoes	Value[a]	
Holliston	345,259	414,484	< 2,500
South Reading	342,708	318,013	< 2,500
Georgetown	339,540	336,320	< 2,500
Beverly	287,600	171,000	6,154
Reading	287,000	191,500	2,662
Raynham	250,000	250,000	< 2,500
Southborough	249,800	202,100	< 2,500
Sutton	229,500	197,800	< 2,500
Brookfield	225,000	272,000	< 2,500
Spencer	205,102	410,204	< 2,500
Duxbury	203,005	153,598	< 2,500
Plymouth	176,050	155,000	< 2,500
West Bridgewater	169,300	176,460	< 2,500
Bridgewater	166,600	125,700	< 2,500
Middleborough	161,285	161,336	< 2,500
Hanson	147,558	158,230	< 2,500
Hanover	145,204	233,282	< 2,500
Groveland	141,870	152,039	< 2,500
Webster	141,700	111,000	< 2,500
Melrose	130,186	99,428	2,532
Mendon	127,040	209,200	< 2,500
North Reading	127,000	144,000	< 2,500
Easton	125,700	153,200	< 2,500
Braintree	124,713	237,252	3,468
Groton	117,500	108,000	< 2,500
Needham	113,400	118,120	2,658
Ashland	104,444	143,500	< 2,500
Upton	104,000	179,000	< 2,500
Medway	102,275	155,000	< 2,500
Northbridge	100,000	120,000	< 2,500
Total for major supplying places	38,182,786	$31,175,797	—
Massachusetts total	45,066,828	$37,501,723	—

Sources: Secretary of the Commonwealth, *Statistical Information Relating to Certain Branches of Industry in Massachusetts* (Boston, 1856); *Eighth Census, Population of the United States in 1860* (Washington, D.C., 1864); and *Census of Population: 1960* (Washington, D.C., 1961), vol. I, part A.

a. Examination will reveal a significant place-to-place variation in average value per pair of boots and shoes produced. This reflects the local specialization of output. For example, Randolph, which had a comparatively high value per pair ($1.79) specialized in "the finer quality of boots for gentlemen" ("Special Report of Mr. George Wallis," p. 255).

b. Some of the places whose 1860 population is indicated as being below 2,500 actually may have had a greater number of inhabitants. The places in question belonged to townships of the same name, and the 1860 census only provided a population total for those townships as a whole.

Table A.6. Leather shipments to Boston, 1852.

Place of origin	Sides	Bundles
New York and Albany	180,109	2,686
Baltimore	19,314	20,137
Philadelphia	11,648	8,084
Western Railroad[a]	110,771	35,405
New Orleans	—	3,148
Other domestic sources	75,576	23,690
Direct foreign imports[b]	210	297
Total	397,628	93,447

Source: *DBR,* 14 (1853), 257.

a. The Western Railroad provided Boston with a rail connection to Albany. Presumably, most of the leather arriving from this source originated in New York State and states farther to the west, rather than within Massachusetts.

b. On the basis of what is known about the magnitude of foreign "sole and upper leather" imports to New York in subsequent years, it may be assumed that a good portion of the leather reaching Boston through the hands of New York wholesalers was ultimately of foreign origin. *HMM,* 45 (July–December 1861), 37.

Table A.7. Shipments of boots and shoes from Boston to major urban centers, 1859.

Major center	Estimated cases	Estimated number of pairs[a]	Percentage of all domestic shipments to points outside New England[b]
New York	182,207	9,110,350	25.38%
San Francisco	63,887	3,194,350	8.90
Baltimore	62,464	3,123,200	8.70
Philadelphia	59,119	2,955,950	8.23
St. Louis	55,774	2,788,700	7.77
Cincinnati	44,882	2,244,100	6.25
New Orleans	37,686	1,884,300	5.25
Louisville	21,119	1,055,950	2.94
Chicago	19,168	958,400	2.67
Charleston	17,177	858,850	2.39
Richmond	3,000-5,000	150,000-250,000	0.41-0.70
Detroit	3,000-5,000	150,000-250,000	0.41-0.70
Buffalo	3,000-5,000	150,000-250,000	0.41-0.70
Pittsburgh	3,000-5,000	150,000-250,000	0.41-0.70
Milwaukee	3,000-5,000	150,000-250,000	0.41-0.70
Albany (+Troy)	3,000-5,000	150,000-250,000	0.41-0.70
Rochester	2,000-3,000	100,000-150,000	0.28-0.41
Syracuse	1,000-2,000	50,000-100,000	0.14-0.28
Washington, D.C.	53	2,650	0.01
Total	584,538-598,536	29,226,800-29,926,800	81.37-83.38%

Source: HMM, 42 (January–June 1860), 611.

a. Obtained in each instance by multiplying the number of reported cases by fifty, since the source asserted this was the average number of pairs per case. However, an account of a few years earlier stated that cases held five boxes, each containing one dozen pairs, or a total of sixty pairs to the case. "Special Report of Mr. George Wallis," p. 255.

b. Foreign exports of boots and shoes from Boston were insignificant, the 2,920 cases going to Australia having constituted "more than half" the total shipped abroad. For shipments within New England, see text.

Table A.8. Shipments of boots and shoes from Boston to nonhinterland urban places of intermediate and small size, 1859.

Urban place	1860 population	Cases	Estimated number of pairs[a]
Memphis	22,623	3,000-5,000	150,000-250,000
Nashville	16,988	13,781	689,050
Savannah	22,292	2,000-3,000	100,000-150,000
Indianapolis	18,611	2,000-3,000	100,000-150,000
New Albany, Ind.	12,647	200,300	100,000-150,000
Lexington, Ky.	9,521	2,000-3,000	100,000-150,000
St. Joseph, Mo.	8,932	2,000-3,000	100,000-150,000
Keokuk, Iowa	8,136	2,000-3,000	100,000-150,000
Alton, Ill.	6,332	2,000-3,000	100,000-150,000
Portsmouth, Ohio	6,268	2,000-3,000	100,000-150,000
Dayton, Ohio	20,081	1,000-2,000	50,000-100,000
Columbus, Ohio	18,854	1,000-2,000	50,000-100,000
Norfolk, Va.	14,620	1,000-2,000	50,000-100,000
Quincy, Ill.	13,718	1,000-2,000	50,000-100,000
Dubuque, Iowa	13,000	1,000-2,000	50,000-100,000
Evansville, Ind.	11,484	1,000-2,000	50,000-100,000
Portsmouth, Va.	9,496	1,000-2,000	50,000-100,000
Lafayette, Ind.	9,387	1,000-2,000	50,000-100,000
Galena, Ill.	8,196	1,000-2,000	50,000-100,000
Burlington, Iowa	6,706	1,000-2,000	50,000-100,000
Galesburg, Ill.	4,953	1,000-2,000	50,000-100,000
Paducah, Ky.	4,590	1,000-2,000	50,000-100,000

Sources: *HMM,* 42 (January–June 1860), 611; *Eighth Census, Population of the United States in 1860; Census of Population: 1960,* vol. I, part A.
   a. See note a, table A.7.

Table A.9. Coastal shipments of cotton goods from Boston to domestic destinations, 1845-1846.[a]

Destination	Number of bales and cases	Percentage of domestic total[b]
New York	22,574	36.01%
Philadelphia	19,669	31.37
Baltimore	8,254	13.17
Washington, D.C.[c]	105	0.17
New Orleans	5,454	8.70
Charleston	4,530	7.23
Richmond	904	1.44
Mobile	670	1.07
Apalachicola, Fla.	110	0.18
Galveston	19	0.03
Savannah	15	0.02
Norfolk	10	0.02
Eastport and Calais, Maine	248	0.40
Salem, Mass.	50	0.08
Hartford[d]	44	0.07
Belfast, Maine	13	0.02
Camden, Maine	10	0.02
Thomaston, Maine	6	0.01
Castine, Maine	4	0.01
Portland, Maine	1	e
Undetermined	5	0.01
Total	62,695	100.00%

Sources: *DBR*, 2 (1847), 389; and *HMM*, 15 (July–December 1846), 40–41.

a. Year ending May 31, 1846.

b. Exclusive of any shipments by railroad either to western centers via Albany or to inland hinterland urban places (see text). The percentages indicated make no allowance for variations in the value of bales or cases. However, since there was a wide range in the quality of cotton cloths, it is not unlikely that figures for the value of shipments, if available, would yield a somewhat different percentage distribution among the receiving ports. See Robert Brooke Zevin, "The Growth of Cotton Textile Production after 1815," in Robert W. Fogel and Stanley L. Engerman, eds., *The Reinterpretation of American Economic History* (New York: Harper & Row, 1971), p. 127.

c. Actually received at Georgetown, which was not yet incorporated in Washington, D.C.

d. See note 30 to chap. 4.

e. Percentage negligible.

f. During the same period another 29,297 bales and cases were shipped out of the country from Boston, largely to the Orient and Latin America.

Table A.10. Cotton shipments to Boston, 1840-1843, 1849, 1850, and 1852.

Place of origin	1840 Bales	1840 Percentage of total	1841 Bales	1841 Percentage of total	1842 Bales	1842 Percentage of total	1843 Bales	1843 Percentage of total
New Orleans	65,070	46.91%	72,966	55.34%	56,343	47.08%	73,022	48.19%
Mobile	19,944	14.38	28,100	21.31	19,204	16.05	24,861	16.41
Charleston	22,889	16.50	12,228	9.27	19,586	16.37	16,739	11.05
Savannah	9,137	6.59	5,721	4.34	11,334	9.47	15,565	10.27
Apalachicola	14,499[a]	10.45	10,466[a]	7.94	11,201[a]	9.36	20,704[a]	13.66
Natchez	3,278	2.36	950	0.72	253	0.21	0	—
New York	3,296	2.38	493	0.38	891	0.74	505	0.33
Philadelphia	183	0.13	162	0.12	274	0.23	25	0.02
Baltimore	0	—	45	0.03	76	0.06	1	c
North Carolina[b]	38	0.03	33	0.03	42	0.04	17	0.01
Virginia[b]	118	0.09	2	c	50	0.04	10	0.01
Other places	257	0.19	692	0.52	416	0.35	74	0.05
Total	138,709	100.00%	131,860	100.00%	119,670	100.00%	151,523	100.00%

Place of origin	1849		1850		1852	
	Bales	Percentage of total	Bales	Percentage of total	Bales	Percentage of total
New Orleans	111,390	45.98%	98,681	50.58%	131,877	46.90%
Mobile	43,678	18.03	22,350	11.46	42,935	15.27
Charleston	25,896	10.69	20,799	10.66	12,929	4.60
Savannah	26,545	10.97	26,387	13.53	30,660	10.90
Apalachicola	31,138	12.85	22,325	11.44	37,626	13.38
Galveston	2,468	1.02	1,103	0.57	18,809	6.69
Other places[d]	1,164	0.48	3,341	1.76	6,330	2.25
Total	242,279	100.00%	195,076	100.00%	281,166	100.00%

Sources: HMM, 10 (January–June 1844), 289, 425; 24 (January–June 1851), 227; DBR, 7 (1850), 556; 11 (1851), 253.
a. Figures given for 1840–1843 are actually the totals reported for the entire state of Florida. Based on the 1849, 1850, and 1852 data, it may be assumed that almost all of these earlier Florida shipments were from Apalachicola.
b. Ports of origin unspecified.
c. Percentage negligible.
d. Ports of origin unspecified, but presumably including reshipments from New York and Philadelphia as well as scattered direct arrivals from the South.

Table A.11. Ice shipments from Boston, 1845 and 1846.[a]

Destination	1845		1846	
	Tons	Percentage of domestic total	Tons	Percentage of domestic total
New Orleans	22,244	71.09%	22,061	70.16%
Mobile	4,367	13.96	3,380	10.75
Charleston	3,218	10.28	2,841	9.04
Savannah	890	2.84	1,205	3.83
Norfolk	80	0.26	100	0.32
Wilmington, N.C.	181	0.58	475	1.51
Pensacola, Fla.	150	0.48	480	1.53
Key West, Fla.	100	0.32	100	0.32
Apalachicola, Fla.	0	—	200	0.64
St. Marks, Fla.	60	0.19	0	—
Beaufort, S.C.	0	—	100	0.32
New York	0	—	200	0.64
Baltimore	0	—	300	0.95
Total[b]	31,290	100.00%	31,442	100.00%

Source: *HMM,* 15 (July–December 1846), 40.

a. Years ending May 31.

b. In 1845 17,049.5 additional tons were shipped out of the country, and in 1846 that export figure reached 19,348 tons.

Table A.i2. Flour shipments to Boston, 1841, 1842, 1848, 1849, 1852, and 1860.

Place of origin	1841		1842		1848[a]		1849[a]	
	Barrels	Percentage of total	Barrels	Percentage of total	Barrels	Percentage of total	Barrels	Percentage of total
New York	289,114	46.31%	140,739	23.35%	196,686	20.78%	100,166	9.69%
Philadelphia	42,893	6.87	53,481	8.87	11,917	1.26	31,592	3.06
Baltimore	62,740	10.05	46,744	7.76	24,687	2.61	53,236	5.15
Washington, D.C.[b]	30,978	4.96	23,018	3.82	19,655	2.08	36,736	3.55
Albany	76,691	12.29	90,248	14.98	65,299	6.90	76,849	7.43
Western Railroad	0[c]	–	100,000	16.59	387,803	40.96	293,760	28.42
New Orleans	62,834	10.07	96,833	16.07	195,251	20.62	323,318	31.28
Richmond	17,031	2.73	8,014	1.33	16,836	1.78	70,893	6.86
Fredericksburg, Va.	31,900	5.11	36,574	6.07	23,183	2.45	41,252	3.99
Norfolk	676	0.11	3,895[d]	0.65	4,021[d]	0.42	550[d]	0.05
Petersburg, Va.	5,002	0.80	e		e		e	
Kingston, N.Y.	34	0.01	e	–	e	–	e	–
Delaware[f]	1,027	0.16	e	–	e	–	e	–
New Jersey[f]	100	0.02	e	–	e	–	e	–
Massachusetts[f]	2,070	0.33	e	–	e	–	e	–
Maine[f]	619	0.10	e	–	e	–	e	–
New Hampshire[f]	70	0.01	e	–	e	–	e	–
Connecticut[f]	458[g]	0.07	e	–	e	–	e	–
Other places	0	–	3,092	0.51	1,395	0.15	5,416	0.52
Total	624,237[h]	100.00%	602,638[h]	100.00%	946,733[h]	100.00%	1,033,768	100.00%

Sources: HMM, 6 (January–June 1842), 183; 8 (January–June 1843), 229; 21 (July–December 1849) 539; 44 (January–June 1861), 181; DBR, 7 (1850), 557; 14 (1853), 254–255.
  a. Year ending August 31.
  b. Combined figures for Georgetown, which was not yet incorporated into Washington, D.C., and Alexandria, Va., across the Potomac. Cf. chap. 2 at note no. 20.
  c. Some flour moved from Albany to Boston via the Western Railroad during the final months of 1841, but no data are available. On October 9, 1841, when the railroad began operation, bread made from flour brought from Albany was served at a Boston dinner celebrating the commencement of operations. Arthur M. Johnson and Barry E. Supple, *Boston Capitalists and Western Railroads* (Cambridge: Harvard University Press, 1967), p. 43.

Table A.12 (continued)

Place of origin	1852		1860	
	Barrels	Percentage of total	Barrels	Percentage of total
New York	57,997	6.47%	25,381	2.18%
Philadelphia	14,038	1.57	105,515	9.06
Baltimore	40,721	4.54	156,481	13.61
Washington, D.C.[b]	37,406	4.17	22,646	1.94
Albany	15,065	1.68	260	0.02
Western Railroad	250,811	27.98	302,462	25.97
New Orleans	67,460	7.53	11,212	0.97
Richmond	67,364	7.51	77,876	6.69
Fredericksburg, Va.	32,483	3.62	7,852	0.67
Norfolk and other Virginia ports[i]	5,120	0.57	1,973	0.17
Northern Railroad	45,669	5.09	60,587	5.20
Delaware[f]	0	–	8,723	0.74
Fitchburg Railroad	148,292	16.54	35,737	3.07
Boston and Maine Railroad	98,817	11.02	14,808	1.27
Boston and Providence Railroad	0	–	85,492	7.34
Fall River Railroad	0	–	1,173	0.10
Portland	0	–	217,897	18.71
Other places	15,211[j]	1.70	26,657	2.29
Total	896,454	100.00%	1,164,732	100.00%

d. Includes Petersburg, which was listed separately only in 1841. Other smaller Virginia ports also may be included in this figure.
e. Shipments, if any, are included in the figure given for "Other places."
f. Ports of origin unspecified.
g. These shipments presumably came predominantly or entirely from Hartford, for an account of 1844–1845 flour shipments to Boston indicated that Hartford was the sole Connecticut source. NWR, 69 (Nov. 15, 1845), 163. See note 30 to chapter 4.
h. This total represents the sum of shipments given for all places of origin, rather than the total figure reported in the source. Whether this discrepancy is due to a typographical error or some other factor cannot be determined.
i. The unnamed Virginia ports presumably include Petersburg.
j. Presumably includes smaller ports in Delaware, New Jersey, Massachusetts, Maine, New Hampshire, and Connecticut.

Table A.13. Shipments of corn to Boston, 1841, 1843, 1844, 1845, 1852, and 1860.

Place of origin	1841 Bushels[a]	1841 Percentage of total	1843 Bushels[a]	1843 Percentage of total	1844 Bushels[a]	1844 Percentage of total	1845 Bushels[a]	1845 Percentage of total
New York	154,404	8.17%	137,726	8.94%	104,256	5.40%	122,719	5.17%
Philadelphia	559,511	27.81	298,841	19.40	395,325	20.46	470,049	19.82
Baltimore	537,956	26.74	378,839	24.60	664,524	34.39	638,620	26.93
Washington, D.C.[b]	0	–	46,153	3.00	84,910	4.39	110,322	4.65
Albany	12,792	0.64	13,816	0.90	4,295	0.22	0	–
Western Railroad	0	–	8,004	0.52	2,636	0.14	808	0.03
New Orleans	36,733	1.83	399,750	25.95	33,063	1.71	257,657	10.87
Charleston	3,000	0.15	0	–	0	[c]	0	–
Mobile	0	–	1,192	0.08	40		0	–
Fredericksburg, Va.	162,691	8.09	92,380	6.00	90,067	4.66	128,789	5.43
Norfolk	160,870	8.00	0	–	325,774	16.86	326,325	13.76
Rappahannock, Va.	50,685	2.52	19,400	1.26	65,960	3.41	94,683	3.99
Other Virginia ports[d]	83,114	4.13	12,833	0.83	6,442	0.33	60,943	2.57
Elizabeth City, N.C.[e]	71,594	3.56	13,097	0.85	26,200	1.36	25,400	1.07
Salem, N.J.[f]	50,645	2.52	40,165	2.61	51,500	2.67	62,250	2.63
Delaware[g]	111,956	5.57	65,510	4.25	70,580	3.65	66,921	2.82
New York[h]	4,600	0.23	12,600	0.82	0	–	0	–
Maryland[i]	0	–	0	–	4,280	0.22	1,000	0.04
Massachusetts[g]	0	–	0	–	1,500	0.08	0	–
New Hampshire[g]	0	–	0	–	1,000	0.05	0	–
Rhode Island[g]	500	0.02	0	–	0	–	0	–
Connecticut[g]	500	0.02	0	–	0	–	4,900	0.21
Total	2,011,451	100.00%	1,540,306	100.00%	1,932,352	100.00%	2,371,406	100.00%

Sources: *DBR*, 1 (1847), 483; 14 (1853), 256; *HMM*, 10 (January–June 1844), 287; 44 (January–June 1861), 181; *NWR*, 67 (Jan. 26, 1845), 325; 69 (Jan. 24, 1846), 334.

a. Bushel figures may not be completely comparable for the entire 1841–1860 period. The "customary" weight for a bushel of corn in 1857 was fifty-six pounds. Only three years later the "established" weight for a bushel of corn was placed at seventy pounds. *DBR*, 22 (1857), 520; *HMM*, 43 (July–December 1860), 526.

Table A.13 (continued)

Place of origin	1852		1860	
	Bushels[a]	Percentage of total	Bushels[a]	Percentage of total
New York and the Western Railroad[j]	688,014	32.49%	862,417	41.10%
Philadelphia[k]	165,453	7.81	186,235	8.88
Baltimore[l]	404,945	19.12	296,886	14.15
New Orleans	434,535	20.52	52,350	2.49
Virginia[m]	353,345	16.69	234,616	11.18
Delaware	31,300	1.48	79,344	3.78
Other places[n]	39,847	1.88	386,402	18.42
Total	2,117,439[o]	100.00%	2,098,250	100.00%

b. Figures for 1843 and 1844 are known to be for Georgetown, D.C., and Alexandria, Va. Those for 1841 and 1845 are presumed to be for the same two places. See note b to table A.12.

c. Percentage negligible.

d. Other unspecified ports presumably do not include Alexandria in either 1841 or 1845.

e. Figure for 1843 is known to be for Elizabeth City. Since the North Carolina datum in one source and the Elizabeth City figure in another exactly corresponded with each other, it is assumed that the North Carolina data for 1841, 1844, and 1845 are also for Elizabeth City.

f. Figure for 1843 is known to be for Salem. Since the New Jersey datum in one source and the Salem figure in another exactly corresponded with each other, it is assumed that the New Jersey data for 1841, 1844, and 1845 are also for Salem.

g. Ports of origin unspecified.

h. Minor ports other than New York City and Albany.

i. Minor ports other than Baltimore.

j. Assumed to be primarily from New York, although there is no available breakdown. The standard work on the Western Railroad, Stephen Salsbury's The State, the Investor, and the Railroad: The Boston & Albany, 1825–1867 (Cambridge: Harvard University Press, 1967), gives no indication that the line conducted a major traffic in corn during the 1850s.

k. The 1852 and 1860 sources actually provide data for "Pennsylvania." However, since Boston had no other Pennsylvania source prior to 1852, it is assumed that the figures refer to Philadelphia.

l. The 1852 and 1860 sources actually provide data for "Maryland." However, since Baltimore had accounted for 99.36 to 100 percent of all Maryland shipments to Boston in previous years, it is assumed that those data are for Baltimore.

m. Assumed to be primarily from Norfolk. Cf. 1844 and 1845 data.

n. Presumably includes Washington, D.C., Salem, N.J., and Elizabeth City, N.C., as well as other ports in Delaware and New England.

o. See note h, table A.12.

Table A.14. Production and shipment to market of anthracite coal from Philadelphia's hinterland, 1840-1860 (in thousands of short tons).

Year	Production	Shipment to market[a]
1840	1,129	867.0
1841	1,262	964.3
1842	1,441	1,108.1
1843	1,656	1,263.5
1844	2,128	1,631.7
1845	2,626	2,023.1
1846	3,032	2,344.0
1847	3,726	2,982.3
1848	4,001	3,089.2
1849	4,112	3,242.9
1850	4,327	3,356.9
1851	5,814	4,429.5
1852	6,412	4,993.5
1853	6,653	5,195.2
1854	7,668	[b]
1855	8,607	[b]
1856	8,960	6,751.5
1857	8,618	6,431.4
1858	8,808	6,524.8
1859	10,092	7,517.5
1860	10,984	[b]

Sources: U.S. Bureau of the Census, *Historical Statistics of the United States, Colonial Times to 1957* (Washington, D.C., 1960), p. 360; *DBR,* 7 (1850), 366; *BM,* 9 (1855), 473; *ARJ,* 32 (1859), 84; 33 (1860), 70.

a. Shipments to market seem to have amounted to only about 75–78 percent of production, mostly because of consumption by the iron industry and by other manufacturing activities within the coal-mining areas.

With the passage of time increasing numbers of mining areas were shipping coal to market, and therefore it became ever more difficult for contemporary sources to give accurate shipments totals. As a result, shipment-to-market totals varied from source to source for several of the years shown here. In every instance the highest figures reported have been used, on the assumption that they represent more completeness rather than exaggeration.

b. Not available.

Table A.15. Anthracite coal shipments to New York via the Delaware and Raritan Canal, 1842-1846, 1850, 1851, 1854, and 1858 (in short tons).

Year	Total anthracite receipts at New York via the Delaware and Raritan Canal	(A) Delaware and Raritan anthracite shipments from Philadelphia	(B) Schuylkill anthracite received at Philadelphia	(A/B)
1842	171,754	a	540,892	—
1843	198,352	a	677,295	—
1844	267,496	a	839,934	—
1845	372,072	a	1,083,796	—
1846	339,924	a	1,237,002	—
1850	568,404	589,867[b]	1,712,607	34.44%
1851	769,602	a	2,184,240	—
1854	1,283,148	1,011,456	2,895,208	34.94
1858	1,050,000	a	2,886,133	—

Sources: *ARJ,* 20 (1847), 118; 25 (1852), 24; 28 (1855), 75; 32 (1859), 516; Wheaton J. Lane, *From Indian Trail to Iron Horse: Travel and Transportation in New Jersey, 1620–1860* (Princeton: Princeton University Press, 1939), p. 264.

a. Not separable from smaller quantities of Lehigh anthracite also moving over this route.

b. The slight excess of Philadelphia shipments over the total Delaware and Raritan anthracite traffic to New York probably is due to small way shipments, although there may have been a misprint in one of the two 1850 sources.

Table A.16. Anthracite coal shipments from Philadelphia to Boston, 1841-1843, 1848-1850, and 1852 (in short tons).

Year	(A) Anthracite receipts at Boston from Philadelphia	(B) Schuylkill anthracite received at Philadelphia	(A/B)
1841	92,838	585,540	15.86%
1842	76,604	540,892	14.16
1843	103,295	677,295	15.25
1848	271,978	1,652,835	16.46
1849	253,668	1,605,126	15.80
1850	255,470	1,714,607	14.92
1852	360,869	2,405,950	15.00

Sources: *HMM,* 6 (January–June 1842), 183; 8 (January–June 1843), 279; 10 (January–June 1843), 287; *DBR,* 7 (1850), 556; 14 (1853), 253; *ARJ,* 24 (1851), 21; 32 (1859), 516.

Table A.17. Number employed and value of production (in thousands of dollars) for Philadelphia's leading manufacturing branches, 1860.

Manufacturing branch	Number employed	Value of production
Clothing	14,387	$9,984.5
Sugar refining	478	6,456.7
Boots and shoes	8,434	5,329.9
Cured meats	238	4,575.8
Provision curers and packers	238	4,575.8
Cotton goods, cloths[a]	4,793	4,347.6
Print works (textiles)	925	4,048.9
Leather	1,326	4,022.9
Cotton and woollen goods[b]	3,258	3,593.3
Flour mills	198	3,098.3
Carpets	2,680	2,915.3
Chemicals	737	2,769.3
Book publishing	844	2,260.4
Breweries	596	2,223.4
Bread and crackers	912	2,214.9
Soap and candles	376	2,076.6
Tanners and curriers	340	2,037.0
Machinery, general (iron)	1,613	1,862.0
Furniture	1,627	1,854.4
Gas works	863	1,837.5
Newspapers	944	1,741.1
Hosiery, woollen	2,285	1,738.4
Morocco leather	939	1,727.8
Gold watch cases and chains	624	1,714.8
Gas fixtures, chandeliers, "etc."	1,131	1,680.2
Distillers and rectifiers	136	1,499.0
Printers, job and card	853	1,435.4
Locomotives	1,255	1,420.0
Shirts, collars, "etc."	3,290	1,335.0
Iron stoves and hollowware	956	1,306.7
Silk fringes and trimmings	1,219	1,260.7
Shipbuilding (iron and wood)	958	1,253.0
Cigars	1,290	1,228.2
Bricks	1,876	1,212.2
Umbrellas and parasols	1,094	1,207.3
Hats	998	1,164.2
Iron rolling mills[c]	605	1,110.0
Paints and colors	148	1,109.7
Glass	825	1,069.0
Woollens	673	1,062.8
Carriages and coaches	1,038	1,051.4
Marble cutting	744	1,019.1
Total: all industries[d]	98,397	$141,048.7

Source: *Revised returns of the Eighth Census, Manufacturing of the United States in 1860,* as reproduced in Bishop, *American Manufactures,* III, 14–17.

a. Power-driven cotton factories only. Does not include figures for eighteen establishments using hand looms.

b. Only power-driven plants producing goods of both cotton and wool. Does not include figures for five establishments using hand looms.

c. Includes mills producing bar, sheet, and plate iron, but not mills turning out tubes and flues. Mills of the latter type were placed in a separate category.

d. Total also includes all industrial branches whose 1860 output was valued at less than $1.0 million.

Table A.18. Manufactured goods shipped westward from Philadelphia by the Main Line and manufactured goods arriving by the Main Line at Pittsburgh, 1843-1845 (in short tons).[a]

Class of goods	Shipments from Philadelphia		
	1848[b]	1844[b]	1845[b]
"Merchandise"[c]	14,739.4	19,857.3	19,079.1
Bar and sheet iron	363.0	514.1	232.7
Drugs and dyes	181.5	501.5	590.7
Leather	51.0	8.6	61.7

Class of goods	Arrivals at Pittsburgh[d]		
	1843	1844	1845
"Merchandise"[c]	14,184.4	21,399.3	19,249.5
Bar and sheet iron	11,396.9	9,412.1	7,666.4
Drugs and dyes	384.5	860.9	424.4
Leather	186.2	207.9	239.5

Sources: *HMM,* 14 (January–June 1846), 430; and Catherine Elizabeth Reiser, *Pittsburgh's Commercial Development, 1800-1850* (Harrisburg: Pennsylvania Historical and Museum Commission, 1951), p. 219.

  a. Original data in pounds.
  b. Year ending September 30.
  c. For articles included in the catchall "merchandise" category, see text.
  d. The tonnage of arrivals at Pittsburgh does not correspond exactly with the tonnage shipments from Philadelphia because of way traffic and the three-month difference between the bookkeeping years of the two sources. The largest discrepancy, that with respect to bar and sheet iron, was caused by the considerable production of those items in the hinterlands of both Philadelphia and Pittsburgh, much of which moved westward. Some leather also was transported from places in Philadelphia's hinterland westward to Pittsburgh.

Table A.19. Principal manufactured goods shipped from Philadelphia to Pittsburgh via the Pennsylvania Railroad, 1857 and 1858 (in short tons).[a]

Class of goods	1857	1858
Boots, shoes, hats, "etc."	2,240.7	3,284.9
Books and stationery	1,180.3	1,132.5
Brown sheetings and bagging	2,687.4	2,138.2
"Dry goods" (textiles and clothing)	24,221.2	23,700.4
Drugs, medicines, and dyestuffs	3,532.1	3,480.3
Furniture and oilcloth	1,252.2	1,081.5
Glass and glassware	434.5	222.9
Hardware	5.004.5	4,110.6
Hemp and cordage	667.3	803.7
Iron, rolled, hammered, "etc."	108.9	343.9
Iron rails	194.5	421.6
Iron blooms and pigs	0	146.7
Leather	1,214.1	1,559.4
Machinery and castings	3,398.3	1,704.8
Marble and cement	1,288.9	957.0
Paper[b]	851.4	1.069.9
Queensware[c]	2,464.2	1,931.3

Sources: Edwin T. Freedley, *Philadelphia and Its Manufactures: A Hand-Book Exhibiting the Development, Variety, and Statistics of the Manufacturing Industry of Philadelphia in 1857* (Philadelphia, 1859), p. 75; *HMM*, 41 (July–December 1859), 501–502.

a. Original data in pounds.

b. Includes rags.

c. Probably consisted largely of imported items acquired via New York, because local Philadelphia production was extremely limited.

Table A.20. Cost of raw materials consumed by leading manufacturing branches of Philadelphia, 1860 (in thousands of dollars).

Manufacturing branch	Cost of raw materials
Sugar refiners	$5,472.7
Clothing	5,147.3
Cured meats	3,510.4
Provision curers and packers	3,510.4
Iron products and machinery[a]	3,059.9
Print works (textiles)	2,848.4
Leather	2,661.3
Flour mills	2,648.6
Cotton goods, cloths[b]	2,053.7
Cotton and wollen goods[c]	2,021.8
Boots and shoes	1,912.7
Chemicals	1,544.3
Tanners and curriers	1,443.7
Soaps and candles	1,421.1
Carpets	1,393.8
Bread and crackers	1,314.5
Distillers and rectifiers	1,171.5
Gold watch cases and chains	1,103.9
Breweries	1,102.7
Morocco leather	1,043.7
Total: all industries[d]	$72,333.8

Source: See table A.17.

a. This category is a combination of the following branches, which are listed separately in the source: building foundries; gas and water pipe; general foundries; stoves and hollow ware; iron railings; iron rolling mills, bar, sheet and plate; iron rolled tubes, flues, etc.; iron wire and ornamental work; machinery, general (iron); nails; and iron roofs. However, it does not include locomotives, machine tools, iron shipbuilding, or other branches in which iron was an input of varying importance.

b. Power-driven cotton factories only. Does not include figures for eighteen establishments using hand looms.

c. Only power-driven plants producing goods of both cotton and wool. Does not include figures for five establishments using hand looms.

d. Total also includes all industrial branches whose 1860 raw material costs were under $1.0 million.

Table A.21. Principal raw materials for manufacturing shipped from Pittsburgh to Philadelphia via the Pennsylvania Railroad, 1857 and 1858 (in short tons).[a]

Class of goods[b]	1857	1858
Cotton	366.8	2,840.2[c]
Wool and woollen yarn	2,489.1	2,725.0
Flour	32,581.5	40,340.1
Grain, of all kinds	5,648.3	13,252.8
Hides and hair	1,362.4	1,414.0
Livestock	20,028.0	30,729.2
Lard, lard oil, and tallow	3,578.0	5,376.1

Sources: See table A.19.

a. Original data in pounds.

b. See chapter 4, note 121, on use of arriving goods for other than local manufacturing purposes.

c. By 1860, the volume of cotton carried from Pittsburgh to Philadelphia by the Pennsylvania Railroad had grown to about 14,350 tons. Alfred D. Chandler, Jr., *The Railroads: The Nation's First Big Business* (New York: Harcourt, Brace & World, 1965), p. 22.

Table A.22. Principal commodity classes arriving by lake at Buffalo from Chicago, Cleveland, Detroit, Milwaukee, and Toledo, 1851.

Class of commodity by (i) value (in dollars)[a] (ii) percentage of value of arrivals from all U.S. ports		(A) Chicago	(B) Cleveland	(C) Detroit	(D) Milwaukee	(E) Toledo	(A-E) Five ports combined	All U.S. ports[b]
Lumber (sawed pine and whitewood)[d]	(i)	$11,660	$20,256	$984,909	0	$177,850	$1,194,675	$4,663,967[c]
	(ii)	0.25%	0.43%	21.12%	0	3.81%	25.61%	100.00%
Flour	(i)	186,029	1,260,207	946,929	$280,088	763,767	3,437,020	4,216,250
	(ii)	4.41	29.89	22.46	6.64%	18.11	81.52	100.00
Wool	(i)	283,680	1,634,850	469,020	61,890	237,780	2,687,220	3,683,100
	(ii)	7.70	44.39	12.73	1.68	6.46	72.96	100.00
Wheat	(i)	220,919	471,382	358,931	58,521	561,795	1,671,548	2,764,058
	(ii)	7.99	17.05	12.99	2.12	20.33	60.47	100.00
Corn	(i)	1,058,350	206,326	100,442	10,597	822,826	2,198,521	2,672,432
	(ii)	39.60	7.72	3.76	0.40	30.79	82.27	100.00
Leather	(i)	42,635	281,877	13,525	27,677	200,099	565,813	758,813
	(ii)	5.63	37.18	1.78	3.65	26.39	74.63	100.00
High wines[e]	(i)	20,860	222,183	41,560	0	109,540	394,143	627,800
	(ii)	3.32	35.39	6.62	0	17.45	62.78	100.00
Hogs	(i)	3,042	175,715	43,271	0	194,857	416,885	625,563
	(ii)	0.49	28.09	6.92	0	31.15	66.64	100.00
Beef	(i)	296,567	73,044	2,376	14,795	55,913	442,695	521,843
	(ii)	56.83	14.00	0.46	2.84	10.71	84.83	100.00
Bacon and hams	(i)	218,039	50,544	9,922	1,178	105,034	384,717	405,765
	(ii)	53.74	12.46	2.45	0.29	25.89	94.81	100.00
Pork	(i)	110,580	61,068	3,432	15,996	111,108	302,184	393,768
	(ii)	28.08	15.51	0.87	4.06	28.22	76.74	100.00
Cheese	(i)	45,972	0	51	0	1,386	47,409	346,256
	(ii)	13.28	0	0.01	0	0.40	13.69	100.00

Table A.22 (continued)

Class of commodity by (i) value (in dollars)[a] (ii) percentage of value of arrivals from all U.S. ports		(A) Chicago	(B) Cleveland	(C) Detroit	(D) Milwaukee	(E) Toledo	(A-E) Five ports combined	All U.S. ports[b]
Oats	(i)	143,816	21,267	14,339	0	21,119	200,541	339,430
	(ii)	42.37	6.27	4.22	0	6.22	59.08	100.00
Stoves	(i)	1,800	3,360	47,850	0	29,670	82,680	319,170
	(ii)	0.56	1.05	14.99	0	9.30	25.90	100.00
Sundries[f]	(i)	65,880	56,070	64,395	19,620	45,540	251,505	311,580
	(ii)	21.14	18.00	20.67	6.30	14.62	80.72	100.00
Ashes	(i)	7,990	32,194	60,414	10,774	76,288	187,660	285,961
	(ii)	2.79	11.26	21.13	3.77	26.68	65.52	100.00
Sand	(i)	106,432	72,684	548	0	86,631	266,295	282,130
	(ii)	37.72	25.76	0.19	0	30.71	94.39	100.00
Copper (smelted)	(i)	1.589	202,312	48,275	212	265	252,653	266,395
	(ii)	0.60	75.94	18.12	0.08	0.10	94.84	100.00
Furs	(i)	55,100	27,600	40,400	8,800	43,700	175,600	244,800
	(ii)	22.51	11.27	16.50	3.59	17.85	71.73	100.00
Horned cattle	(i)	39,210	112,560	17,800	50	24,990	194,620	242,910
	(ii)	16.14	46.34	7.33	0.02	10.29	80.12	100.00
Butter	(i)	8,370	71,365	2,215	2,630	26,405	111,035	232,519
	(ii)	3.60	30.69	0.95	1.15	11.36	47.75	100.00
Tobacco	(i)	5,351	47,014	0	0	128,009	180,374	207,888
	(ii)	2.57	22.62	0	0	61.56	86.76	100.00
Hides	(i)	93,977	30,923	6,723	3,229	26,033	160,885	188,765
	(ii)	49.79	16.38	3.56	1.71	13.79	85.23	100.00
Buffalo robes	(i)	160,800	900	550	50	0	162,300	162,300
	(ii)	99.08	0.55	0.34	0.03	0	100.00	100.00

Table A.22 (continued)

Class of commodity by (i) value (in dollars)[a] (ii) percentage of value of arrivals from all U.S. ports		(A) Chicago	(B) Cleveland	(C) Detroit	(D) Milwaukee	(E) Toledo	(A-E) Five ports combined	All U.S. ports[b]
Horses	(i)	5,580	55,200	42,600	1,140	20,640	125,160	157,800
	(ii)	3.54	34.98	27.00	0.72	13.08	79.32	100.00
Oil (lard oil and linseed oil)	(i)	218	23,033	872	363	115,045	139,531	151,503
	(ii)	0.14	15.20	0.58	0.24	75.94	92.10	100.00
Sheepskins	(i)	8,851	30,206	15,292	202	23,771	78,322	136,345
	(ii)	6.49	22.15	11.22	0.15	17.43	57.44	100.00
Merchandise[g]	(i)	6,294	38,954	22,550	5,650	8,326	81,774	113,302
	(ii)	5.56	34.38	19.90	4.99	7.35	72.17	100.00
Iron[h]	(i)	3,936	32,372	1,991	78	102	38,479	105,826[i]
	(ii)	3.72	30.59	1.88	0.07	0.10	36.36	100.00
Barley	(i)	7,256	308	0	61,995	0	69,559	102,961
	(ii)	7.05	0.30	0	60.21	0	67.56	100.00
Total[j]	(i)	3,398,704	5,719,659	3,451,832	670,491	4,204,905	17,481,591	27,026,247
	(ii)	12.58	21.16	12.77	2.48	15.69	64.68	100.00

Source: Israel Andrews, *Report . . . on the Trade and Commerce of the British North American Colonies*, U.S. Senate Document no. 112, 32nd Cong., 1st sess., 1853, pp. 97–139.

a. Determined, commodity class by commodity class, by taking the average value per unit of weight or per unit of shipment for total lake shipments of that class arriving at Buffalo and applying it to the weight or shipment-unit figures given for each separate port. Some value-assignment errors may have crept in because of quality and price differences among shipments of the same type arriving from different ports. However, given the nature of the commodities, such errors are not likely to have been large in most of the individual cases.

b. Chicago, Cleveland, Detroit, Milwaukee, Toledo, and twenty-eight smaller U.S. ports on the Great Lakes. Additional commodity arrivals came to Buffalo from Canada. See chapter 4, note 128.

c. Lumber arrivals from Canada were valued at another $4,331,133. Thus, lumber shipments were responsible for over 89 percent of the value of all commodities arriving at Buffalo from Canada.

d. Not including other minor lumber categories ("lumber, black walnut," "oak timber," "ship-plank," "shingle bolls," "laths," and "shingles"), which together accounted for another 59,424 dollars' worth of arrivals from U.S. ports.

e. Not including $1,246 in arrivals from U.S. ports merely classified as "wine."

f. Apparently consisting of miscellaneous manufactured items.

g. Catchall category including textiles, shoes, hats, etc. See text.

h. Includes iron shipped as pigs, as well as in other forms.

i. This is the only commodity class of consequence in which Canadian shipments ($195,610) exceeded those arriving from U.S. ports. In this instance, the shipments actually originated in England and came by way of Canada.

j. Includes the 30 commodity classes listed, as well as 104 other classes, each of which provided arrivals whose total value was

Table A.23. Shipments of sawed lumber arriving by lake at Buffalo from smaller nonhinterland ports, 1851.

Nonhinterland port	1850 population[a]	Value of shipments (in dollars)	Percentage of value of arrivals from all U.S. ports
Conneaut, Ohio	<2,500	$626,738	13.44%
Saginaw, Mich.	<2,500	433,240	9.29
Ashtabula, Ohio	<2,500	328,473	7.04
St. Clair, Mich.	<2,500	218,793	4.69
Monroe, Mich.	2,813	192,020	4.12
Grand Haven, Mich.	<2,500	108,020	2.32
Madison Dock, Ohio	<2,500	95,854	2.06
Huron, Ohio plus	<2,500	71,506	1.53
Milan, Ohio	<2,500		
Fairport, Ohio	<2,500	44,596	0.96
Trenton, Mich.	<2,500	34,011	0.73
Sandusky, Ohio	5,087	33,545	0.72
Gibraltar, Mich.	<2,500	29,810	0.64
Black River, Ohio	<2,500	28,160	0.60
Vermillion, Ohio	<2,500	21,230	0.46
St. Joseph, Mich.	<2,500	18,040	0.39
Fremont, Ohio	1,464	13,342	0.29
Total	—	2,297,378	49.26

Sources: Andrews, *Report . . . on the Trade and Commerce,* pp. 121, 138; U.S. Bureau of the Census, *Seventh Census of the United States: 1850* (Washington, D.C., 1853).

a. Since only the populations of Saginaw, Monroe, Sandusky, and Fremont exceeded 2,500 by the census of 1860, the 1850 population of each of the other thirteen places listed must have been well under 2,500.

Table A.24. Shipments of wheat, wool, flour, and corn arriving by lake at Buffalo from smaller nonhinterland ports, 1851.

Nonhinterland port	Wheat		Wool		Flour		Corn	
	Value of shipments (in dollars)	% of value of arrivals from all U.S. ports	Value of shipments (in dollars)	% of value of arrivals from all U.S. ports	Value of shipments (in dollars)	% of value of arrivals from all U.S. ports	Value of shipments (in dollars)	% of value of arrivals from all U.S. ports
Sandusky, Ohio	$433,670	15.69%	$501,360	13.61%	$319,918	7.59%	$133,701	5.00%
Monroe, Mich.	118,065	4.27	62,160	1.69	276,420	6.56	8,827	0.33
Huron, Ohio, plus Milan, Ohio	187,410	6.78	65,880	1.79	7,042	0.17	99,023	3.71
Racine, Wisc.[a]	73,431	2.66	23,640	0.64	62,024	1.47	4,310	0.16
Kenosha, Wisc.[a]	67,126	2.43	9,000	0.24	6,696	0.16	2,924	0.11
Michigan City, Ind.[a]	67,768	2.45	12,240	0.33	413	0.01	143,263	5.36
Conneaut, Ohio	0	0	4,440	0.12	0	0	5,454	0.20
Ashtabula, Ohio	0	0	13,260	0.36	84	0.002	0	0
Madison Dock, Ohio	0	0	9,360	0.25	0	0	585	0.02
Fairport, Ohio	0	0	52,380	1.42	2,163	0.05	990	0.04
Black River, Ohio	0	0	53,220	1.44	1,953	0.05	5,940	0.22
Vermillion, Ohio	20,033	0.72	10,800	0.29	24,332	0.58	13,674	0.51
Fremont, Ohio	30,957	1.12	1,500	0.04	2,272	0.05	19,683	0.74
Trenton, Mich.	0	0	0	0	0	0	945	0.04
Saginaw, Mich.	0	0	720	0.02	1,400	0.03	0	0
Mackinaw City, Mich.[a]	0	0	0	0	116	0.003	0	0
Grand Haven, Mich.	21,543	0.78	9,960	0.27	28,998	0.69	0	0
St. Joseph, Mich.	14,374	0.52	60	0.002	22,614	0.54	9,408	0.35
Sheboygan, Wisc.[a]	0	0	660	0.02	1,771	0.04	0	0
Waukegan, Ill.[a]	57,713	2.09	8,940	0.24	7,413	0.18	5,688	0.21
Total	$1,092,090	39.51%	$839,580	22.80%	$765,629	18.16%	$454,415	17.00%

Source: Andrews, *Report . . . on the Trade and Commerce*, pp. 108, 121, 133–134, 137–139.
a. The 1850 populations of places not listed in Table A.23 were as follows: Racine, 5,107; Kenosha, 3,455; Michigan City, 999; Mackinaw City, <2,500; Sheboygan, <2,500; and Waukegan, <2,500.

Table A.25. Annual steamboat arrivals at and departures from Cincinnati, 1847-1857.[a]

Arrivals

Date	New Orleans		Pittsburgh		St. Louis		Other nonhinterland and hinterland ports[b]		Total	
	Number	Percentage	Number	Percentage	Number	Percentage	Number	Percentage	Number	Percentage
1847-1848[a]	319	7.99%	880	22.04%	295	7.39%	2,449	62.58%	3,993	100.00%
1848-1849	319	9.82	728	22.40	278	8.56	1,924	59.22	3,249	100.00
1849-1850	260	7.11	750	20.53	276	7.56	2,367	64.80	3,653	100.00
1850-1851	288	7.79	658	17.79	214	5.79	2,538	68.63	3,698	100.00
1851-1852	219	5.98	574	15.66	218	5.95	2,654	72.41	3,665	100.00
1852-1853	254	6.26	619	15.25	233	5.74	2,952	72.75	4,058	100.00
1853-1854	206	5.30	531	13.66	216	5.56	2,934	75.48	3,887	100.00
1854-1855	159	5.92	407	15.18	210	7.83	1,906	71.07	2,687	100.00
1855-1856	143	5.11	530	18.96	279	9.98	1,844	65.95	2,796	100.00
1856-1857	127	4.70	385	14.23	315	11.65	1,878	69.43	2,705	100.00

Departures

Date	New Orleans		Pittsburgh		St. Louis		Other nonhinterland and hinterland ports[b]		Total	
	Number	Percentage	Number	Percentage	Number	Percentage	Number	Percentage	Number	Percentage
1847-1848	297	8.42%	762	21.60%	309	8.76%	2,159	61.21%	3,527	100.00%
1848-1849	281	9.54	612	20.79	313	10.63	1,738	59.04	2,944	100.00
1849-1850	237	6.61	679	18.93	320	8.92	2,350	65.53	3,586	100.00
1850-1851	249	7.56	547	16.62	222	6.74	2,274	69.08	3,292	100.00
1851-1852	326	9.05	498	13.82	241	6.69	2,536	70.42	3,601	100.00
1852-1853	250	6.03	567	13.68	288	6.95	3,401	73.35	4,146	100.00
1853-1854	197	5.01	495	12.58	275	6.99	2,967	75.42	3,934	100.00
1854-1855	133	4.85	400	14.57	316	11.51	1,896	69.07	2,745	100.00
1855-1856	146	5.25	453	16.28	374	13.44	1,810	65.04	2,783	100.00
1856-1857	101	3.31	393	14.82	376	14.18	1,781	67.18	2,651	100.00

Sources: *HMM*, 21 (July–December 1849), 468; 23 (July–December 1850), 469; 25 (July–December 1851), 506; 29 (July–December 1853), 751; 31 (July–December 1854), 636; 37 (July–December 1857), 759; *WrJ*, 7 (1851), 44; *ARJ*, 25 (1852), 134; *DBR*, 14 (1853), 183.

a. Years ending August 31.

b. Including Louisville.

Table A.26. Shipments of major selected commodities from Cincinnati to New Orleans and other destinations, 1850-1851[a]

Commodity	Via river New Orleans Volume	Percentage	Via river Other down-river ports[b] Volume	Percentage	Upriver ports[c] Volume	Percentage	Via canals and railroads[d] Volume	Percentage	Total[e] Volume	Percentage
Beef (barrels)	19,319	89.66%	68	0.32%	314	1.46%	236	1.10%	21,548	100.00%
Beef (tierces)	8,677	91.80	8	0.08	657	6.95	14	0.14	9,452	100.00
Butter (barrels)	1,850	56.78	867	26.61	1	0.06	539	16.54	3,258	100.00
Butter (firkins, kegs)[g]	32,500	96.16	959	2.84	15	0.04	8	0.02	33,797	100.00
Corn (sacks)[h]	15,672	77.83	3,519	17.48	156	0.77	790	3.92	20,137	100.00
Cheese[i]	69,258	56.46	48,432	39.48	2,165	1.76	1,900	1.55	122,675	100.00
Candles[j]	76,245	66.92	20,272	17.79	10,695	9.39	6,195	5.44	113,929	100.00
Flour (barrels)[j]	281,609	57.94	95,943	19.74	7,719	1.59	4,859	1.00	486,007	100.00
Iron (pieces)	6,608	6.10	54,894	50.71	6,634	6.13	40,119	37.06	108,225	100.00
Iron (bundles)	1,503	3.41	25,281	57.31	2,182	4.95	15,144	34.33	44,100	100.00
Iron (tons)	64	0.64	1,341	13.42	219	2.19	8,152	81.58	9,993	100.00
Lard (barrels)[k]	22,854	70.95	117	0.36	3,277	10.17	4,143	12.86	32,212	100.00
Lard (kegs)[k]	56,380	78.43	5,358	7.45	5,739	7.98	2,823	3.93	71,887	100.00

Lard oil (barrels)	13,617	52.15	1,547	5.92	3,726	14.27	7,220	27.65	26,110	100.00
Linseed oil[i]	4,443	56.81	1,362	17.41	1,042	13.32	974	12.45	7,821	100.00
Pork (hogsheads)[l]	19,044	60.40	1,313	4.16	8,809	27.94	1,054	3.34	31,532	100.00
Pork (tierces)[l]	11,341	54.51	18	0.09	8,759	42.10	644	3.10	20,804	100.00
Pork (barrels)[l]	112,622	89.48	1,055	0.83	3,801	3.02	4,608	3.66	175,867	100.00
Pork (pounds)	1,345,860	25.49	755,860	14.11	1,559,280	29.53	1,092,553	20.70	5,279,773	100.00
Soap (boxes)	9,425	43.02	6,440	29.40	3,600	16.43	2,068	9.44	21,908	100.00
Whiskey (barrels)	140,661	56.42	56,164	22.53	31,231	12.53	3,268	1.31	249,304	100.00

Source: *HMM*, 25 (July–December 1851), 488.

a. Year ending August 31.

b. Including St. Louis and Louisville, as well as various nonhinterland and hinterland ports of intermediate and small size.

c. Including Pittsburgh, as well as various nonhinterland and hinterland ports of intermediate and small size.

d. Shipments under this category confined to hinterland and nonhinterland destinations north of the Ohio River, since Cincinnati had no direct connections to the south by these modes of transportation.

e. For most categories the total includes additional shipments by flatboat. Although not specified, in most instances either all flatboat shipments or the great majority of them were destined for New Orleans.

f. Although units of measurement were not uniform, tierces usually were equivalent to about 1.5 barrels.

g. Barrels of butter normally contained 200 pounds, while firkins and kegs usually only held 100 and 25 pounds respectively.

h. A sack of cork was roughly equivalent to two bushels of about 56 pounds each.

i. Units of measurement not specified.

j. Barrels of flour normally weighed about 216 pounds.

k. A barrel of lard usually held 225 pounds, while kegs generally weighed but 45 pounds.

l. The capacity of pork containers was normally as follows: hogsheads, 800 pounds; tierces, 304 pounds; and barrels, 200 pounds. See chapter 4, note 154.

Table A.27. Average annual volume of grocery imports at Cincinnati for five-year periods, 1846-1860.

Commodity	1846-1850	1851-1855	1856-1860
Sugar (tons)[a]	12,450	25,830	22,660
Molasses (barrels)	44,300	82,500	77,800
Coffee (tons)[b]	5,392	8,024	9,344

Source: Thomas Senior Berry, *Western Prices before 1861: A Study of the Cincinnati Market* (Cambridge: Harvard University Press, 1943), p. 320, as derived from annual reports of the Cincinnati Chamber of Commerce.

a. Converted from statistics for hogsheads, barrels, and boxes, with respective average weights of 1,000, 200, and 600 pounds.

b. Converted from statistics for sacks averaging 160 pounds in weight.

Table A.28. Annual foodstuff shipments from New Orleans to New York, Philadelphia, Baltimore, and Boston, 1850-1851, 1853-1854, and 1859-1860.[a]

Commodity	Year	New York	Philadelphia	Baltimore	Boston	Total
Pork	1850-1851	55,849	5,538	13,421	77,806	152,614
(barrels)[b]	1853-1854	43,616	968	6,925	62,401	113,910
	1859-1860	868	0	0	2,097	2,965
Bacon	1850-1851	9,856	2,763	1,843	6,503	20,965
(hogsheads)[b]	1853-1854	2,963	98	138	5,970	9,169
	1859-1860	271	0	0	91	362
Lard	1850-1851	209,825	41,045	32,585	224,333	507,788
(kegs)[b]	1853-1854	87,088	1,541	0	106,221	194,850
	1859-1860	48,699	1,120	0	5,309	55,128
Flour	1850-1851	72,584	418	0	88,925	161,927
(barrels)[b]	1853-1854	33,129	91	0	7,181	40,401
	1859-1860	10,862	0	0	41,524	52,386
Beef	1850-1851	3,055	421	955	13,435	17,866
(barrels)	1853-1854	5,081	60	76	7,934	13,151
	1859-1860	9,878	10	0	1,699	11,597
Whiskey	1850-1851	1,381	268	1,542	2,242	5,433
(barrels)	1853-1854	1,293	58	77	597	2,025
	1859-1860	1,007	158	248	1,447	2,860

Sources: *HMM*, 25 (July-December 1851), 605; 31 (July-December 1854), 477; *DBR*, 29 (1860), 784.
a. Years ending August 31.
b. For normal equivalent weights per unit of measurement see notes j, k, and l to table A.26. Average weight per hogshead of bacon was identical with that per hogshead of pork.

Table A.29. Annual cotton shipments from Charleston, 1849-1860.[a]

Destination	1849-1850[a]		1850-1851		1851-1852		1852-1853	
	Bales[b]	Percentage of total[c]	Bales[b]	Percentage of total[c]	Bales[b]	Percentage of total[c]	Bales[b]	Percentage of total[c]
New York	101,886	66.10%	104,185	73.14%	147,237	72.58%	119,285	70.68%
Boston	22,720	14.74	16,784	11.78	19,993	9.86	18,535	10.98
Philadelphia	15,564	10.10	11,138	7.82	24,548	12.10	18,346	10.87
Baltimore[d]	9,236	5.99	7,890	5.54	10,336	5.10	11,682	6.92
Providence[e]	4,754	2.97	2,454	1.72	736	0.36	400	0.24
Other U.S. ports	152	0.10	0	—	0	—	529	0.31

Destination	1853-1854		1854-1855		1855-1856		1856-1957	
	Bales[b]	Percentage of total[c]	Bales[b]	Percentage of total[c]	Bales[b]	Percentage of total[c]	Bales[b]	Percentage of total[c]
New York	154,578	78.35	162,757	79.68	104,776	73.40	110,601	65.27
Boston	16,712	8.47	12,185	5.97	9,058	6.35	22,174	13.09
Philadelphia	13,015	6.60	19,118	9.36	16,208	11.35	17,326	10.22
Baltimore[d]	12,387	6.27	9,393	4.60	9,928	6.95	12,719	7.51
Providence[e]	493	0.25	711	0.34	2,667	1.87	6,461	3.81
Other U.S. ports	102	0.05	102	0.05	118	0.08	168	0.10

Place of destination	1857–1858		1858–1859		1859–1860	
	Bales[b]	Percentage of total[c]	Bales[b]	Percentage of total[c]	Bales[b]	Percentage of total[c]
New York	88,399	74.94	82,734	53.50	100,285	62.94
Boston	9,284	8.33	35,328	22.85	30,234	18.97
Philadelphia	8,983	7.62	19,497	12.61	17,835	11.19
Baltimore[d]	10,748	9.11	9,225	5.97	8,101	5.08
Providence[e]	10	0.01	7,643	4.94	2,884	1.81
Other U.S. ports	0	—	208	0.13	0	—

Sources. *HMM*, 25 (July–December 1851), 490; 27 (July–December 1852), 618; 31 (July–December 1854), 605; 33 (July–December 1855), 605; *DBR*, 12 (1852), 86; 19 (1855), 460; 21 (1856), 518; 23 (1857), 504; 25 (1858), 471; 27 (1859), 598; 29 (1860), 527; 31 (1861), 460.

a. Years ending August 31.

b. Includes both upland cotton from Charleston's interior hinterland and Sea Island cotton from the city's coastal hinterland. In every case upland shipments accounted for well over 90 percent of the total.

c. Total refers to domestic shipments only. In each of the observed years cotton exports going directly to foreign ports were far in excess of those to domestic centers.

d. Shipments actually listed for "Baltimore and Norfolk," since the packets sailing from Charleston to Baltimore during these years normally called also at Norfolk. However, it is assumed that the vast bulk of these shipments went on to Baltimore since Norfolk did not possess any large-scale textile mills.

e. Shipments actually listed for "Rhode Island, etc." There are some indications that some of these shipments went to Bristol, R.I., and it may be surmised that others went to the textile center of Fall River, Mass., and perhaps to other nearby manufacturing ports.

Table A.30. Annual rice shipments from Charleston, 1849-1860.[a]

Destination	1849-1850[a]		1850-1851		1851-1852		1852-1853	
	Short tons[b]	Percentage of total[c]	Short tons[b]	Percentage of total[c]	Short tons[b]	Percentage of total[c]	Short tons[b]	Percentage of total[c]
New York	8,913.7	51.45%	8,339.2	45.26%	6,292.9	42.95	13,609.6	52.87%
Boston	2,299.0	13.27	2,771.0	15.04	1,230.9	8.40	2,734.6	10.62
Philadelphia	1,411.6	8.15	1,608.2	8.73	1,386.3	9.46	2,681.0	10.42
Baltimore[d]	1,211.6	6.99	1,430.8	7.76	978.8	6.68	1,378.0	5.35
Providence[e]	43.2	0.25	5.5	0.03	5.5	0.04	110.0	0.43
New Orleans[f]	3,378.1	19.50	4,203.1	22.81	4,750.4	32.43	4,862.8	18.89
Other U.S. ports	68.8	0.39	68.8	0.37	5.2	0.04	354.7	1.42

Destination	1853-1854		1854-1855		1855-1856		1856-1857	
	Short tons[b]	Percentage of total[c]	Short tons[b]	Percentage of total[c]	Short tons[b]	Percentage of total[c]	Short tons[b]	Percentage of total[c]
New York	11,857.1	52.38	9,035.1	48.39	15,107.4	56.38	11,969.6	47.97
Boston	1,860.7	8.22	1,205.3	6.46	2,028.1	7.57	3,024.5	12.12
Philadelphia	1,315.8	5.81	1,585.9	8.49	1,967.9	7.34	1,387.9	5.56
Baltimore[d]	2,804.2	12.39	2,058.3	11.02	2,331.5	8.70	2,444.8	9.79
Providence[e]	0	—	0	—	13.8	0.05	26.1	0.10
New Orleans[f]	4,448.4	19.65	4,714.1	25.25	5,177.7	19.32	5,658.1	22.68
Other U.S. ports	351.7	1.55	71.5	0.38	169.0	0.63	440.1	1.76

Destination	1857-1858		1858-1859		1859-1860	
	Short tons[b]	Percentage of total[c]	Short tons[b]	Percentage of total[c]	Short tons[b]	Percentage of total[c]
New York	14,822.8	55.11	14,743.6	53.17	12,391.4	46.84
Boston	2,846.5	10.58	2,298.8	8.29	2,532.3	9.57
Philadelphia	1,927.5	7.17	2,133.5	7.69	2,590.8	9.79
Baltimore[d]	1,626.4	6.05	2,422.5	8.74	2,820.4	10.66
Providence[e]	18.7	0.07	68.5	0.25	0	–
New Orleans[f]	5,002.3	18.60	5,348.2	19.29	5,226.7	19.76
Other U.S. ports	650.7	2.42	713.1	2.57	894.6	3.38

Sources: *HMM*, 25 (July–December 1851), 490; 27 (July–December 1852), 618–619; 31 (July–December 1854), 605; 33 (July–December 1855), 605; *DBR*, 12 (1852), 86; 19 (1855), 460; 21 (1856), 518–519; 23 (1857), 504; 25 (1858), 471–472; 27 (1859), 598–599; 29 (1860), 527; 31 (1861), 460–461.

a. Years ending August 31.

b. Tonnage figures arrived at by assigning a weight of 550 pounds to each tierce of milled rice shipped (based on Berry, *Western Prices*, p. 154), and by following the standard practice of equating 21 bushels of rice shipped in the "rough" form to one tierce (based on J. B. De Bow, *Encyclopedia of the Trade and Commerce of the United States*, (London, 1894), p. 250). Milled rice accounted for 95 percent or more of Charleston's rice shipments in each of the observed years.

c. Total refers to domestic shipments only. The only observed year in which rice shipments from Charleston to foreign ports exceeded those from Charleston to domestic ports was 1849–1850.

d. Cf. note d, table A.29. Although rice was a consumer's good, it may be assumed that only a very small share of the shipments of that staple to "Baltimore and Norfolk" went to the latter city, since its population in 1860 (14,620) was less than 7 percent of Baltimore's and it commanded a much smaller and less populous hinterland than the Maryland major center.

e. Cf. note e, table A.29.

f. In most, but not all, of the observed years shipments were listed as going to "New Orleans, etc.," rather than solely to New Orleans. Apparently then, some rice was occasionally unloaded at Mobile or some other Gulf port before the carrying vessels arrived at the Louisiana city. Since the population of New Orleans (and its hinterland) was so much greater than that of any other Gulf port, it may be assumed that all but a small fraction of the rice bound for "New Orleans, etc." actually did reach New Orleans.

Table A.31. Annual lumber shipments from Charleston, 1849-1860.[a]

Destination	1849-1850[a]		1850-1851		1851-1852		1852-1853	
	Feet	Percentage of total[b]	Feet	Percentage of total[b]	Feet	Percentage of total[b]	Feet	Percentage of total[b]
New York	750,500	5.38%	1,033,234	7.12%	1,585,848	11.64%	1,285,097	7.34%
Boston	209,005	1.50	647,312	4.46	1,811,778	13.30	3,287,347	18.79
Philadelphia	5,918,304	42.43	5,017,334	34.59	1,781,749	13.08	4,064,892	23.23
Baltimore[c]	1,283,407	9.20	3,321,060	22.90	2,370,162	17.40	3,546,920	20.27
Providence[d]	2,413,760	17.31	2,462,758	16.98	4,818,429	35.37	4,101,123	23.44
Other U.S. ports	3,372,168	24.18	2,023,800	13.95	1,256,724	9.22	1,211,600	6.92

Destination	1853-1854		1854-1855		1855-1856		1856-1857	
	Feet	Percentage of total[b]	Feet	Percentage of total[b]	Feet	Percentage of total[b]	Feet	Percentage of total[b]
New York	1,428,361	8.34	1,135,198	6.87	738,062	6.78	137,783	1.47
Boston	4,190,779	24.48	1,623,466	9.83	2,550,770	23.43	809,009	8.62
Philadelphia	2,993,416	17.49	3,535,205	21.41	3,851,661	35.38	3,380,199	36.00
Baltimore[c]	2,799,369	16.35	2,577,531	15.61	1,624,068	14.92	2,542,866	27.08
Providence[d]	4,846,103	28.31	6,405,655	38.79	1,827,733	16.79	2,112,869	22.50
Other U.S. ports	858,977	5.02	1,236,709	7.49	293,620	2.70	406,783	4.33

	1857-1858		1958-1859		1859-1860	
Destination	Feet	Percentage of total[b]	Feet	Percentage of total[b]	Feet	Percentage of total[b]
New York	2,150,885	24.00	785,052	11.49	1,384,478	18.84
Boston	1,212,471	13.53	0	—	299,976	4.08
Philadelphia	892,400	9.96	1,147,386	16.79	1,400,349	19.60
Baltimore[c]	2,901,379	32.37	2,294,966	33.58	1,371,321	18.66
Providence[d]	1,052,938	11.75	1,828,149	26.75	1,335,835	18.18
Other U.S. ports	753,152	8.40	777,801	11.38	1,517,561	20.65

Sources: HMM, 27 (July–December 1852), 619; 31 (July–December 1854), 605; 33 (July–December 1855), 606; 42 (January–June 1860), 97; DBR, 12 (1852), 86; 19 (1855), 460; 21 (1856), 519; 25 (1858), 472; 27 (1859), 599; 29 (1860), 527; 31 (1861), 461.

a. Years ending August 31.

b. Total refers to domestic shipments. Until the last four observed years domestic lumber shipments from Charleston were two to four times greater than foreign lumber exports. During the lumber trade's decline in the final four years the ratio of domestic to foreign shipments averaged about 1.3 to 1.

c. Cf. note d, table A.29. Since Norfolk's population grew by only 294 between 1850 and 1860, thereby suggesting that there was little construction-based lumber demand in the city, and since Baltimore grew by well over 43,000 during the same period (table 2.1) and had sizable wood-demanding industries, such as shipbuilding, coopering, and furniture making, it may be assumed that nearly all of the shipments denoted as going to "Baltimore and Norfolk" actually went to the former place, especially because Norfolk also had some pine exports of its own. HMM, 41 (July–December 1859), 473.

d. Cf. note e, table A.29.

Table A.32. Annual wheat and flour shipments from Charleston, 1855-1856 and 1857-1858.[a]

| | Wheat | | | |
| | 1855-1856 | | 1857-1858 | |
Destination	Bushels[b]	Percentage of total[c]	Bushels[b]	Percentage of total[c]
New York	475,820	81.32%	264,947	90.44%
Boston	13,108	2.24	878	0.30
Philadelphia	19,298	3.30	23,610	8.06
Baltimore[d]	7,362	1.26	3,490	1.19
Other U.S. ports	69,525	11.88	16	0.01
Total	585,113	100.00%	292,941	100.00%

| | Flour | | | |
| | 1855-1856 | | 1857-1858 | |
Destination	Barrels[e]	Percentage of total[c]	Barrels[e]	Percentage of total[c]
New York	23,499	76.87	35,355	83.99
Boston	2,627	8.59	1,809	4.30
Philadelphia	505	1.65	5	0.01
Baltimore[d]	0	—	10	0.02
Other U.S. ports	3,937	12.88	4,917	11.68
Total	30,568	100.00%	42,096	100.00%

Sources: *DBR,* 21 (1856), 517; 25 (1858), 471.

a. Years ending August 31.

b. The average weight of a bushel of wheat was 60 pounds.

c. Totals refer to domestic shipments only. During the late 1850s, shipments of wheat and flour from Charleston to foreign ports usually were only a fraction of those to domestic ports.

d. Cf. note d, table A.29. Since the quantities involved were small in percentage terms, there is no need to conjecture what share of shipments labeled as going to "Baltimore and Norfolk" actually went to the former place.

e. A barrel of flour normally contained about 216 pounds.

Table A.33. Annual sugar and molasses shipments from New Orleans to Charleston and northeastern major centers, 1842-1860.[a]

		Sugar			
		Charleston		New York, Boston, Philadelphia, and Baltimore combined[b]	
Date	Total coastwise shipments from New Orleans (in short tons)[c]	Short tons[c]	% of coast-wise total	Short tons[c]	% of coast-wise total[d]
1842-1843[a]	33,250.0	655.9	1.97%	28,655.6	86.87%
1843-1844	17,351.9	751.0	4.33	12,900.1	74.34
1844-1845	53,306.2	2,222.5	4.17	45,653.9	85.64
1845-1846	42,753.3	1,825.8	4.27	34,391.4	80.44
1846-1847	25,601.6	1,897.7	7.41	17,730.8	69.26
1847-1848	45,785.2	1,731.4	3.78	36,165.9	78.99
1848-1849	48,383.1	1,899.5	3.93	38,848.9	80.29
1849-1850	47,754.2	2,575.3	5.39	37,297.4	78.10
1850-1851	22,937.9	1,824.5	7.95	15,809.6	69.36
1851-1852	26,049.9	1,930.5	7.41	15,804.5	60.67
1852-1853	47,287.2	1,952.2	4.12	34,454.6	72.86
1853-1854	90,374.5	2,738.5	3.03	74,319.9	82.24
1854-1855	65,790.1	2,510.0	3.82	53,955.0	82.01
1855-1856	26,397.3	1,844.9	7.07	14,968.3	57.36
1856-1857	4,938.5	87.0	1.76	565.0	11.44e
1857-1858	36,340.5	1,759.9	4.78	27,785.0	75.42
1858-1859	53,466.8	2,710.6	5.07	40,050.5	74.91
1859-1860	23,208.3	1,305.9	5.63	13,725.7	59.14

Sources: *DBR* 4 (1847), 393; 7 (1850), 422; 10 (1851), 449; 13 (1852), 512; 23 (1857), 374; 25 (1858), 566; 27 (1859), 477; 29 (1860), 784; 31 (1861), 456; *HMM*, 25 (July–December 1851), 604; 31 (July–December 1854), 477; 33 (July–December 1855), 604.

a. Years ending August 31.

b. Insignificant quantities of sugar also were sent to Providence in 1852–1853, 1853–1854, and 1858–1859.

c. Tonnage figures arrived at by assigning a weight of 1,000 pounds to each reported hogshead of shipment, and a weight of 200 pounds to each barrel shipped. Based on Berry, *Western Prices*, p. 154.

Table A.33 (continued)

		Molasses			
	Total coastwise shipments from New Orleans (in barrels)[g]	Charleston		New York, Boston, Philadelphia, and Baltimore combined[f]	
Date		Barrels[g]	% of coast-wise total	Barrels[g]	% of coast-wise total[d]
1842-1843[a]	86,377.5	4,085.2	4.73%	67,308.8	77.92%
1843-1844	48,331.2	5,467.0	11.31	30,634.7	63.38
1844-1845	121,338.1	5,610.0	4.62	94,629.3	77.99
1845-1846	74,621.2	6,331.5	8.48	44,459.9	59.58
1846-1847	48,591.5	3,238.0	6.66	29,270.1	60.24
1847-1848	109,327.0	6,660.0	6.09	72,651.7	66.45
1848-1849	97,944.8	6,659.0	6.80	68,426.0	69.86
1849-1850	116,992.7	10,531.0	9.00	76,908.0	65.74
1850-1851	68,025.7	7,045.2	10.36	36,216.7	53.24
1851-1852	95,025.2	9,519.0	10.02	45,928.2	48.33
1852-1853	122,210.5	10,621.0	8.69	70,772.5	57.91
1853-1854	263,694.8	13,020.0	4.94	175,941.1	66.72
1854-1855	257,863.0	17,829.0	6.91	175,533.0	68.07
1855-1856	142,967.0	12,932.0	9.05	84,619.0	59.19
1856-1857	24,556.0	1,330.0	5.42	10,699.0	43.57
1857-1858	136,705.9	10,247.0	7.50	73,637.0	53.87
1858-1859	144,386.0	8,878.0	6.15	86,212.0	59.71
1859-1860	118,690.0	7,395.0	6.23	64,535.0	54.37

d. The remaining percentage of coastwise shipments was split in various ways among Savannah, Norfolk, Richmond, Petersburg, Va., Alexandria, Mobile, Apalachicola, and Pensacola, Fla., and "Other ports."

e. During the aberrant year 1856–1857, in which Louisiana had two successive crop failures, Mobile received 51.17 percent of the very small total of sugar shipped from New Orleans.

f. In most of the indicated years molasses was also shipped to Providence in quantities of varying importance.

g. Barrels arrived at by adding statistics given in that measure to hogshead data, with each hogshead converted to 1.575 barrels. (Barrels of molasses normally contained 40 gallons, and the capacity of a hogshead was 63 gallons.)

Table A.34. Annual foodstuff shipments from New Orleans to Charleston as a share of total domestic foodstuff exports from New Orleans, 1844-1851.[a]

Class of commodity (i) to Charleston (ii) total domestic exports[b] (iii) Charleston as percentage of total (i/ii)		1844-1845	1845-1846	1846-1847	1847-1848	1848-1849	1849-1850	1850-1851
Flour (barrels)[c]	(i)	1,100	11,476	37,270	6,235	4,086	2,034	6,175
	(ii)	199,459	286,169	223,418	363,850	559,419	184,319	319,062
	(iii)	0.55%	4.01%	16.88%	1.71%	0.73%	1.10%	1.94%
Pork (barrels)[c]	(i)	1,038	2,828	1,044	2,328	1,754	4,059	1,003
	(ii)	172,711	242,960	189,034	271,103	410,901	435,764	176,507
	(iii)	0.60%	1.16%	0.55%	0.86%	0.43%	0.43%	0.93%
Bacon (hogsheads)[c]	(i)	2,533	1,962	2,874	4,128	3,502	4,246	2,872
	(ii)	11,842	20,368	21,836	43,790	63,806	60,933	43,809
	(iii)	21.39%	9.63%	13.16	9.63%	5.49%	6.96%	6.56%
Lard (kegs)[c]	(i)	9,332	5,677	5,362	9,777	5,988	2,098	2,769
	(ii)	338,526	529,947	470,261	848,486	867,795	859,592	550,603
	(iii)	2.76%	1.07%	1.14%	1.15%	0.69%	0.24%	0.50%
Beef (barrels)[c]	(i)	24	275	150	311	60	229	119
	(ii)	14,802	13,973	22,433	20,324	26,720	34,178	21,770
	(iii)	0.16%	1.97%	0.67%	1.53%	0.22%	0.67%	0.55%
Corn (sacks)[c]	(i)	4,382	87,953	800	6,937	909	1,501	23,978
	(ii)	143,676	729,915	310,787	603,993	317,203	117,409	376,769
	(iii)	3.05%	12.05%	0.26%	1.15%	0.29%	1.28%	6.36%

Sources: *DBR*, 4 (1847), 392; *HMM*, 19 (July–December 1848), 516–517; 21 (July–December 1849), 538; 25 (July–December 1851), 605.

a. Years ending August 31.

b. Includes shipments from New Orleans to Mobile and intermediate points via the Pontchartrain Railroad and the New Canal.

c. For normal equivalent weights per unit of measurement see notes j, k, and l to table A.26, and note b to table A.28. A sack of corn was equivalent to two bushels of about 70 pounds each, or roughly 140 pounds.

Table A.35. Annual cotton shipments from Savannah to Charleston as a share of total domestic cotton exports from Savannah, 1846-1847 and 1850-1860[a] (in bales).

Date	(A) Shipments to Charleston[b]	(B) Total domestic exports[b]	(A/B)
1846-1847[a]	16,397	108,454	15.12%
1850-1851	3,649	163,787	2.23
1851-1852	18,759	228,614	8.21
1853-1854	17,271	215,030	8.03
1854-1855	7,468	203,188	3.68
1855-1856	15,970	207,772	7.69
1856-1857	5,026	168,819	2.98
1858-1859	9,758	205,759	4.74
1859-1860	21,007	209,282	10.04

Sources: *DBR,* 2 (1847), 418; 19 (1855), 461; 29 (1860), 670; *HMM,* 27 (July–December 1852), 619; 29 (July–December 1853), 62; 33 (July–December 1855), 607.

a. Years ending August 31.

b. Includes both upland and Sea Island cotton. In each year upland cotton accounted for over 90 percent of total domestic exports.

Except for the last two years, domestic cotton exports from Savannah exceeded foreign shipments from that port.

Table A.36. New York's share of U.S. foreign trade, five-year periods, 1841-1860 (in millions of dollars).

Period	(A) Imports via New York	(B) Total U.S. imports	(A/B)	(C) Exports via New York	(D) Total U.S. exports	(C/D)	New York imports and exports as a percentge of U.S. foreign trade
1841-1845[a]	$298	$516	57.8%	$144	$534	27.0%	42.1%
1846-1850	455	746	61.0	235	721	32.6	47.0
1851-1855	780	1,264	61.7	486	1,207	40.3	51.2
1856-1860	1,101	1,656	66.5	623	1,768	35.2	50.4

Source: Robert Greenhalgh Albion, *The Rise of New York Port, 1815-1860* (New York: Scribner's, 1939), pp. 390-391, as derived from U.S. Secretary of the Treasury, *Reports on Commerce and Navigation, 1841-1860.*

a. The 1843 statistics included in each of the 1841-1845 figures refer to only a nine-month portion of that year.

Table A.37. Bank capital of major centers, 1850 and 1860.[a]

| Center | 1850 | | 1860[a] | |
	Bank capital	Bank capital per capital [b]	Bank capital	Bank capital per capita[b]
New York [c]	$28,840,670	$44.07	$72,390,475	$66.24
Philadelphia[c]	10,600,000	31.17	11,963,260	21.12
Boston[c]	22,610,000	108.01	33,710,000 [d]	113.25
Baltimore	7,075,794	41.86	10,328,243	48.62
Albany (+Troy)	3,680,700	46.27	7,715,710	75.94
Providence	8,173,437	196.89	15,503,000	305.98
Rochester	880,000	24.17	2,324,820	48.23
Hartford	4,062,300	299.69	7,578,202	281.54
St. Louis[c]	603,751	7.63	7,311,274	44.37
Cincinnati	1,682,026	14.57	540,400	3.36
Pittsburgh[c]	2,618,865	35.71	4,464,700	47.82
Buffalo	952,000	22.53	2,388,850	29.44
Louisville	2,960,000	68.53	5,310,000	78.05
Detroit	762,000	36.25	786,465	17.24
Cleveland	400,000	23.48	677,100	15.60
Chicago	—	0.00	150,000	1.34
San Francisco	—	0.00	—	0.00
Milwaukee	225,000	11.22	982,000	21.70
New Orleans[c]	13,600,000	116.86	24,551,666	140.70
Richmond[c]	2,114,000	76.68	3,959,450	97.28
Charleston	9,153,583	212.95	11,124,251	274.32
Mobile	2,000,000	97.49	2,500,000	85.45
Newark	1,408,650	36.22	2,258,650	31.40
Washington, D.C.	1,182,300	29.56	1,282,330	20.98
New Haven	1,681,875	82.67	3,442,056	87.66
Lowell	1,100,000	32.95	1,500,000	40.73
Jersey City[c]	—	0.00	630,400	17.29
Syracuse	610,000	27.39	1,273,800	45.30

Sources: BM, 5 (1850–1851), 627–631; 12 (1857–1858), 648; 15 (1860–1861), 768–776.
a. Unless otherwise noted, 1860 data actually represent conditions as of January 1861.
b. Based on populations indicated in table 2.1.
c. See table 2.1 for municipal units included.
d. Based on 1860 data for Cambridge, Charlestown, Chelsea, Dorchester, and Roxbury, and on an 1858 datum for Boston.

Table A.38. Total value of real estate in selected major centers, 1846 and 1853.

Center	1846	1853	Absolute increase	Percentage increase
Cleveland	$2,764,128	$13,723,414	$10,959,286	396.3%
Chicago	3,664,425	13,130,677	9,466,252	258.3
Cincinnati	27,136,752	56,275,430	29,138,678	107.4

Sources: HMM, 30 (January–June 1854), 484; 31 (January–June 1855), 683.

Table A.39. Characteristics of horse-drawn street railways in selected major centers, 1860.

Characteristic	New York[a]	Philadelphia	Boston[a]	St. Louis[a]	Cincinnati
Miles of track	141.71	148.00	67.39	26.30	17.38
Cost of roads, equipment, depots	$7,074,513	$3,811,700	$2,964,875	$576,590	$403,162
Miles of track per thousand capita[b]	0.13	0.26	0.23	0.16	0.11
Cost per thousand capita[b]	$6,474	$6,740	$9,959	$3,499	$2,504
Cost per mile of track	$49,944[c]	$25,755	$43,996	$21,924	$23,197
Number of passengers carried	44,943,292	d	11,880,877[e]	d	3,257,160[f]
Annual passengers per mile of track	317,143	—	184,371[g]	—	187,409
Annual trips per capita [b]	41.1	—	39.9	—	20.2

Sources: *Eighth Census, 1860, Mortality and Miscellaneous Statistics* (Washington, D.C., 1866), p. 332; *Boston Evening Transcript*, June 5, 1860; *HMM*, 45 (July-December 1861), 295; *ARJ*, 33 (1860), 234.
a. See table 2.1 for municipal units included.
b. Based on populations indicated in table 2.1.
c. The high cost per mile of track was in some measure due to the political corruption associated with right-of-way speculation and purchases. George Rogers Taylor, "The Beginnings of Mass Transportation in Urban America," *Smithsonian Journal of History*, 1 (Fall 1966), 43.
d. Not available.
e. Figure is actually for 1859.
f. Estimate based on seven-month total.
g. Computed on basis of 64.44 miles of track in operation at the time passenger data were collected in Boston.

Table A.40. Growth of U.S. newspaper publication, 1840-1860.

Data category	(A) 1840	(B) 1850	(C) 1860	(C/A) 1860/1840
U.S. population (thousands)	17,069	23,192	31,443	1.84
Newspapers published	1,404	2,302	3,725	2.65
Daily newspapers	138	254	387	2.80
Editions per week[a]	2,281	3,833	5,990	2.63
Annual circulation (thousands)	186,438[b]	405,617	885,796	4.75
Annual newspaper copies per capita	10.9	17.5	28.2	2.59

Sources: U.S. Bureau of the Census, *Census of Population: 1970, Number of Inhabitants—United States Summary* (Washington, D.C., 1971), p. 42; *Seventh Census, 1850, Statistical View of the United States* (Washington, D.C., 1854), pp. 155–158; *Eighth Census, 1860, Mortality and Miscellaneous Statistics of the United States* (Washington, D.C., 1866), p. 322; Alfred McClung Lee, *The Daily Newspaper in America: The Evolution of a Social Instrument* (New York: Macmillan, 1937), p. 718.

a. Obtained by assigning a weight of six to dailies, three to triweeklies, two to semiweeklies, and one to weaklies.

b. Estimate based on known circulation of newspapers and periodicals.

Table A.41. Annual circulation of newspapers and news-bearing periodicals published in reported major centers, 1850.

Major center	Number of newspapers and news-bearing publications	Annual circulation	(A) Percentage of 1850 U.S. population	(B) Percentage of 1850 annual circulation	(B/A) Location quotient
New York	104	78,747,600	2.22[a]	18.47	8.32
Boston	113	54,482,644	0.90	12.78	14.20
Philadelphia	51	48,457,240	1.46	11.36	7.78
Baltimore	31	20,711,100	0.73	4.86	6.66
Albany	8	16,050,460	0.22[b]	3.76	17.09
New Orleans	18	11,260,860	0.50	2.64	5.28
Cincinnati	39	8,753,200	0.50	2.05	4.10
Charleston	12	5,675,800[c]	0.18	1.33	7.00
St. Louis	18	4,890,030	0.34	1.15	3.38
Louisville	23	3,186,638	0.19	0.75	3.95
Chicago	17	1,886,952[d]	0.13	0.44	3.38
Mobile	4	1,002,000	0.09	0.23	2.56
Reported center total	438	255,104,524	7.47	59.83	8.01
U.S. total	2,516[e]	426,409,978[f]	100.00	100.00	—

Sources: Seventh Census, 1850, Statistical View of the United States (Washington, D.C., 1854), pp. 156, 158; BM, 10 (1856), 280.

a. Not including the population of Brooklyn (138,882), since that politically independent unit had numerous additional newspapers with a considerable, but unspecifiable, circulation. All other percentages indicated in this column are based on the populations given in table 2.1.

b. Based on the population of Albany only, since Troy had newspapers of its own whose annual circulation is not available. See note e, table 2.1.

c. Not including the annual circulation of weekly and triweekly editions.

d. Not including the annual circulation of one daily and three weekly newspapers.

e. Includes 214 semimonthly, monthly, and quarterly periodicals not included in the 1850 newspaper total given in table A.40.

f. The news-bearing periodicals mentioned in note e accounted for 20,694,788 of this total.

Table A.42. Growth of U.S. postal services, 1840-1860.

Data category	(A) 1840	(B) 1850	(C) 1860	(C/A) 1860/1840
U.S. population (thousands)	17,069	23,192	31,443	1.84
Post offices	13,468	18,417	28,498	2.12
Population per post office	1,267	1,259	1,103	—
Miles of post roads	155,739	178,672	240,594	1.54
Number of letters carried (thousands)	27,536	69,426	161,802[a]	5.88
Number of letters carried per capita	1.61	2.99	5.15	3.20

Sources: U.S. Bureau of the Census, *Historical Statistics of the United States: Colonial Times to 1957* (Washington, D.C., 1960), p. 497; *HMM*, 21 (July–December 1849), 412; 39 (July–December 1858), 620; *BM*, 12 (1857), 438; Lee, *Daily Newspaper*, 746.

a. Estimate based on letter total reported for 1856 (131,450,409) and the ratio of 1860 to 1856 total U.S. Post Office receipts. Such an estimate appears justified since the set of postage rates prevailing in 1860 was identical to that prevailing in 1856.

Table A.43. Number of letters received and sent at reported major centers, 1852.[a]

Major center[b]	Letters received	Letters sent	Local total[c]	Percentage of total letters carried by U.S. Post Office[d]
New York[e]	9,105,312	12,357,118	21,462,430	22.41
Philadelphia[e]	3,019,364	4,760,395	7,779,759	8.12
Boston[e]	2,842,435	4,485,245	7,327,680	7.65
New Orleans	1,982,252	1,835,708	3,817,960	3.99
Baltimore	1,400,252	1,732,743	3,132,995	3.27
San Francisco	1,187,920	1,303,824	2,491,744	2.60
Reported center total	19,537,535	26,475,033	[f]	—

Source: U.S. Senate, *Report of the Postmaster General,* Executive Documents, vol. I, 32nd Cong., 2nd sess., 1852, p. 683.

a. Year ending June 30, 1852.

b. Data were also reported for Washington, D.C., but those figures are not included here; most of the letters entering and leaving Washington went free of charge because of congressional and executive privileges.

c. According to indications in the source, local totals apparently do not include any intraurban letters distributed from the single post office in each of the reported centers.

d. The total number of letters carried was 95,790,524. Location quotients are not computed here, as they were in table A.41, because of the absence of 1852 population figures.

e. The politically defined urban unit, not the functionally defined unit employed in table 2.1 and elsewhere.

f. The local totals of the reported centers cannot be summed without falling victim to double accounting, since some letters undoubtedly went from one reported major center to another. However, it is clear that the number of letters both received and sent from each of the six centers was several times greater than would be expected in view of their shares of the 1850 national population total.

Table A.44. Annual number of letters sent per capita, selected geographic units, 1856.

Geographic unit	Annual letters per capita
United States as a whole	4.9
Southern "country districts"	1.6
Northern "country districts"	3.5
All of the southern states	2.9
All of the northern states	6.1
New Orleans	19.7
Cincinnati	21.2
New York[a]	30.0
Boston[a]	40.8

Source: *BM,* 12 (1857), 437.

a. The politically defined urban unit, not the functionally defined unit employed in table 2.1 and elsewhere.

Table A.45. Letters and papers conveyed to and from foreign places, for reported major centers, 1854.[a]

Major center	Letters	Percentage of U.S. total	Newspapers	Percentage of U.S. total
New York[b]	1,904,268	61.48%	2,657,956	74.50%
Boston[b]	405,348	13.09	169,849	4.76
New Orleans	362,243	11.70	467,505	13.10
Chicago	181,337	5.85	35,876	1.01
Charleston[c]	74,974	2.42	17,928	0.50
Philadelphia	64,362	2.08	119,224	3.34
Baltimore	29,983	0.97	23,502	0.66
Washington, D.C.	17,640	0.57	37,494	1.05
Mobile	1,454	0.05	6	[d]
Other[e]	55,769	1.80	38,273	1.07
U.S. total	3,097,378	100.00	3,567,613	100.00

Source: U.S. Senate, *Report of the Postmaster General*, Executive Documents, vol. II, 33rd Cong., 2nd sess., 1854, p. 661.
a. Year ending June 30, 1854.
b. The politically defined urban unit, not the functionally defined unit employed in table 2.1 and elsewhere.
c. Roughly 85 percent of the letters and newspapers conveyed between Charleston and foreign ports either originated or terminated in Havana, Cuba.
d. Percentage negligible.
e. Includes Savannah, Ga., and other unspecified places.

Table A.46. Passengers arriving at and departing from major midwestern centers, 1850-1851.[a]

Major center	By steamboat	By railroad	By canal	(A) By stage	1850 Total	(B) Ratio of population	(A) to (B)
Cincinnati	270,796[b]	159,287	[c]	[c]	430,083	115,435	3.73:1
St. Louis	318,713[b]	0	0	18,582	337,295[d]	79,061	4.27:1
Pittsburgh	428,745[b]	0	[c]	[c]	428,745	73,341[e]	5.85:1
Louisville	120,000[b]	36,500	0	[c]	156,500	43,194	3.62:1
Buffalo	171,557[b]	381,586	43,000	[c]	596,143	42,261	14.11:1
Chicago	85,800	71,253	42,770	[c]	199,823	29,963	6.67:1
Detroit	369,430[b]	197,399	0	[c]	566,829	21,019	26.97:1

Source: Israel Andrews, *Report . . . on the Trade and Commerce of the British North American Colonies*, U.S. Senate Document no. 112, 32nd Cong., 1st sess., pp. 735-736.
a. Year ending June 30, 1851. Data for Cleveland and Milwaukee not reported in source.
b. Not including local traffic carried by steam ferryboats.
c. Datum not available.
d. Largely because of migrant traffic, the number of passengers borne by steamboats to and from St. Louis grew to over one million for the year ending Sept. 30, 1855. *HMM*, 33 (July–December 1855), 637.
e. See note g, table 2.1.

Table A.47. Multiwire telegraph services, 1852.

Termini locations	Number of wires
New York-Philadelphia	14
New York-Baltimore-Washington	7
New York-Buffalo	7
New York-Boston	6
New York-New Orleans[a]	2
New York-Dunkirk, N.Y.[b]	2
Buffalo-Milwaukee (via Chicago)	2
Pittsburgh-Cleveland	2
Bittsburgh-Cincinnati	2
Cleveland-Cincinnati	2
Cincinnati-St. Louis	2
Chicago-St. Louis	2
Boston-Portland, Maine[c]	2

Sources: U.S. Senate, *Report of the Superintendent of the Census, December 1, 1852,* Executive Document no. 1, 32nd Cong., 2nd sess., 1853, I, 571–572; Alexander Jones, *Historical Sketch of the Electric Telegraph: Including Its Rise and Progress in the United States* (New York, 1852), p. 87.

a. There were two different routes, one proceeding from Washington via Richmond, Charleston, and Mobile, and the other continuing onward from Pittsburgh via Cincinnati, Louisville, and Nashville.

b. One of these wires was owned and operated by the New York and Erie Railroad, which pioneered in the use of the telegraph for railroad-service coordination. The other wire was part of a "back door" line between New York and Pittsburgh.

c. Two wires were necessary between Boston and Portland because of the importance of the traffic in news and private messages to and from Europe via Halifax, Nova Scotia, where the telegraph terminated and the steamship took over.

Table A.48. Dispatches sent and received by the Pittsburg, Cincinnati, and Louisville Telegraph Company, 1850.

Office location	Dispatches sent and received	Percentage of company total
Cincinnati	156,000	42.87%
Louisville	74,660	20.52
Pittsburgh	73,900	20.31
Major center subtotal	304,560	83.70
All other places	59,319	16.30
Total	363,879	100.00%

Source: Jones, *Electric Telegraph,* pp. 103–104.

Table A.49. Mentions of nonlocal places made in an economic context: Daily newspapers published in nine major centers, 1851.

Major center of publication	(A) Total nonlocal place mentions[a]	(B) Total mentions of other major centers	(B) as a percentage of (A)	Number of additional hinterland and non-hinterland places mentioned once mentions	(C) Total other hinterland and non-hinterland mentions	(C) as a percentage of (A)
New York	1,610	849	52.73%	282	761	47.27%
Philadelphia	1,305	536	41.07	260	769	58.93
Boston	1,195	598	50.04	148	597	49.96
New Orleans	1,190	567	47.65	174	623	52.35
Cincinnati	1,423	728	51.16	179	695	48.84
St. Louis	1,565	824	52.65	149	741	47.35
Chicago	1,267	564	44.51	224	703	55.49
Cleveland	1,115	585	52.47	145	530	47.53
San Francisco	1,100	525	47.73	116	575	52.27

Sources: *New York Daily Tribune*, Jan. 15, May 24, 1851; *New York Daily Times*, Sept. 29, Nov. 27, 1851; *Philadelphia Public Ledger*, Jan. 15, Apr. 9, July 23, Nov. 10, 1851; *Boston Evening Transcript*, Jan. 8, May 9, Aug. 29, 1851; *New Orleans Times Pica-yune*, Jan. 14, July 2, 1851; *Cincinnati Enquirer*, Jan. 29, June 12, Aug. 12, 1851; *St. Louis Intelligencer*, Jan. 6, Apr. 12, July 23, Oct. 7, 1851; *Chicago Daily Democrat*, Jan. 6, Apr. 10, Aug. 15, 1851; *Cleveland Plain Dealer*, Jan. 14, May 14, 1851; and (San Francisco) *Daily Alta California*, Jan. 7, Mar. 14, May 29, Aug. 20, Oct. 27, 1851.

a. The following types of mentions are not included in this total: nonlocal places mentioned in a political or other noneconomic context; all foreign places, whether or not mentioned in an economic context; and all domestic references not refined below the state level. In the content analyses performed for the first three centers (New York, Philadelphia, and Boston), any mention of urban units included in their functional definitions was not regarded as nonlocal (see notes b, c, and d to table 2.1).

Table A.50. Mentions of other major centers (by region) made in an economic context: Daily newspapers published in nine major centers, 1851.

Major center mentioned	New York		Philadelphia		Boston		New Orleans	
	No.	% of total[a]	No.	% of total[a]	No.	% of total[a]	No.	% of total[a]
New York	b	b	203	15.56%	208	17.41%	178	14.96%
Philadelphia	141	8.76%	b	b	68	5.69	46	3.87
Boston	156	9.69	75	5.74	b	b	51	4.29
Baltimore	66	4.10	57	4.37	36	3.01	36	3.03
Albany (+Troy)[c]	60	3.73	2	0.15	26	2.18	3	0.25
Providence	40	2.48	3	0.23	32	2.68	3	0.25
Washington, D.C.	32	1.99	33	2.52	6	0.50	23	1.93
Rochester	7	0.43	8	0.61	0	—	0	—
Hartford	19	1.18	1	0.08	8	0.67	0	—
Other north-eastern major centers[d]	47	2.92	24	1.84	34	2.85	4	0.34
All northeastern major centers	568	35.28	406	31.11	418	34.98	344	28.91
Cincinnati	13	0.81	13	1.00	4	0.33	27	2.27
St. Louis	7	0.43	10	0.77	3	0.25	38	3.19
Pittsburgh	17	1.06	23	1.76	3	0.25	17	1.43
Louisville	4	0.25	4	0.31	3	0.25	31	2.61
Buffalo	17	1.06	2	0.15	12	1.00	4	0.34
Chicago	10	0.62	0	—	4	0.33	1	0.08
Detroit	3	0.19	1	0.08	2	0.17	0	—
Milwaukee	0	—	1	0.08	1	0.08	0	—
Cleveland	5	0.31	2	0.15	2	0.17	0	—
All midwestern major centers	76	4.72	56	4.29	34	2.85	118	9.92
New Orleans	96	5.96	37	2.83	56	4.69	b	b
Charleston	35	2.17	14	1.07	21	1.76	20	1.68
Richmond	20	1.24	8	0.61	6	0.50	1	0.08
Mobile	13	0.81	6	0.46	18	1.51	50	4.20
All southern major centers	164	10.19	65	4.98	101	8.45	71	5.97
San Francisco	41	2.55	9	0.69	45	3.76	34	2.86

| Cincinnati | | St. Louis | | Chicago | | Cleveland | | San Francisco | |
No.	% of total[a]	No.	% of total[a]	No.	% of total[a]	No.	% of total[a]	No.	% of total[a]
143	10.05%	180	11.50%	199	15.71%	125	11.21%	197	17.91%
59	4.15	62	3.96	32	2.53	30	2.69	61	5.55
42	2.95	77	4.92	68	5.37	31	2.78	80	7.27
15	1.05	55	3.51	4	0.32	3	0.27	34	3.09
24	1.69	4	0.26	50	3.95	34	3.05	3	0.27
0	—	1	0.06	0	—	0	—	2	0.18
16	1.12	7	0.45	2	0.16	2	0.18	14	1.27
6	0.42	7	0.45	5	0.39	5	0.45	0	—
32	2.25	10	0.64	9	0.71	5	0.45	1	0.09
9	0.63	6	0.38	4	0.32	6	0.54	2	0.18
346	24.31	409	26.13	373	29.44	241	21.61	394	35.82
b	b	56	3.58	8	0.63	109	9.78	12	1.09
59	4.15	b	b	44	3.47	5	0.45	24	2.18
52	3.65	69	4.41	4	0.32	38	3.41	3	0.27
85	5.97	54	3.45	0	—	2	0.18	3	0.27
41	2.88	8	0.51	57	4.50	71	6.37	2	0.18
6	0.42	13	0.83	b	b	71	6.37	0	—
4	0.28	2	0.13	41	3.24	30	2.69	0	—
2	0.14	3	0.19	13	1.03	7	0.63	0	—
40	2.81	2	0.13	10	0.79	b	b	0	—
289	20.31	207	13.23	177	13.97	333	29.87	44	4.00
70	4.92	201	12.84	12	0.95	9	0.81	76	6.91
5	0.35	1	0.06	1	0.08	0	—	7	0.64
3	0.21	1	0.06	0	—	0	—	2	0.18
3	0.21	2	0.13	0	—	0	—	2	0.18
81	5.69	205	13.10	13	1.03	9	0.81	87	7.91
12	0.84	3	0.19	1	0.08	2	0.18	b	b

Sources: See table A.49.
a. See column (A), table A.49, for total used.
b. Not applicable.
c. See note e, table 2.1.
d. Newark, Lowell, Syracuse, New Haven, and Jersey City.

Table A.51. Comparative aspects of nonlocal place mentions made in an economic context: daily newspapers published in Boston and Cincinnati, 1851 and 1860.

| Place-mention category | Boston | | | | Cincinnati | | | |
| | 1851 | | 1860 | | 1851 | | 1860 | |
	No.	% of total	No.	% of total	No.	% of total	No.	% of Total
All other major centers	598	50.04%	484	46.72%	728	51.16%	732	45.66%
All hinterland places[a]	524	43.85	458	44.21	499	35.07	508	31.69
of which hinterland major centers	58	4.85	38	3.67	0	—	0	—
Nonhinterland lesser cities, towns, and settlements	131	10.96	132	12.74	196	13.77	363	22.65
Total	1.195[c]	100.00%[c]	1,036[c]	100.00%[c]	1,423	100.00%	1,603	100.00%

Sources: *Boston Evening Transcript*, Jan. 8, May 9, Aug. 29, 1851; Feb. 1, June 5, Sept. 8, Nov. 24, 1860; *Cincinnati Enquirer*, Jan. 29, June 12, Aug. 12, 1851; Jan. 31, June 12, Oct. 3, 1860.

a. All places occurring within the liberally defined hinterlands shown in maps 6.2–6.5. See note 64 to chapter 6 for further comment.

b. As defined here, the Boston hinterland encompassed the major centers of Providence, Lowell, and Hartford.

c. Total obtained by counting Providence, Lowell, and Hartford once rather than twice.

Notes

1. The Questions and Their Setting

1. The argument that urban population size is dependent on the provision of goods and services to smaller places lies at the core of Walter Christaller's central-place theory. Those unfamiliar with classical central-place theory and its recent modifications are directed to: Brian J. L. Berry and Allan Prod, *Central Place Studies. A Bibliography of Theory and Applications,* 2d ed. (Philadelphia: Regional Science Research Institute, 1965); Brian J. L. Berry, *Geography of Market Centers and Retail Distribution* (Englewood Cliffs, N.J.: Prentice-Hall, 1967). For a translation of Christaller's original work, which first appeared in German in 1933, see Walter Christaller, *Central Places in Southern Germany* (Englewood Cliffs, N.J.: Prentice-Hall, 1966).

2. Allan Pred, *Major Job-Providing Organizations and Systems of Cities* (Washington, D.C.: Association of American Geographers, 1974); idem, "The Interurban Transmission of Growth in Advanced Economies: Empirical Findings versus Regional-Planning Assumptions," *Regional Studies,* 10 (1976), 151–171; idem, *City-Systems in Advanced Economies: Past Growth, Present Processes and Future Development Options* (London: Hutchinson University Library, 1977).

3. Gunnar E. Törnqvist, "Spatial Organization of Activity Spheres," in H. Swain and R. D. Mackinnon, eds., *Issues in the Management of Urban Systems* (Schloss Laxenburg: International Institute for Applied Systems Analysis, 1975), pp. 226–265; idem, "The Geography of Economic Activities: Some Critical Viewpoints on Theory and Application," *Economic Geography,* 52 (1977), 153–162.

4. For example, see Gerald Karaska, "Manufacturing Linkages in the Philadelphia Economy: Some Evidence of Agglomeration Economies," *Geographical Analysis,* 1 (1969), 354–369; Walter Isard and Thomas W. Langford, *Regional Input-Output Study: Recollections and Diverse Notes on the Philadelphia Experience* (Cambridge: MIT Press, 1971); William B. Beyers, "On Geographical Properties of Growth Center Linkage Systems," *Economic Geography,* 50 (1974), 203–218; Roland A. Earickson, "The Spatial Pattern of Income Generation in Lead Firm, Growth Area Linkage Systems," *Economic Geography,* 51 (1975), 17–26.

5. Brian J. L. Berry, "Cities as Systems within Systems of Cities," *Papers of the Regional Science Association,* 13 (1964), 147–163; Olof Wärneryd, *Interdependence in Urban Systems* (Göteborg: Regionkonsult Aktiebolag, 1968); and L. S. Bourne, *Urban Systems: Strategies for Regulation—A Comparison of Policies in Britain, Sweden, Australia, and Canada* (London: Oxford University Press, 1975). In order to avoid confusion the terms system of cities and city-system are used rather than the term urban system. Although all three terms are often used interchangeably by geog-

raphers and others, urban system is also applied frequently to individual cities, in which case the city is conceptualized as being composed of various interacting and interdependent components.

6. For comments on the attributes of complex social systems see Walter Buckley, *Sociology and Modern Systems Theory* (Englewood Cliffs, N.J.: Prentice-Hall, 1967).

7. Carl H. Madden, "On Some Indications of Stability in the Growth of Cities in the United States," *Economic Development and Cultural Change,* 4 (1955–1956), 236–252; Fred Lukermann, "Empirical Expressions of Nodality and Hierarchy in a Circulation Manifold," *East Lakes Geographer,* 2 (1966), 17–44.

8. Allan Pred, *Urban Growth and the Circulation of Information: The United States System of Cities, 1790–1840* (Cambridge: Harvard University Press, 1973), pp. 3–7; idem, *City-Systems in Advanced Economies,* pp. 34–36.

9. U.S. Bureau of the Census, *Census of Population: 1970, Number of Inhabitants—United States Summary* (Washington, D.C., 1971), p. 42. In comparison, the next highest decennial rate of registered urban population growth (63.7 percent) had been attained between 1830 and 1840.

10. Pred, *Urban Growth;* idem, *The Spatial Dynamics of U.S. Urban-Industrial Growth, 1800–1914: Interpretive and Theoretical Essays* (Cambridge: MIT Press, 1966).

11. George Rogers Taylor, *The Transportation Revolution, 1815–1860* (New York: Holt, Rinehart and Winston, 1951), p. 348. See also Douglas C. North, *The Economic Growth of the United States, 1790–1860* (New York: W. W. Norton, 1966), pp. 212–214; and George Van Vleck, *The Panic of 1857* (New York: Columbia University Press, 1943).

12. Alfred D. Chandler, Jr., *The Railroads: The Nation's First Big Business* (New York: Harcourt, Brace & World, 1965), p. 21; Taylor, *Transportation Revolution,* pp. 85–86; Henry V. Poor, *History of the Railroads and Canals of the United States of America* (New York, 1860); John F. Stover, *Iron Road to the West: American Railroads in the 1850s* (New York: Columbia University Press, 1978). Also note Albert Fishlow, *American Railroads and the Transformation of the Ante-Bellum Economy* (Cambridge: Harvard University Press, 1965), on the failure of the railroads to forge a truly integrated national market by 1860.

13. These points do not necessarily vitiate completely Fogel's arguments that canal technology has been underrated, that the superiority of the railroads has been overstated, and that American economic growth could have achieved nearly the same levels without the railroad. See Robert William Fogel, *Railroads and American Economic Growth: Essays in Econometric History* (Baltimore: Johns Hopkins University Press, 1964).

14. Israel Andrews, *Report . . . on the Trade and Commerce of the British North American Colonies,* U.S. Senate Document no. 112, 32nd Cong., 1st sess., 1853, p. 50; Louis C. Hunter, *Steamboats on the Western Rivers* (Cambridge: Harvard University Press, 1949); Harry N. Scheiber, *Ohio Canal: A Case Study of Government and the Economy, 1820–1861* (Athens: Ohio University Press, 1969); Erik F. Haites, James Mak, and Gary M. Walton, *Western River Transportation: The Era of Early Internal Development, 1810–1860* (Baltimore: Johns Hopkins University Press, 1975).

15. See Allan Pred, "The Impact of Technological and Institutional Innovations on Life Content: Some Time-Geographic Observations," *Geographical Analysis,* 10 (1978), 345–372.

16. Railroad demand was such that by 1860 "the four largest American iron works . . . were all integrated rail mills." Glenn Porter and Harold C. Livesay, *Merchants and Manufacturing: Studies in the Changing Structure of Nineteenth-Century Marketing* (Baltimore: Johns Hopkins University Press, 1971), p. 58.

17. See Alfred D. Chandler, Jr., "Anthracite Coal and the Beginnings of the Industrial Revolution in the United States," *Business History Review,* 46 (1972), 141–181.

18. Ibid., p. 169.

19. Pred, *Spatial Dynamics;* idem, *Urban Growth;* Jeffrey G. Williamson and Joseph A. Swanson, "The Growth of Cities in the American Northeast, 1820–1870," *Explorations in Entrepreneurial History,* 2d ser., 4, no. 1 (1966–1967); and Simeon J. Crowther, "Urban Growth in the Mid-Atlantic States, 1785–1850," *Journal of Economic History,* 3 (1976), 624–644.

20. See Porter and Livesay, *Merchants and Manufacturing,* pp. 62–78.

21. See John B. Sharpless, "The Economic Structure of Port Cities in the Mid-Nineteenth Century, Boston and Liverpool, 1840–1860," *Journal of Historical Geography,* 2 (1976), 131–143.

22. Diane Lindstrom, *Economic Development in the Philadelphia Region, 1810–1850* (New York: Columbia University Press, 1978), pp. 41–54. However, despite Lindstrom's census-based claims, there are considerable difficulties in establishing the exact relative importance of manufacturing and wholesaling-trading activities for specific cities throughout the 1840–1860 period. Contemporaries asserted that commercial employment was often either understated or inconsistently reported in the 1840 census. With respect to business matters in general, it was contended that "little reliance" was "to be placed upon the accuracy of 1840 and 1850 returns." Moreover, owing to the inadquate instructions given 1840 census marshals and their assistants, urban manufacturing totals were distorted by the inclusion of establishments whose primary function was to perform repair services, and workshops that sold directly to the household consumer. *HMM,* 12 (January–June 1845), 129; Andrews, *Report . . . on the Trade and Commerce,* p. 718; and Meyer H. Fishbein, "The Censuses of Manufactures, 1810–1890," *National Archives Accessions,* no. 57 (June 1963), 7–9.

23. Lindstrom, *Economic Development,* p. 49. For comments on Boston's functional shift see Oscar Handlin, *Boston's Immigrants: A Study in Acculturation* (Cambridge: Harvard University Press, 1959); David Ward, *Cities and Immigrants: A Geography of Change in Nineteenth-Century America* (New York: Oxford University Press, 1971); Sharpless, "Economic Structure of Port Cities."

24. U.S. Bureau of the Census, *Eighth Census of the United States, 1860, Mortality and Miscellaneous Statistics* (Washington, D.C., 1866), p. xviii.

25. Taylor, *Transportation Revolution,* p. 389.

26. *Eighth Census, 1860, Mortality and Miscellaneous Statistics,* p. xviii; Pred, *Spatial Dynamics,* p. 20. Note that the nature of published census re-

turns requires that manufacturing employment be computed as a percentage of a city's population rather than as a percentage of a city's total labor force.

27. Chandler, "Anthracite Coal," p. 178.

28. *ARJ,* 23 (1850), 654; "New York Industrial Exhibition, Special Report of Mr. Joseph Whitworth, Presented to the House of Commons by Command of Her Majesty in Pursuance of Their Address of February 6, 1854," in Nathan Rosenberg, ed., *The American System of Manufactures* (Edinburgh: Edinburgh University Press, 1969), p. 331; and *San Francisco Mercantile Gazette and Prices Current,* Jan. 13, 1860. Also see 1860 descriptions of various iron foundries and machine works in J. Leander Bishop, *A History of American Manufactures from 1608 to 1860* (Philadelphia, 1863), III.

29. See Eric E. Lampard, "The Evolving System of Cities in the United States: Urbanization and Economic Development," in Harvey S. Perloff and Lowdon Wingo, Jr., eds., *Issues in Urban Economics* (Baltimore: Johns Hopkins University Press, 1968), pp. 100–101. Also see items listed in note 3.

30. Victor S. Clark, *History of Manufactures in the United States* (New York: McGraw-Hill, 1929), I, 487, 491; Chandler, "Anthracite Coal," p. 177; Edwin T. Freedley, *Philadelphia and its Manufactures* (Philadelphia, 1859), p. 251.

31. Fred Bateman and Thomas Weiss, "Comparative Regional Development in Antebellum Manufacturing," *Journal of Economic History,* 35 (1975), 182–208; Percy W. Bidwell, "Population Growth in Southern New England," *Publications of the American Statistical Association,* 15, n.s., no. 120 (December 1917), 832. Also see related findings in Paul John Uselding, *Studies in the Technological Development of the American Economy during the First Half of the Nineteenth Century* (New York: Arno Press, 1975). There were almost certainly a few more states whose twenty largest establishments averaged more than 164 workers in 1860, since the Bateman and Weiss sample did not include Pennsylvania, Rhode Island, and Ohio.

2. The Pattern of Urban Growth, 1840–1860

1. In both the national and the northeastern computations the populations of New York, Philadelphia, and Boston have been allowed to include subsequently annexed suburbs as specified in table 2.1.

2. Computed from U.S. Bureau of the Census, *Census of Population: 1970, Number of Inhabitants—United States Summary* (Washington, D.C., 1971), p. 49. See John Burk Sharpless, *City Growth in the United States, England and Wales, 1820–1861: The Effects of Location, Size and Economic Structure on Inter-Urban Variations in Demographic Growth* (New York: Arno Press, 1977), pp. 128–129. The sources from which urban population shares have been determined are identical with those given in table 2.1.

3. Nevertheless, the size rank that Syracuse had reached within the northeastern regional city-system by 1850—ninth, exclusive of Newark and other places that subsequently became part of a larger Standard Metropolitan Statistical Area (SMSA) or Standard Consolidated Area—was little different from the rank position (tenth) held by its 1970 metropolitan area counterpart.

4. Compare the top and bottom rows of table 2.2.

5. It is sometimes, but far from always, recognized that, regardless of any urban-place definition problems, most measures of growth within a system of cities are sensitive to the addition of new system members. Generally, the smaller the system the more likely are new units to create distortions. See Jeffrey G. Williamson and Joseph A. Swanson, "The Growth of Cities in the American Northeast, 1820–1870," *Explorations in Entrepreneurial History,* 2d ser., 4, no. 1 (1966–1967), 9; Brian T. Robson, *Urban Growth: An Approach* (London: Methuen, 1973); Peter Haggett, "Measuring Instability in the Growth of Urban Systems: A Biproportional Index," in *General Problems of Geography and Geosystems Modelling* (Moscow, 1976), pp. 116–121.

6. *HMM,* 8 (January–June 1843), 511; Israel Andrews, *Report . . . on the Trade and Commerce of the British North American Colonies,* U.S. Senate Document no. 112, 32nd Cong., 1st sess., 1853, p. 694; Edward K. Muller, "Selective Urban Growth in the Middle Ohio Valley, 1800-1860," *Geographical Review,* 66 (1976), 178–199. Cf. Eric E. Lampard, "The Evolving System of Cities in the United States: Urbanization and Economic Development," in Harvey S. Perloff and Lowdon Wingo, Jr., eds., *Issues in Urban Economics* (Baltimore: Johns Hopkins University Press, 1968), p. 122.

7. See *HMM,* 8 (January–June 1843), 511. A few previously unenumerated newcomers, such as Santa Fe, N. Mex., and San Antonio, Tex., could not have appeared in the 1840 census because the territories to which they belonged were not yet part of the United States.

8. U.S. Bureau of the Census, *Seventh Census of the United States: 1850* (Washington, D.C., 1853); U.S. Bureau of the Census, *Census of Population: 1960* (Washington, D.C., 1961), I, part A; and *Webster's Geographical Dictionary* (Springfield, Mass.: Merriam, 1949), pp. 173, 692, 838, 907. Among the other comparatively large, previously unenumerated newcomers in 1850 were Lawrence, Mass. (8,262), and Watervliet, N.Y. (7,564).

9. The combined 1860 population of Minneapolis, St. Paul, and St. Anthony (16,223) was 0.83 percent of the 1970 Minneapolis-St. Paul SMSA population. Denver's 1860 population (2,749) was 0.39 percent of that inhabiting the Denver SMSA in 1970. Salt Lake City's 8,236 inhabitants of 1860 represented 1.17 percent of the 1970 Salt Lake City–Ogden SMSA population.

10. *Eighth Census, Population of the United States in 1860* (Washington, D.C., 1864); *Census of Population: 1960,* I, part A; *Webster's Geographical Dictionary,* pp. 769, 1,020; and Robert Greenhalgh Albion, *The Rise of New York Port 1815-1860* (New York: Scribner's, 1939), p. 55. Among other relatively large, previously unenumerated newcomers in 1860 were the New York centers of Binghamton (8,325) and Yonkers (8,218).

11. See Sharpless, *City Growth,* pp. 52–53.

12. Ibid., p. 57; Williamson and Swanson, "Growth of Cities," p. 28.

13. Adna Ferrin Weber, *The Growth of Cities in the Nineteenth Century: A Study in Statistics,* Columbia University Studies in History, Economics and Public Law, vol. XI (New York, 1899); Wilson H. Grabill, Clyde V. Kiser, and Pascal K. Whelpton, *The Fertility of American Women* (New York: John Wiley, 1958), pp. 16–19; Everett S. Lee and Michael Lalli, "Population," in David T. Gilchrist, ed., *The Growth of the Seaport Cities, 1790–1825* (Charlottesville: University of Virginia Press, 1967), p. 32. Also see compari-

son of 1840 and 1850 median child/woman ratios for Philadelphia with those of surrounding rural areas in Diane Lindstrom, *Economic Development in the Philadelphia Region, 1810–1850* (New York: Columbia University Press, 1978), p. 225.

14. U.S. Bureau of the Census, *Historical Statistics of the United States, Colonial Times to 1957* (Washington, D.C., 1960), p. 57; Douglas C. North, *The Economic Growth of the United States, 1790–1860* (New York: W. W. Norton, 1966), p. 206; David Ward, *Cities and Immigrants: A Geography of Change in Nineteenth-Century America* (New York: Oxford University Press, 1971), pp. 55–65; Lee and Lalli, "Population," p. 33; Bayard Still, *Urban America: A History with Documents* (Boston: Little, Brown, 1974), pp. 118–119.

15. James P. Allen, "Changes in the American Propensity to Migrate," *Annals of the Association of American Geographers,* 67 (1977), 577–587 (quotation on 577). As defined by Allen (p. 578): "A persistence rate for any area is the percentage of the population of the area at the beginning of any time period (the base year) who were still living in that area at the end of the period . . . Thus, persistence rates are highly and inversely correlated with rates of outmigration." See Peter R. Knights, *The Plain People of Boston, 1830–1860: A Study in City Growth* (New York: Oxford University Press, 1971), pp. 62–63; Susan E. Hirsch, *Roots of the American Working Class: The Industrialization of Crafts in Newark, 1800–1860* (Philadelphia: University of Pennsylvania Press, 1978), p. 92; Alan Dawley, *Class and Community: The Industrial Revolution in Lynn* (Cambridge: Harvard University Press, 1976), pp. 135, 169.

16. Lindstrom, *Economic Development,* pp. 24–25.

17. See Carl H. Madden, "Some Temporal Aspects of the Growth of Cities in the United States," *Economic Development and Cultural Change,* 6(1957–1958), 165; and Lindstrom, *Economic Development,* pp. 24, 153, 178–179.

18. The combined 1840–1850 actual absolute increase of previously recognized urban places and previously enumerated newcomers approached 343,-000 (table 2.4, column B). If the registered absolute increase for newcomers that had not been previously enumerated was overstated by as little as 5 percent—which it most certainly was—then less than 225,000 could be added to the figure of approximately 343,000, thus making a grand combined total well under 571,000.

19. According to an evaluation that appeared in *Hunt's Merchants' Magazine:* "There is no doubt that the population of the city [Philadelphia] is much larger than the figures returned by the Deputy United States Marshal would denote. The returns were collected in the summer, when, as in New York and Boston, very many families were absent from the city. Their houses being closed, the marshals were unable to obtain the desired statistics when they made their regular rounds and thousands were missed in this way. An evidence of these serious omissions is furnished by the fact that the census returns give the number of deaths which occurred in the city year ending June 1st 1860 as 6,076; while the records of the board of health prove that during that period the deaths really numbered 10,000." *HMM,* 44 (January–June 1861), 70. Although there may have been some similar underenumera-

tion in some of the 204 cities that have been grouped together, it is unlikely that it aggregately would have been of similar dimensions; for probably few places in that group contained a large class of people who both desired and could afford to leave their urban residences during the summer months.

20. Although Newark and Jersey City are listed separately in tables 2.1 and 2.2, much of their absolute growth during the 1840s and 1850s may be regarded as spillover growth from New York, especially because of the New York manufacturing investments made in those places and the frequent ferry service between the two New Jersey centers and Manhattan.

21. The share of the total registered absolute increase in urban population captured by major centers also would be augmented if it were allowed to include the absolute population increases occurring in opposite-bank spillover growth centers that had not acquired 2,500 inhabitants by an earlier census. For example, for the 1850–1860 period this would involve the absolute increases of newcomers such as Rahway, N.J., opposite New York, and Jeffersonville, Ind., opposite Louisville.

22. Simeon J. Crowther, "Urban Growth in the Mid-Atlantic States," *Journal of Economic History*, 36 (1976), 624–644.

23. Other answers can be obtained by using measures other than the one employed in table 2.6. However, sample calculations seem to indicate that the use of a "continuity formula" (which utilizes interpolated decade midpoint values in making comparisons) or other alternatives would, in this case, provide answers that were only slightly different. See Sharpless, *City Growth*, pp. 54–55; Robson, *Urban Growth*, p. 71.

24. As indicated in table 2.6, the absolute population increases of San Francisco, Milwaukee, and Syracuse have also been included in computing $U_{t2} - U_{t1}$ for 1840–1850.

25. Sharpless, *City Growth*, p. 179.

3. Antebellum Urban Growth and Regional Interdependence: Conventional and Recent Views

1. Probably the most notable of the earlier works of this genre was Bessie L. Pierce, *A History of Chicago*, vol. I, *The Beginning of a City, 1673–1848*, and vol. II, *From Town to City, 1848–1871* (New York: Alfred Knopf, 1937, 1940).

2. Constance McLaughlin Green, *Washington, Village and Capital, 1800–1878* (Princeton: Princeton University Press, 1962); Bayrd Still, *Milwaukee: The History of a City* (Madison: State Historical Society of Wisconsin, 1965); Blake McKelvey, *Rochester*, vol. I, *The Water-Power City, 1812–1854;* and vol. II, *The Flour City, 1855–1890* (Cambridge: Harvard University Press, 1945, 1949). See also Charles N. Glaab, "The Historian and the American City," in Leo F. Schnore and Philip M. Hauser, eds., *The Study of Urbanization* (New York: John Wiley, 1965), pp. 53–80.

3. For example: J. Thomas Sharf and Thompson Westcott, *History of Philadelphia* 3 vols.; (Philadelphia, 1884); J. Thomas Scharf, *The Chronicles of Baltimore* (Baltimore, 1874); idem, *History of St. Louis City and County* (Philadelphia, 1883).

4. Robert Greenhalgh Albion, *The Rise of New York Port, 1815–1860* (New York: Charles Scribner's Sons, 1939); Oscar Handlin, *Boston's Immigrants: A Study in Acculturation* (Cambridge: Harvard University Press, 1959); Peter R. Knights, *The Plain People of Boston, 1830–1860: A Study in City Growth* (New York: Oxford University Press, 1971); Sam Bass Warner, Jr., *The Private City: Philadelphia in Three Periods of Its Growth* (Philadelphia: University of Pennsylvania Press, 1968); Susan E. Hirsch, *Roots of the American Working Class: The Industrialization of Crafts in Newark, 1800–1860* (Philadelphia: University of Pennsylvania Press, 1978); Carl W. Condit, *The Railroad and the City: A Technological and Urbanistic History of Cincinnati* (Columbus: Ohio State University Press, 1977); Catherine Elizabeth Reiser, *Pittsburgh's Commercial Development, 1800–1850* (Harrisburg: Pennsylvania Historical and Museum Commission, 1951).

5. There is no full consensus on this criticism. See, e.g., Eric E. Lampard, "American Historians and the Study of Urbanization," *American Historical Review*, 65 (1961), 49–61; idem, "Two Cheers for Quantitative History: An Agnostic Forward," in Leo F. Schnore, ed., *The New Urban History* (Princeton: Princeton University Press, 1975), pp. 12–14; Leo F. Schonore, "Further Reflections on the 'New' Urban History: A Prefatory Note," *ibid.*, pp. 3–11; H. J. Dyos, "Agenda for Urban Historians," in idem, ed., *The Study of Urban History* (New York: St. Martin's Press, 1968), p. 7; Glaab, "The Historian," pp. 58–60.

6. An exception is Albion's *New York Port.*

7. An important exception is Diane Lindstrom's *Economic Development in the Philadelphia Region, 1810–1850* (New York: Columbia University Press, 1978).

8. James Weston Livingood, *The Philadelphia-Baltimore Trade Rivalry, 1780–1850* (Harrisburg: Pennsylvania Historical and Museum Commission, 1947); Wyatt Winton Belcher, *The Economic Rivalry between St. Louis and Chicago, 1850–1880* (New York: Columbia University Press, 1947). Also see Harry N. Scheiber, "Urban Rivalry and Internal Improvement in the Old Northwest, 1820–1860," *Ohio History,* 71 (1962), 227–239; J. Christopher Schnell and Patrick E. McLear, "Why the Cities Grew: A Historiographical Essay on Western Urban Growth, 1850–1880," *Bulletin of the Missouri Historical Society,* 28 (1971–1972), 162–177.

9. Quotation of Louis B. Schmidt in Douglas C. North, *The Economic Growth of the United States, 1790–1860* (New York: W. W. Norton, 1966), p. 103. Also see Guy S. Callender, "The Early Transportation and Banking Enterprises of States in Relation to the Growth of Corporations," *Quarterly Journal of Economics,* 17 (1902), 111–162; Louis B. Schmidt, "Internal Commerce and the Development of a National Economy before 1860," *Journal of Political Economy,* 47, (1939), 798–822.

10. Robert Gallman, "Self-Sufficiency in the Cotton Economy of the Antebellum South," *Agricultural History,* 44 (1970), 5–24; Diane Lindstrom, "Southern Dependence upon Interregional Grain Supplies: A Review of the Trade Flows, 1840–1860," *Agricultural History,* 44 (1970), 101–113; William Hutchinson and Samuel Williamson, "The Self-Sufficiency of the Antebellum South: Estimates of the Food Supply," *Journal of Economic History,* 31 (1971), 591–612.

11. Albert Fishlow, "Antebellum Interregional Trade Reconsidered," *American Economic Review,* 54 (May 1964), 352; Lindstrom, *Economic Development,* p. 6. For a dissenting view (which predates the trade-flow and consumption-estimate studies cited in note 10), see Robert W. Fogel, "A Personal View of the 'New Economic History,' " and "American Interregional Trade in the Nineteenth Century," in Ralph L. Andreano, ed., *New Views on American Economic Development* (Cambridge, Mass.: Schenkman, 1965), pp. 201–209, 213–224.

12. Lawrence A. Herbst, "Interregional Commodity Trade from the North to the South and American Economic Development in the Antebellum Period," *Journal of Economic History,* 35 (1975), 268 (italics added); Paul J. Uselding, "A Note on the Inter-Regional Trade in Manufactures in 1840," *Journal of Economic History,* 36 (1976), 435.

13. Fishlow, "Antebellum Interregional Trade," p. 360; idem, *American Railroads and the Transformation of the Ante-Bellum Economy* (Cambridge: Harvard University Press, 1965).

14. On interior entrepôts see James E. Vance, Jr., *The Merchant's World: The Geography of Wholesaling* (Englewood Cliffs, N.J.: Prentice-Hall, 1970), pp. 83–90. On natural avenues and gateways see A. L. Kohlmeier, *The Old Northwest as the Keystone of the Arch of American Federal Union* (Bloomington, Ind.: Principia Press, 1938), p. 2; Erik F. Haites, James Mak, and Gary M. Walton, *Western River Transportation: The Era of Early Internal Development, 1810-1860* (Baltimore: Johns Hopkins University Press, 1975), pp. 5–11. The first (northeastern) avenue went less frequently by way of the St. Lawrence River.

15. George D. Green, comments in *Journal of Economic History,* 35 (1975), 215.

16. See C. A. Vapnarsky, "On Rank Size Distributions of Cities: An Ecological Approach," *Economic Development and Cultural Change,* 17 (1969), 584–595; Allan Pred, *City-Systems in Advanced Economies: Past Growth, Present Processes and Future Development Options* (London: Hutchinson University Library, 1977), pp. 14–16.

17. Fishlow, "Antebellum Interregional Trade," p. 363; *HMM,* 8 (January–June 1843), 322.

18. Haites, Mak, and Walton, *Western River Transportation,* p. 117. Ransom has argued that, up to 1840, manufacturing growth in the West was not attributable to the development of a large intraregional market. Roger L. Ransom, "A Closer Look at Canals and Western Manufacturing," *Explorations in Economic History,* 8 (1970–1971), 501–508. However, for evidence of interurban trade within the West prior to 1840, see Allan Pred, *Urban Growth and the Circulation of Information: The United States System of Cities, 1790-1860* (Cambridge: Harvard University Press, 1973), pp. 132–139.

19. Diane Lindstrom, "Demand, Markets, and Eastern Economic Development: Philadelphia, 1815-1840," *Journal of Economic History,* 35 (1975), 271–273; idem, *Economic Development.*

20. The decline in canal, river, and Great Lakes freight rates during the 1840s was general, although it is difficult to specify briefly because of seasonal fluctuations and variations by commodity. Representatively, between 1839 and 1850 the charges for shipping one barrel of flour (212 pounds) on the Erie

Canal from Buffalo to Albany were reduced from $0.75 to $0.53; during a similar period (1841–1850) spring steamboat freight rates from Cincinnati to Pittsburgh declined from $0.25 per pound to $0.12½ or less per pound. *HMM,* 28 (January–June 1853), 386–388; Thomas Senior Berry, *Western Prices before 1860: A Study of the Cincinnati Market* (Cambridge: Harvard University Press, 1943), p. 560.

21. Fishlow, *American Railroads,* p. 291 (quotation); Kohlmeier, *Old Northwest,* pp. 149–151; Henry N. Scheiber, *Ohio Canal Era: A Case Study of Government and the Economy, 1820–1861* (Athens: Ohio University Press, 1969), pp. 325–328; John G. Clark, *The Grain Trade in the Old Northwest* (Urbana: University of Illinois Press, 1966), pp. 216–236.

22. Scheiber, *Ohio Canal Era,* p. 333 (quotation). Also note J. Richard Peet, "The Spatial Expansion of Commercial Agriculture in the Nineteenth Century," *Economic Geography,* 45 (1969), 283–301.

23. Thomas D. Odle, "The American Grain Trade of the Great Lakes, 1825–1873," part 8, *Inland Seas,* 9 (1953), 165–168. For example, in 1860, there were almost 12.2 million bushels of wheat and well over 13.6 million bushels of corn exported eastward from Chicago, but only 3.1 percent of the former and 4.2 percent of the latter went by rail. In the same year 65.1 percent of Chicago's eastward flour shipments were moved by rail, but the city's total export of this commodity amounted to only 626,823 barrels. Fishlow, *American Railroads,* p. 266.

24. See Edward K. Muller, "Regional Urbanization and the Selective Growth of Towns in North American Regions," *Journal of Historical Geography,* 3 (1977), 29–30.

25. See Lindstrom, *Economic Development,* pp. 112, 121, 122, 145.

26. Haites, Mak, and Walton, *Western River Transportation,* p. 10.

27. Scheiber, *Ohio Canal Era,* pp. 103, 128–130, 213, 216–217, 250, 289–290; *ARJ,* 23 (1852), 110; Henry V. Poor, *History of the Railroads and Canals of the United States of America* (New York, 1860), p. 493; Arthur M. Johnson and Barry E. Supple, *Boston Capitalists and Western Railroads* (Cambridge: Harvard University Press, 1967), p. 114; Clark, *Grain Trade,* p. 91; and Belcher, *Economic Rivalry,* pp. 65–66.

28. Jeffrey C. Williamson and Joseph A. Swanson, "The Growth of Cities in the American Northeast, 1820–1870," *Explorations in Entrepreneurial History,* 2d ser., 4, no. 1 (1966–1967). Also see idem, "A Model of Urban Capital Formation and the Growth of Cities in History," ibid., 2d ser., 8 (1970–1971), 213–222.

29. Williamson and Swanson, "Growth of Cities," p. 67.

30. Robert Higgs, "Williamson and Swanson on City Growth: A Critique," *Explorations in Entrepreneurial History,* 2d ser., 8 (1970–1971), 203–211.

31. Higgs, "Williamson and Swanson," p. 204 (quotation). Although they apologize somewhat for it, the test run by Williamson and Swanson on the growth consequences of the preexisting proportion of the population engaged in manufacturing activities also ignores the fact that no two cities have the same manufacturing mix and that different industries have different growth impacts. See John R. Sharpless, "The Economic Structure of Port Cities in the Mid-Nineteenth Century: Boston and Liverpool," *Journal of Historical Geography,* 2 (1976), 135, 145.

32. The conceptual problems that Williamson and Swanson have with "urban scale [or agglomeration] economies" external to the firm can be traced in part to their not making the conventional distinction between localization and urbanization economies. "Localization economies [occur] for all firms in a single industry [activity] consequent upon the enlargement of the total output of that industry at that location [most usually taking the form of cost-reducing backward and forward linkages with other activities] . . . Urbanization economies [occur] for all firms in all industries at a single location, consequent upon the enlargement of the total economic size (population, income, output, or wealth) of that location, for all industries taken together." Walter Isard, *Location and Space-Economy* (New York: John Wiley, 1956), p. 173.

33. Williamson and Swanson, "Growth of Cities," p. 41 (quotation). For further discussion of the naive qualities of this hinterland-impact measure see Higgs, "Williamson and Swanson," pp. 209–210.

34. See comments by John Burk Sharpless in *City Growth in the United States, England and Wales, 1820–1861: The Effects of Location, Size and Economic Structure on Inter-Urban Variations in Demographic Growth* (New York: Arno Press, 1977), pp. 52, 184–187, 253–255.

35. North and other authorities consider the pre-1840 census data on manufacturing utilized by Williamson and Swanson to be "so poor that they are almost worthless." Haites, Mak, and Walton, *Western River Transportation,* p. 117. Also see note 22, chapter 1, on the weaknesses of 1840 statistics.

36. Muller, "Regional Urbanization," pp. 21–39. Also see Edward K. Muller, "Selective Urban Growth in the Middle Ohio Valley," *Geographical Review,* 66 (1976), 178–179.

37. Muller, "Regional Urbanization," pp. 24–25.

38. Ibid., pp. 25–26.

39. Ibid., p. 26 (quotation). Also see note 22 above.

40. Muller, "Regional Urbanization," pp. 26–27.

41. Vance, *Merchant's World,* p. 83. Also see A. F. Burghardt, "A Hypothesis about Gateway Cities," *Annals of the Association of American Geographers,* 61 (1971), 269–285.

42. Vance's (and Muller's) emphasis on regional entrepôts that predate considerable hinterland settlement is in keeping with the widespread evidence from the U.S. historical record, which shows that the towns of the westward-shifting settlement frontier either preceded or were concurrent with surrounding hinterland settlement. Fred Lukermann, "Empirical Expressions of Nodality and Hierarchy in a Circulation Manifold," *East Lakes Geographer,* 2 (1966), 36. See also Richard C. Wade, *The Urban Frontier: Pioneer Life in Early Pittsburgh, Cincinnati, Lexington, Louisville, and St. Louis* (Chicago: University of Chicago Press, 1964); Kenneth W. Wheeler, *To Wear a City's Crown: The Beginnings of Urban Growth in Texas, 1836–1865* (Cambridge: Harvard University Press, 1968), pp. 161–166. However, this evidence and Muller's model run counter to Sharpless's completely unsubstantiated assertion that "the integration of urban systems during economic development actually takes place in waves—first at subregional, then regional and only lastly at the national." Sharpless, *City Growth,* p. 159.

43. For more elaborate comments on the hierarchical nesting of market

areas, and the relationship of this concept to the threshold and range of a good (or service), see the basic works on central-place theory cited in note 1, chapter 1.

44. Michael P. Conzen, "A Transport Interpretation of the Growth of Urban Regions: An American Example," *Journal of Historical Geography,* 1 (1975), 381.

45. Cf. concepts earlier expressed in Allan Pred, *The Spatial Dynamics of U.S. Urban-Industrial Growth, 1800–1914: Interpretive and Theoretical Essays* (Cambridge: MIT Press, 1966); idem, *Urban Growth.*

46. Lindstrom, *Economic Development,* pp. 8–9. Cf. related, but different, ideas on the growth of Philadelphia and Baltimore and the areas surrounding them as expressed by Joseph A. Pratt, "Regional Development in the Context of National Economic Growth," in Glenn Porter, ed., *Regional Economic History: The Mid-Atlantic Area since 1700* (Wilmington: Eleutherian Mills–Hagley Foundation, 1976), pp. 25–40.

47. Lindstrom, *Economic Development,* pp. 9, 13.

48. However, some idea of the nature of such flows and linkages can be extracted from Lindstrom's empirical discussion of the Philadelphia case.

49. In discussing the Philadelphia case upon which her model is based, Lindstrom says little of the considerable overlap of Philadelphia's and Baltimore's hinterlands in the Susquehanna valley. See Livingood, *Philadelphia-Baltimore Trade Rivalry.*

50. This is also true of Lindstrom's empirical materials, which in some ways specify Philadelphia's trade with New York, Boston, and Baltimore, but otherwise present the Quaker City's intraregional, nonhinterland linkages in terms of totals for states and groups of states.

51. Lindstrom, *Economic Development,* p. 18.

52. For example, see Brian J. L. Berry, "Hierarchical Diffusion: The Basis of Development Filtering and Spread in a System of Cities," in Niles M. Hansen, ed., *Growth Centers in Regional Economic Development* (New York: Free Press, 1972), pp. 108–130; idem, *Growth Centers in the American Urban System* (Cambridge, Mass.: Ballinger, 1973), esp. I, 63–81; J. R. Lasuén, "Multi-Regional Economic Development: An Open-System Approach," in Torsten Hägerstrand and Antoni Kuklinski, eds., *Information Systems for Regional Development,* Lund Studies in Geography, ser. B, no. 37 (Lund: Gleerup, 1971), pp. 169–211; idem, "Urbanization and Development—The Temporal Interaction between Geographical and Sectoral Clusters," *Urban Studies,* 10 (1973), 163–188; Brian Robson, *Urban Growth: An Approach* (London: Methuen, 1973), esp. pp. 131–185.

53. For example, see Poul Ove Pedersen, "Innovation Diffusion within and between National Urban Systems," *Geographical Analysis,* 2 (1970), 203–254. The few empirical studies attempting to link diffusion with the interurban spread of growth have in most cases examined innovations that are artifacts of growth, such as television ownership, rather than true growth-inducing innovations, such as new manufactures and services, new production and transportation technology, and new commercial and business practices.

54. For this evidence, as well as somewhat more formal and elaborate arguments against hierarchical-diffusion interpretations of city-system growth transmission, see Allan Pred, "Large-City Interdependence and the Preelec-

tronic Diffusion of Innovations in the U.S.," *Geographical Analysis,* 3 (1971), 165–181; idem, *Urban Growth,* pp. 227–277; idem, "The Growth and Development of Systems of Cities in Advanced Economies," in Allan Pred and Gunnar E. Törnqvist, *Systems of Cities and Information Flows: Two Essays,* Lund Studies in Geography, ser. B, no. 38 (Lund: Gleerup, 1973), pp. 27–37. Also see Pred, *City-Systems,* pp. 121–123, for a critique of the related hinterland-spread view of interurban growth transmission, which holds that the employment multipliers and other growth impacts of large-scale investments will be concentrated within the city of investment and its trading hinterland, or the set of smaller places dependent upon it for higher-order retailing and service activities.

4. Snapshots of Antebellum City-System Interdependence

1. See introduction to chapter 1.

2. See Fred Lukermann, "Empirical Expressions of Nodality and Hierarchy in a Circulation Manifold," *East Lakes Geographer,* 2 (1966), 38–39.

3. Even under modern circumstances it is virtually impossible to specify the full set of economic flows within any city-system because of massive data-collection problems. Moreover, the current data available on the movement of goods, services, and monetary payments are frequently beset with locational inadequacies and imprecision. See Derek Thompson, "Spatial Interaction Data," *Annals of the Association of American Geographers,* 64 (1974), 560–575; Allan Pred, *City-Systems in Advanced Economies: Past Growth, Present Processes and Future Development Options* (London: Hutchinson University Library, 1977), pp. 125–127.

4. Such an assertion is contained in John Burk Sharpless, *City Growth in the United States, England and Wales, 1820–1861: The Effects of Location, Size and Economic Structure on Inter-Urban Variations in Demographic Growth* (New York: Arno Press, 1977), p. 92.

5. Michael P. Conzen, "The Maturing Urban System in the United States, 1840–1910," *Annals of the Association of American Geographers,* 67 (1977), 88–108.

6. Clarence H. Danhof, *Change in Agriculture: The Northern United States, 1820–1870* (Cambridge: Harvard University Press, 1969), p. 30. See also Fred Mitchell Jones, *Middlemen in the Domestic Trade of the United States, 1800–1860,* Illinois Studies in the Social Sciences, vol. XXI, no. 3 (Urbana: University of Illinois Press, 1937), pp. 45–46; John G. Clark, *The Grain Trade in the Old Northwest* (Urbana: University of Illinois Press, 1966), pp. 41–42, 120; Lewis E. Atherton, *The Pioneer Merchant in Mid-America* (Columbia: University of Missouri Press, 1939).

7. Danhof, *Change in Agriculture,* p. 31 (quotation); Thomas D. Odle, "The American Grain Trade of the Great Lakes, 1825–1873," part 8, *Inland Seas,* 9 (1953), 162–163; Paul W. Gates, *The Farmer's Age: Agriculture 1815–1860* (New York: Holt Rinehart and Winston, 1960), pp. 162–163; Morton Rothstein, "Antebellum Wheat and Cotton Exports: A Contrast in Marketing Organization and Economic Development," *Agricultural History,* 40 (1966), 95–96.

8. Norman Sydney Buck, *The Development of the Organization of Anglo-American Trade, 1800-1860* (New Haven: Yale University Press, 1925), pp. 66–93; Rothstein, "Antebellum Wheat and Cotton Exports," pp. 94, 97–98; Gates, *Farmer's Age,* pp. 152–153 (quotation). "The cotton factor, or commission merchant, who took a commission for each of his services, also purchased and shipped goods for the planter, [and] advanced him credit, but insisted that all the planter's cotton be consigned to him." Gates, *Farmer's Age,* p. 153. At times, an initial middleman transaction took place at an inland collection port, such as Augusta, Ga.

9. Glenn Porter and Harold C. Livesay, *Merchants and Manufacturers: Studies in the Changing Structure of Nineteenth-Century Marketing* (Baltimore: Johns Hopkins University Press, 1971), pp. 28–29. For a comment on long-term credit see *HMM,* 33 (July–December 1855), 263.

10. Porter and Livesay, *Merchants and Manufacturers,* pp. 7, 8, 24; Jones, *Middlemen in the Domestic Trade,* pp. 24, 52–53, 65–66; Buck, *Organization of Anglo-American Trade.*

11. Porter and Livesay, *Merchants and Manufacturers,* pp. 96–115 (quotation from 115).

12. *Eighth Census, Manufactures of the United States in 1860* (Washington, D.C., 1865), pp. lxxiii, 733–742; J. Leander Bishop, *A History of American Manufactures from 1608 to 1860* (Philadelphia, 1868), II, 453.

13. *Manufactures of the United States in 1860,* p. lxxii; *NWR,* 73 (Jan. 1, 1848), 288; *WJ,* 1 (1848), 401–402; Massachusetts, Secretary of the Commonwealth, *Statistical Information Relating to Certain Branches of Industry in Massachusetts* (Boston, 1856), p. 639.

14. *ARJ,* 32 (1859), 28; Jones, *Middlemen in the Domestic Trade,* p. 48; *Manufactures of the United States in 1860,* p. lxxiii (quotation); Edgar M. Hoover, Jr., *Location Theory and the Shoe and Leather Industries* (Cambridge: Harvard University Press, 1937), p. 218.

15. Jones, *Middlemen in the Domestic Trade,* p. 14; *BM,* 9 (1854), 233; *Tenth Census, 1880,* vol. XVIII, *Report on the Social Statistics of Cities* (Washington, D.C., 1886), p. 156 (quotation); Hoover, *Location Theory,* p. 174.

16. Hoover, *Location Theory,* pp. 174–175 (quotation), 216, 265–269; Robert G. Leblanc, *Location of Manufacturing in New England in the 19th Century,* Geography Publications at Dartmouth, no. 7 (Hanover, N.H., 1969), p. 62; Victor S. Clark, *History of Manufactures in the United States* (New York: McGraw-Hill, 1929), I, 443–445; Bishop, *American Manufactures,* II, 500–501; "New York Industrial Exhibition, Special Report of Mr. George Wallis, Presented to the House of Commons by Command of Her Majesty, in Pursuance of Their Address of February 6, 1854," in Nathan Rosenberg, ed., *The American System of Manufactures* (Edinburgh: Edinburgh University Press, 1969), pp. 254–257; Alan Dawley, *Class and Community: The Industrial Revolution in Lynn* (Cambridge: Harvard University Press, 1976), pp. 26–29, 47, 76–77, 138, 223, 227.

17. *Report on the Social Statistics of Cities,* p. 156.

18. It is quite likely that all but a small fraction of Boston's leather sales were forwarded to hinterland urban places that produced boots and shoes; Boston's own footwear production was relatively modest (212,000 pairs in

1855), and the total raw material purchases of its boot and shoe industry and saddlery and harness workshops amounted to $233,700 in 1860 (or the equivalent of less than 1 percent of local leather sales in 1858). Secretary of the Commonwealth, *Statistical Information,* p. 457; Bishop, *American Manufactures,* III, 276–277. Also note Hoover, *Location Theory,* pp. 219–220.

19. *HMM,* 42 (January–June 1860), 610; 45 (July–December 1861), 40–41; Hoover, *Location Theory,* p. 174.

20. The *Shoe and Leather Reporter,* which published occasional statistics on Boston's footwear wholesaling, avoided compiling any exact data on the small but "frequent and numerous" railroad shipments within New England because of the "almost impossible task" of making use of the freight records of the different railroad companies in the unaggregated form in which they were available. However, it was estimated that Boston's 1859 sales, which specifically included 717,991 cases sent to places outside New England, "considerably exceed three quarters of a million cases." In other words, shipments within New England may have come to 35,000 cases or more. *HMM,* 43 (July–December 1860), 610.

21. Edwin T. Freedley, *Philadelphia and Its Manufactures* (Philadelphia, 1859), pp. 185–186; *Boston Evening Transcript,* Aug. 29, 1851 (quotation).

22. *WJ,* 1 (1848), 402; Hoover, *Location Theory,* p. 173 (quotation).

23. *HMM,* 23 (July–December 1850), 491; 24 (January–June 1851), 227–228; 44 (January–June 1861), 183; David R. Goldfield, *Urban Growth in the Age of Sectionalism: Virginia, 1847–1861* (Baton Rouge: Louisiana State University Press, 1977), p. 243; *San Francisco Mercantile Gazette and Prices Current,* Mar. 19, 1860.

24. See chap. 2 at note no. 20.

25. In addition to the cities of the South and West identified in table A.8 there were another 397 urban places in those regions that acquired 20 or more cases of boots and shoes from Boston in 1859. Nineteen of those places received 500 to 1,000 cases (25,000–50,000 pairs), 103 received 100 to 500 cases (5,000–25,000 pairs), and the remaining 275 places received 20 to 100 cases (1,-000–5,000 pairs). *HMM,* 43 (July–December 1860), 610–611.

26. The "nesting" of market areas and interdependencies in the central-place theories of both Christaller and Lösch results in regional systems of cities that are *closed* except for interactions with the single highest-order place in the country. See the interdependence diagrams in Allan Pred, "The Growth and Development of Systems in Cities in Advanced Economies," in Allan Pred and Gunnar E. Törnqvist, *Systems of Cities and Information Flows: Two Essays,* Lund Studies in Geography, ser. B, no. 38 (Lund: Gleerup, 1973), pp. 29, 33; Pred, *Urban Growth and the Circulation of Information: The United States System of Cities, 1790–1840* (Cambridge: Harvard University Press, 1973), pp. 229, 232–233.

27. The number of places with cotton mills that sent significant quantities of textiles to Boston for further shipment is too great to list in a format resembling table A.5. In 1855, Worcester County, Mass., alone had twenty-seven such places. Secretary of the Commonwealth, *Statistical Information,* pp. 466–563.

28. In 1846, the Western Railroad garnered close to $460,000 in receipts for the movement of all types of commodities in both directions between

Worcester and Albany. In the first eleven months of that same year, 8,358 tons of goods originating in Boston were carried through to Albany by the Western. How much of this freight income and tonnage was derived from the movement of cotton textiles cannot be determined. Henry V. Poor, *History of the Railroads and Canals of the United States of America* (New York, 1860), p. 163; Stephen Salsbury, *The State, the Investor, and the Railroad: The Boston & Albany, 1825–1867* (Cambridge: Harvard University Press, 1967), p. 307; *HMM,* 16 (January–June 1847), 325.

29. The total shipments to southern ports (18.69 percent of the coastal total) are consistent with comments made in the previous chapter regarding the inadequacies of the Callender-Schmidt-North thesis and the importance of intraregional flows along the major centers of the Northeast vis-à-vis flows between the Northeast as a whole and the South as a whole.

30. This figure includes shipments to Hartford, which, like many other lesser centers located in the Connecticut River valley, was within the overlapping hinterlands, or primary spheres of economic influence, of New York and Boston. See Robert Greenhalgh Albion, *The Rise of New York Port, 1815–1860* (New York: Scribner's, 1939), pp. 77, 156.

31. Cotton goods shipments from Boston to San Francisco fluctuated somewhat after 1853, reaching a low of 1,601 bales and cases in 1854, and a high of 9,992 bales and cases the following year. *HMM,* 44 (January–June 1861), 179.

32. *Report on the Social Statistics of Cities,* p. 156 (quotation); *HMM,* 30 (January–June 1854), 391; Albion, *New York Port,* p. 63 (quotation).

33. Leblanc, *Location of Manufacturing,* pp. 96–99. More specific details on coal shipments from Philadelphia are given later in this chapter.

34. The value of fish production in the Massachusetts portion of Boston's tributary area alone exceeded $2.9 million in 1855. Secretary of the Commonwealth, *Statistical Information,* pp. 613–614.

35. Henry Hall, *The Ice Industry of the United States,* in *Tenth Census, 1880,* XXII (Washington, D.C., 1888), 2–3; Richard O. Cummings, *The American Ice Harvests: A Historical Study in Technology, 1800–1918* (Berkeley: University of California Press, 1949), pp. 8, 22, 34–36, 42, 59.

36. In 1867, ice shipments also went from Boston to Philadelphia, presumably in schooners that had carried coal in the opposite direction. *BM,* 3 (1849), 407.

37. Wilmington, N.C., had a population of 7,264 in 1850, as compared to Savannah's 15,312 and Norfolk's 14,326 in the same year.

38. *BM,* 3 (1849), 407; *NYSL,* July 13, 1844.

39. *DBR,* 14 (1853), 257–258; *BM,* 3 (1849), 407; Hall, *Ice Industry,* p. 3; Cummings, *American Ice Harvests,* pp. 33, 55–57; *HMM,* 11 (July–December 1844), 378.

40. *HMM,* 23 (July–December 1850), 490; 45 (July–December 1861), 124; *BM,* 3 (1849), 409. Another major ice source was the ponds of Cambridge, which is considered here as a part of Boston rather than a part of its hinterland. See note d, Table 2.1.

41. *BM,* 3 (1849), 408; *NYSL,* May 1, 1844.

42. Carl Bode, *Antebellum Culture* (Carbondale: Southern Illinois University Press, 1970), pp. 20–21; John B. Sharpless, "The Economic Structure of

Port Cities in the Mid-Nineteenth Century: Boston and Liverpool, 1840–1860," *Journal of Historical Geography,* 2 (1976), 141; Secretary of the Commonwealth, *Statistical Information,* p. 590; *HMM,* 39 (July–December 1858), 45; *Manufactures of the United States in 1860,* pp. 245–246; Bishop, *American Manufactures,* III, 16, 114, 120, 276–277; *Chicago Daily Democrat,* July 12, 1860.

43. *ARJ,* 28 (1855), 670.

44. The places in question were the Connecticut cities of Bridgeport, New London, New Haven, and Hartford, and the city of Springfield, Mass. See Albion, *New York Port,* pp. 155–164; Edward Chase Kirkland, *Men, Cities and Transportation: A Study in New England History, 1820-1900* (Cambridge: Harvard University Press, 1948), I, 12–13, 138, 256. Also see note 30 above.

45. The intermediate-sized New York cities of Utica, Oswego, and Lockport also clearly belonged to the hinterlands of major cities other than Boston. Lansing, Mich., and Fond du Lac, Wis., with respective 1860 populations of 3,074 and 5,460, were the smallest places obtaining New England Mutual services directly from Boston.

46. Lance E. Davis, "Capital Mobility and American Growth," in Robert W. Fogel and Stanley L. Engerman, eds., *The Reinterpretation of American Economic History* (New York: Harper & Row, 1972), pp. 285–300 (quotation on 285).

47. Arthur M. Johnson and Barry E. Supple, *Boston Capitalists and Western Railroads* (Cambridge: Harvard University Press, 1967), pp. 56 (quotation), 181–182. By the end of 1844, it was estimated that the Boston capital placed in railroads inside and outside of New England amounted to $30 million, while the entire remainder of the country had committed only $100 million to railroad investments. *ARJ,* 18 (1845), 13.

48. Johnson and Supple, *Boston Capitalists,* 47–48, 101; Poor, *Railroads and Canals,* p. 231. At the time of the formation of the New York Central, one Boston investor alone held almost $250,000 in New York railroad securities.

49. Johnson and Supple, *Boston Capitalists,* pp. 84–85, 88–99, 127–130, 156–159; *HMM,* 23 (July–December 1850), 487.

50. Johnson and Supple, *Boston Capitalists,* pp. 50–51, 55 (quotation); *HMM,* 16 (January–June 1847), 210; 23 (July–December 1850), 351, 487.

51. Johnson and Supple, *Boston Capitalists,* pp. 31–47, 56; Kirkland, *Men, Cities and Transportation,* I, 242, 247, 259, 334 (quotation).

52. If shipments of Maryland and Virginia flour from Washington, D.C., are included, the percentages provided by major northeastern centers range from 46.51 (1852) to 80.48 (1841). In 1852, Boston's overseas flour exports corresponded to about 25 percent of the number of barrels received that year. This percentage was higher than that occurring during any of the European crop-failure and famine years of the late 1840s. *DBR,* 14 (1853), 254–255.

53. The Albany figures given in table A.12 are for water shipments only.

54. The volumes of flour carried to Boston by the Western Railroad in 1847 and 1848 were not surpassed until the 1860s. Salsbury, *State, Investor, and Railroad,* p. 278.

55. In 1858 about 1.13 million barrels of flour were shipped eastward from the western termini of the Baltimore and Ohio and the Pennsylvania Rail-

road, some of which must have been unloaded at way stations before reaching Philadelphia or Baltimore. *HMM,* 40 (January–June 1859), 482. The importance of Boston as an outlet to Baltimore flour merchants in 1860 is suggested by an estimate that "perhaps half" of Baltimore's flour found its way to Boston. Albert Fishlow, "Postscript," in Ralph L. Andreano, *New Views on American Economic Development* (Cambridge, Mass.: Schenkman, 1965), p. 212.

56. *HMM,* 21 (July–December 1849), 539–540 (quotation); Salsbury, *State, Investor, and Railroad,* pp. 281, 286. Note in table A.12 the 94,000 barrel decrease in Western Railroad shipments between 1848 and 1849. The Western never succeeded in attracting much of the flour that moved from Albany to New York for export because of the discrepancy between river-barge and railroad freight charges. Kirkland, *Men, Cities and Transportation,* I, 494–496.

57. Odle, "American Grain Trade," part 8, pp. 164–166. However, Clark notes that New Orleans's flour shipments to Boston remained important until 1859, when the Louisiana city provided about 14 percent of Boston's total flour receipts. Clark, *Grain Trade,* p. 234.

58. See chap. 3, second section.

59. By 1847, flour shipments from Massachusetts, Maine, New Hampshire, and Connecticut amounted to only 0.27 percent of Boston's total receipts. *NWR,* 73 (Feb. 5, 1848), 356.

60. Probably these railroads also enabled some hinterland flour producers to seek the Boston market, rather than serving only a narrowly circumscribed local area. Kirkland, *Men, Cities and Transportation,* I, 190.

61. Ibid., pp. 190, 212, 213 (quotation), 214, 363.

62. In 1848 the receipts of flour at Boston via the Western were equal to 64.22 percent of all the flour shipments carried by that railroad from Albany to Massachusetts points. The corresponding figures for 1849, 1852, and 1860 were 55.53, 47.61, and 61.95 percent. In 1852, Boston redistributed only 4.85 percent of its flour receipts through coastwise shipping. Salsbury, *State, Investor, and Railroad,* p. 278; *DBR,* 7 (1853), 254–255.

63. During the period of accentuated European demand in the late 1840s, Boston's corn exports abroad varied between 19.52 percent (1849) and 31.10 percent (1847) of her receipts. *DBR,* 7 (1850), 557.

64. With the inclusion of Washington, D.C., the percentage acquired from major northeastern centers varied from 56.60 percent (1845) to close to 70 percent (1860). (For 1860 it is not possible to separate out a Washington, D.C., figure from the subtotal for "other places".)

65. In 1846, New Orleans's corn shipments to Boston reached 30.90 percent of all Boston's corn receipts. *NWR,* 71 (Jan. 16, 1847), 319; *DBR,* 3 (1847), 274–275.

66. Previously undiscussed interdependencies incorporated into figure 4.2 include the movement of livestock and hams to Boston and the provision of locomotives, other railroad supplies, manufactured goods in general, and mercantile investments and services from Boston. Gates, *Farmer's Age,* pp. 212–213; *Boston Evening Transcript,* Feb. 1, 1860; *ARJ,* 25 (1852), 571, 822; 31 (1858), 111, 190; *DBR,* 14 (1853), 252; James Robertson, *A Few Months in America: Containing Remarks on Some of Its Industrial and Commercial Interests* (London, 1855), p. 202.

67. Hartford was actually within the overlapping hinterlands of New York and Boston. See notes 30 and 44 above.

68. Those eighteen cities and their market areas would have been "nested" within New York's national market area and closed off from Boston, which would have been in a separate nesting arrangement located to the east of New York. See note 26 above.

69. *HMM,* 6 (January–June 1842), 183–184; 8 (January–June 1843), 280; 10 (January–June 1844), 287; 23 (July–December 1850), 490; *NWR,* 67 (Jan. 26, 1845), 325; 72 (June 19, 1847), 247; Clark, *History of Manufactures,* I, 467–469; Porter and Livesay, *Merchants and Manufacturers,* pp. 42, 48; *ARJ,* 24 (1851), 249.

70. Harry N. Scheiber, *Ohio Canal Era: A Case Study of Government and the Economy, 1820–1861* (Athens: Ohio University Press, 1969), pp. 349–350; *ARJ,* 25 (1852), 571; Alfred D. Chandler, Jr., "Anthracite Coal and the Beginnings of the Industrial Revolution in the United States," *Business History Review,* 46 (1972), 166–167.

71. *HMM,* 44 (January–June 1861), 538–539. For additional data and comments reflecting the role of railroads in Boston's hinterland interdependencies see *HMM,* 13 (July–December 1845), 556–557; 15 (July–December 1846), 44–45; 20 (January–June 1849), 548–549; 23 (July–December 1850), 487; 23 (January–June 1851), 638–639; 32 (January–June 1855), 504–505; *DBR,* 13 (1852), 576–578; *ARJ,* 21 (1848), 551; 24 (1851), 251; 25 (1852), 256; Kirkland, *Men, Cities and Transportation,* vol. I.

72. See Kirkland, *Men, Cities and Transportation,* II, 111–131. In the late 1840s, between 6,000 and 7,100 domestic shipping arrivals per year were cleared at Boston's Custom-House from both within and beyond that city's hinterland, with at least another 4,000 smaller vessels (probably almost all of hinterland origin) annually escaping such registration. *HMM,* 21 (July–December 1849), 668.

73. *HMM,* 14 (January–June 1846), 428; *ARJ,* 18 (1845), 46; Chandler, "Anthracite Coal," pp. 152 (quotation), 173. Although anthracite had become popular as a home fuel in some places by 1850, for the country as a whole "wood continued to fulfill the greater portion of domestic demands." With respect to locomotive usage, anthracite was apparently less popular than wood and, later, bituminous coal, "since both the mineral and chemical action of the coal wore out the fire-boxes [and] ran up larger repair bills." Vera F. Eliasberg, "Some Aspects of Development in the Coal Mining Industry, 1839–1918," in *Output, Employment, and Productivity in the United States after 1800* (New York: National Bureau of Economic Research, 1966), pp. 418–419 (quotations); Kirkland, *Men, Cities, and Transportation,* I, 308.

74. For the period considered here, Lindstrom has defined Philadelphia's economic hinterland as including the entire eastern half of Pennsylvania (except for the northern counties of Tioga, Bradford, and Lycoming), all of Delaware, all New Jersey counties fronting on either Delaware Bay or the Delaware River (as well as Atlantic and Monmouth counties) and a small part of Maryland. Diane Lindstrom, *Economic Development in the Philadelphia Region, 1810–1850* (New York: Columbia University Press, 1978), frontispiece and p. 94.

75. *ARJ,* 25 (1852), 23; *DBR,* 3 (1847), 345; *WJ,* 9 (1853), 246; Freedley, *Philadelphia,* 114; Lindstrom, *Economic Development,* p. 58 (quotation).

76. *BM,* 9 (1855), 473; *HMM,* 34 (January–June 1856), 258; *ARJ,* 32 (1859), 515–516; 33 (1860), 70. The freight tariffs received by the short Reading Railroad (93 miles) were enough to make its gross revenues the fifth largest of all the railroads in the country in 1859. *ARJ,* 33 (1860), 1,089.

77. *ARJ,* 25 (1851), 309–310; 32 (1859), 515–516; Wheaton J. Lane, *From Indian Trail to Iron Horse: Travel and Transportation in New Jersey, 1620–1860* (Princeton: Princeton University Press, 1939), pp. 242–244, 263–265; Poor, *Railroads and Canals,* pp. 389–390, 452–453; J. I. Bogen, *The Anthracite Railroads* (New York: Ronald Press, 1927).

78. *ARJ,* 19 (1846), 172; 20 (1847), 104; 21 (1848), 265. The Reading Railroad also delivered Schuylkill anthracite to several other hinterland urban places in addition to Philadelphia's industrial suburbs.

79. Freedley, *Philadelphia,* pp. 87, 101–102; Poor, *Railroads and Canals,* p. 536; *BM,* 9 (1855), 472.

80. *ARJ,* 18 (1845), 46. This source estimated daily steamboat consumption at 500 tons per day. Since some boats did not operate on Sundays, and since the Hudson River traffic was closed by ice during winter months, the lower demand figure of 160,000 tons may be closer to the truth.

81. *ARJ,* 32 (1859), 516.

82. Thus, in 1850, total shipments from Philadelphia by the Delaware and Raritan Canal and coastwise shipping only came to just under 96 percent of the city's Schuylkill anthracite receipts. *ARJ,* 25 (1852), 23–24; 32 (1859), 516.

83. Lane, *Indian Trail,* pp. 264, 296.

84. Because of consumption in Philadelphia, this probably means that Boston's receipts accounted for a slightly higher percentage of the total anthracite tonnage shipped from the Quaker City. See note 82 above, and the observation in the text to which it refers.

85. Kirkland, *Men, Cities and Transportation,* I, 11; Chandler, "Anthracite Coal," pp. 134–156, 169; Peter Temin, *Iron and Steel in Nineteenth-Century America: An Economic Inquiry* (Cambridge: MIT Press, 1964). The glass works in question was actually located in Cambridge, which was a functional part of Boston. See notes b and d to table 2.1.

86. *NYSL,* Nov. 23, 1844; *DBR,* 25 (1858), 113; Kirkland, *Men, Cities and Transportation,* I, 250.

87. *HMM,* 6 (January–June 1842), 475; 16 (January–June 1847), 266; Lindstrom, *Economic Development,* p. 116; Lane, *Indian Trail,* p. 271; Chandler, "Anthracite Coal," pp. 166, 170–172.

88. On the hinterland assignments of places on Long Island Sound and in the Connecticut valley, see notes 30 and 44 above, as well as the text relating to note 44.

89. In 1860, boats on the Susquehanna and Tidewater Canal carried 229,-282 tons of anthracite to Chesapeake Bay, where they either turned northward to Philadelphia via the Chesapeake and Delaware Canal or continued southward to Baltimore. Since the Chesapeake and Delaware Canal carried over 193,000 tons of coal traffic in 1860, about 36,000 tons of anthracite must have moved from centers in Philadelphia's hinterland directly to Baltimore. James Weston Livingood, *The Philadelphia-Baltimore Trade Rivalry,*

1780–1890 (Harrisburg: Pennsylvania Historical and Museum Commission, 1947), pp. 75–80; Poor, *Railroads and Canals,* p. 570.

90. Cumberland semibituminous shipments to Baltimore via the B&O Railroad grew from just under 5,000 tons in 1843 to over 490,000 tons in 1857 before falling off in the wake of the crisis of that year. Milton Reizenstein, *The Economic History of the Baltimore and Ohio Railroad, 1827–1853,* Johns Hopkins University Studies in Historical and Political Science (Baltimore, 1897), p. 88; Poor, *Railroads and Canals,* p. 582.

91. Lane, *Indian Trail,* p. 271; *BM,* 13 (1848), 57; *San Francisco Mercantile Gazette and Prices Current,* Mar. 19, July 10, 1860. The known anthracite receipts in San Francisco for the first six months of 1860 were 20,780 tons.

92. For data on the quantities of Western coal reaching New Orleans, see, for example, *HMM,* 19 (July–December 1848), 510, *DBR,* 31 (1861), 454. Just before the Civil War, New Orleans received about 650,000 dollars' worth of western coal annually. It was not until after 1850 that New Orleans steamboat operators began to employ coal, and even then wood remained the dominant fuel because of the "exorbitant" prices coal commanded in Louisiana and the infeasibility of having a furnace that would burn both types of fuel. Louis C. Hunter, *Steamboats on the Western Rivers* (Cambridge: Harvard University Press, 1949), pp. 268–269.

93. Lindstrom, *Economic Development,* p. 46; Allan Pred, *The Spatial Dynamics of U.S. Urban-Industrial Growth, 1800–1914: Interpretive and Theoretical Essays* (Cambridge: MIT Press, 1966), pp. 167–177; idem, *Urban Growth,* pp. 189–190.

94. These figures, which were for Philadelphia as incorporated in 1854 (see note c to table 2.1), were regarded by proponents of that city as a considerable understatement. *HMM,* 25 (July–December 1851), 128–139; 33 (July–December 1855), 57; 43 (July–December 1860), 561–562; Robertson, *Few Months in America,* p. 27.

95. *Eighth Census, 1860, Mortality and Miscellaneous Statistics* (Washington, D.C., 1866), p. xviii.

96. Lindstrom, *Economic Development,* pp. 78, 95, 105, 130. For a discussion of the factors and processes creating hinterland demand for Philadelphia manufactures, see the same work, pp. 93–105, 121–151, 185.

97. Ibid., pp. 90–91, 184.

98. *HMM,* 43 (July–December 1860), p. 561 (quotation). "Philadelphia goods," a term applied to any of a variety of heavier textile fabrics made in Philadelphia, was used in contrast to "Parisian" or "German" goods, which were more delicate and ornamental but were also made in the same city. The fancier goods were wholesaled in New York to a large degree. See Freedley, *Philadelphia,* pp. 95, 234.

99. *ARJ,* 19 (1846), 224; 33 (1860), 16, 43.

100. Ibid., 28 (1855), 75; Temin, *Iron and Steel,* p. 283; Lane, *Indian Trail,* p. 296. Some of the iron goods moving through the Delaware and Raritan may not have been produced in Philadelphia itself, but in that city's hinterland. All the same, hinterland iron quite likely was handled by Philadelphia commission merchants before being forwarded to New York. The minimum preshipment value of the iron sent via the Delaware and Raritan Canal was

estimated by applying the 1854 price of foundry pig iron in Philadelphia ($36.88 per ton) as indicated by Temin. According to the prices given by Temin, if one-third of the canal shipments had consisted of iron rails or other rolled products, the preshipment value would have risen to about $1.9 million.

101. *New York Journal of Commerce,* Mar. 12, 1860; Freedley, *Philadelphia.* For most of the items mentioned here, the primary importance of shipments to New York is not based on data, but on qualitative statements made by Freedley.

102. *ARJ,* 20 (1847), 618; 25 (1852), 637; Freedley, *Philadelphia.*

103. Lindstrom, *Economic Development,* pp. 66 (quotation), 74; Freedley, *Philadelphia,* pp. 346, 454.

104. The models under discussion would deny the possibility of flows from the second-ranked Philadelphia to the third-ranked Boston because these cities would have been in separate nesting arrangements (see notes 26 and 68 above). The crisscrossing of similar manufacturing flows between Philadelphia and its sister dominants in the Northeast is nowhere better illustrated than in the case of cotton goods. While Philadelphia was sending such textiles to New York, Boston, and Baltimore, her commission merchants were acquiring similar goods in great quantities from those same places for local and nonlocal sale. Table A.9; *HMM,* 43 (July–December 1860), 561–562.

105. Actually, between late 1852, when the Pennsylvania Railroad opened its western division, and 1854, when it completed its own transmountain section, that railroad used the facilities of the Main Line in sending goods to and from Pittsburgh.

106. See note d, table A.18.

107. *HMM,* 33 (July–December 1855), 371; *ARJ,* 31 (1858), 94. The Main Line was sold to the Pennsylvania Railroad in 1857, when it was unable to withstand the competition of the parallel route. The Main Line ceased its through service the following year and completely abandoned its western division in 1864. Odle, "American Grain Trade," part 9, p. 256; Julius Rubin, *Canal or Railroad? Imitation and Innovation in the Response to the Erie Canal in Philadelphia, Baltimore, and Boston, Transactions of the American Philosophical Society,* n.s., 51, (part) 7 (Philadelphia, 1961), 60.

108. *HMM,* 41 (July–December 1859), 501–502.

109. Porter and Livesay, *Merchants and Manufacturers,* pp. 33–34; Elva Tooker, *Nathan Trotter, Philadelphia Merchant, 1787-1853* (Cambridge: Harvard University Press, 1955), pp. 128, 137; Freedley, *Philadelphia,* pp. 142, 377, 449.

110. *ARJ,* 25 (1852), 223, 824; Freedley, *Philadelphia,* pp. 318, 326, 328, 403, 446, 451–453.

111. *HMM,* 14 (January–June 1846), 429; 36 (January–June 1857), 518; Albert Fishlow, *American Railroads and the Transformation of the Ante-Bellum Economy* (Cambridge: Harvard University Press, 1965), pp. 270–271.

112. Freedley, *Philadelphia,* pp. 333, 389 (quotations); *HMM,* 14 (January–June 1846), 426.

113. Other nonhinterland urban places of small and intermediate population that had direct linkages with Philadelphia through manufacturing shipments include Bangor, Maine, Taunton, Mass., Newport, R.I., Oswego and

Schenectady, N.Y., Paterson, N.J., Lexington, Ky., Petersburg, Va., Nashville and Athens, Tenn., Wilmington, N.C., Columbia, S.C., Savannah, Augusta, and Macon, Ga., Montgomery and Selma, Ala., Natchez, Miss., and Galveston, San Antonio, and Indianola, Tex. *ARJ,* 20 (1847), 618; 25(1852) 223, 637; 33 (1860), 300; Freedley, *Philadelphia.*

114. *HMM,* 25 (July–December 1851, 128–129; Bishop, *American Manufactures,* III, 17. A comparison of 1850 raw-material cost figures (for Philadelphia as incorporated in 1854) with those for 1860 shows an increase of about 110 percent. However, the 1850 total may have been understated. See note 94.

115. For a definition of "production systems," see chap. 1 at note 29.

116. *HMM,* 18 (January–June 1847), 311; 43 (July–December 1860), 563; *DBR,* 7 (1850), 356; Freedley, *Philadelphia,* p. 100. The hinterland share of the national total in 1856 would have been much higher if the production of western New Jersey and Delaware had been included.

117. Chandler, "Anthracite Coal," pp. 159, 161; *DBR,* 2 (1847), 212; *HMM,* 43 (July–December 1860), 566.

118. *ARJ,* 23 (1850), 502–503; 25 (1852), 79; Porter and Livesay, *Merchants and Manufacturers,* p. 48; Livingood, *Philadelphia-Baltimore Trade Rivalry,* pp. 74, 80.

119. Freedley, *Philadelphia,* p. 122. See note 104.

120. Tooker, *Nathan Trotter;* Lindstrom, *Economic Development,* pp. 65, 191. Many of the raw materials included in the tonnage arriving from New York were of foreign origin. (This was true to a considerably lesser degree for tonnage from Boston and Baltimore.) The raw material portion of the tonnages arriving from New York, Boston, and Baltimore was also apt to include goods of hinterland as well as local origin.

121. Except for wool, each of the raw materials mentioned here either had not been sent at all from Pittsburgh to Philadelphia via the Main Line in 1850 or had been shipped in much smaller quantities. Catherine Elizabeth Reiser, *Pittsburgh's Commercial Development, 1800–1850* (Harrisburg: Pennsylvania Historical and Museum Commission, 1851), p. 224. Note also that not all of the goods arriving in Philadelphia from Pittsburgh in the late 1850s were for local manufacturing purposes. For example, some flour must have been marketed to local households, and some flour, grains and other items certainly were shipped on to other locations, as should be evident from the previous discussion of Philadelphia's role in Boston's flour and grain trade.

122. *DBR,* 7 (1850), 367, 422; 21 (1856), 512, 518; 31 (1861), 455, 460; *HMM,* 33 (July–December 1855), 603, 605; 37 (July–December 1850), 606. Also see table A.29. In normal years of the late 1840s and early 1850s, New Orleans appears to have provided Philadelphia with more than 35 percent of her cotton imports. However, even in the years when Philadelphia's imports from New Orleans peaked, its receipts were only a fraction of those of New York or Boston (see table A.10). The falloff in cotton flows from New Orleans to Philadelphia is in keeping with the increased volume of cotton shipments to Philadelphia via Pittsburgh that occurred in the late 1850s. Since a bale of cotton averaged about 500 pounds, the 1853 peak shipment from New Orleans corresponded to about 4,840 tons, or roughly one-third of the 1860 quantity sent on from Pittsburgh (see note c, table A.21).

123. *DBR,* 4 (1848), 393; 9 (1850), 367, 422; 21 (1856), 513; 25 (1858), 566; 31

(1861), 456; *HMM,* 33 (July–December 1855), 604. Because of the varied measures used for Philadelphia sugar receipts (hogsheads, barrels, boxes, and bags), it is difficult to ascertain precisely the share of New Orleans's total domestic and foreign shipments that went to the Pennsylvania city. However, it is known that the New Orleans sugar shipments to Philadelphia were consistently much less important than those to New York.

124. *NWR,* 67 (Jan. 18, 1845), 311; *DBR,* 4 (1848), 392; and Freedley, *Philadelphia,* p. 216. The cigar and paint industries did not consume enough raw materials in 1860 (over $500,000 in each case) to be listed in table A.20, but they were important enough to be included in table A.17. Although as many as 188,000 lead ingots had come to Philadelphia from St. Louis via New Orleans in the year ending Aug. 31, 1845, by 1857 the Philadelphia paint industry was obtaining almost all its lead from European sources.

125. *DBR,* 21 (1846), 527. See discussion of cotton shipments to Boston in text following note no. 32.

126. Tooker, *Nathan Trotter,* pp. 94, 97.

127. *HMM,* 14 (January–June 1846), 429; 41 (July–December 1859), 473. The total raw material consumption of Philadelphia shipbuilding amounted to over $543,000 in 1860. Ship's timber was also obtained from lesser ports in Maine, but most commonly from hinterland sources.

128. Other shipments of these commodities worth $4.9 million arrived at Buffalo from an unspecified number of Canadian ports. Israel Andrews, *Report . . . on the Trade and Commerce of the British North American Colonies,* U.S. Senate Document no. 112, 32nd Cong., 1st sess., 1853, pp. 97–139.

129. *DBR,* 16 (1854), 497; *HMM,* 30 (January–June 1854), 301; 38 (January–June 1858), 690–692.

130. Andrews, *Report . . . on the Trade and Commerce,* pp. 93, 96. Although the value of goods forwarded westward in 1851 was higher than that of shipments arriving from the West ($31.9 million in total), the latter shipments weighed much more (over 731,000 tons).

131. Heavy summer usage of the railroads east of Buffalo became more common not long after 1851 due to the reduction of freight rates. However, as late as 1853: "The Erie Canal alone carried eastward from Buffalo . . . four times the salt meat, four times the flour, ten times the wool, ninety times the wheat, and two hundred forty-nine times the corn [carried by] the three railroads that ran eastward out of that place . . ." Clark, *Grain Trade,* p. 285; A. L. Kohlmeier, *The Old Northwest as the Keystone of the Arch of American Federal Union* (Bloomington, Ind.: Principia Press, 1938), p. 112.

132. Clark, *Grain Trade,* pp. 119–121; Odle, "American Grain Trade," part 6, pp. 52–53, 55. Creditors in the Northeast "would not accept western banknotes or credit on non-specie paying western banks, but they would accept credits on the specie-paying Buffalo banks." Odle, "American Grain Trade," part 7, pp. 105–106.

133. *HMM,* 38 (January–June 1858), 692; Andrews, *Report . . . on the Trade and Commerce,* p. 95 (quotation).

134. *HMM,* 16 (January–June 1847), 599; 28 (January–June 1853), 627; Andrews, *Report . . . on the Trade and Commerce,* p. 139; Odle, "American Grain Trade," part 8, p. 167.

135. By 1860, Toledo clearly had established itself among the ranks of intermediate-sized cities, having attained a population of 13,768.

136. Clark, *Grain Trade.*

137. The total value of domestic paper, carriages, furniture, glassware, pig lead, paints, machinery, reapers, and hardware brought by lake to Buffalo in 1851 was $380,852. Of this total, $295,726, or 77.65 percent, came from Chicago, Cleveland, Detroit, Milwaukee, and Toledo. Andrews, *Report . . . on the Trade and Commerce,* pp. 105–138.

138. Pred, *Urban Growth,* p. 139; *HMM,* 6 (January–June 1842), 189, 444; 15 (July–December 1846), 358.

139. Clark, *Grain Trade,* p. 281 (quotation); *Chicago Daily Democrat,* Jan. 2, 1860.

140. *HMM,* 38 (January–June 1858), 694–695. Between 1851 and 1855 Milwaukee's wheat exports shot up from 317,000 bushels to 2,642,000 bushels, and by 1860 they had reached almost 7,600,000 bushels, with Buffalo receiving well over half of these shipments. Clark, *Grain Trade,* p. 269.

141. Kohlmeier, *Old Northwest,* pp. 193, 248; Scheiber, *Ohio Canal Era,* pp. 320–322; Clark, *Grain Trade,* pp. 242–244; Odle, *"American Grain Trade,"* part 2, p. 23 (quotation).

142. See note 135.

143. Scheiber, *Ohio Canal Era,* pp. 220–221, 224, 258; Odle, "American Grain Trade," part 2, p. 24; Kohlmeier, *Old Northwest,* pp. 88–89. A few years after 1851, newly constructed railroads gave additional cause for shipments from Toledo to Buffalo. These railroads ran westward from Toledo into the bountiful farming areas of Illinois and the upper Mississippi valley.

144. Andrews, *Report . . . on the Trade and Commerce,* p. 93; *NWR,* 68 (July 19, 1845), 320; *HMM,* 22 (January–June 1850), 469–470; Thomas Senior Berry, *Western Prices before 1861: A Study of the Cincinnati Market* (Cambridge: Harvard University Press, 1943), pp. 89–92; Scheiber, *Ohio Canal Era,* p. 260; Kohlmeier, *Old Northwest.* p. 126.

145. Erie was not solely within Buffalo's sphere of influence, but within the overlapping hinterlands of Buffalo, Pittsburgh, and Cleveland.

146. Andrews, *Report . . . on the Trade and Commerce,* pp. 121, 138. Dunkirk and Barcelona provided additional sawed lumber worth approximately $98,600.

147. Ibid., p. 102.

148. Odle, "American Grain Trade." part 3, pp. 99–100.

149. The total value of shipments of wheat, wool, flour, and corn arriving at Buffalo from smaller nonhinterland ports ($3,151,714) corresponded to 11.66 percent of the value of all domestic commodities moved by lake to Buffalo during 1851.

150. *HMM,* 25 (July–December 1851), 509–512, and 41 (July–December 1859), 495–498, reprinted from Charles Cist's *Sketches and Statistics of Cincinnati in 1851* and *Sketches and Statistics of Cincinnati in 1859.* Cist's 1859 figure sometimes has been called into question because it is more than double the total value of production reported in the 1860 census. However, the census figure is for Cincinnati alone, exclusive of Covington and Newport, and, as admitted by one of Cist's critics, it was doubtlessly "below the truth" owing to "negligent census officials," who, ironically, were under the direction of

Cist himself. Moreover, the discrepancy "may be explained in part by the fact that production and values [prices] both declined in 1860 compared to the preceding year." Bishop, *American Manufactures*, III, 459; Berry, *Western Prices*, p. 255.

151. *Eighth Census, 1860, Mortality and Miscellaneous Statistics,* p. xviii. Corresponding percentages for other midwestern major centers were as follows: Pittsburgh, 18.0; Louisville, 9.8; Cleveland, 8.0; Buffalo, 6.9; Milwaukee, 7.0; St. Louis, 5.8; Detroit, 5.2; and Chicago, 4.8. See Carl Abbott, "Popular Economic Thought and Occupational Structure: Three Middle Western Cities in the Antebellum Decade," *Journal of Urban History,* 1 (1974–1975), 175–187.

152. *HMM,* 31 (July–December 1854), 549; 42 (January–June 1860), 60; *DBR,* 23 (1857), 488; Andrews, *Report . . . on the Trade and Commerce,* pp. 710–716; Jones, *Middlemen in the Domestic Trade,* pp. 15, 53–54; Scheiber, *Ohio Canal Era,* pp. 232, 325–326; Berry, *Western Prices,* p. 330; Odle, "American Grain Trade," part 1, p. 245. Another official estimate of Cincinnati's 1860 exports placed the total figure as high as $119.6 million. In addition, Cincinnati wholesalers and forwarders increased their share of all mercantile inventories held in Ohio from 25 percent in 1852 to more than 40 percent in 1860. Scheiber, *Ohio Canal Era,* pp. 346, 350.

153. Odle, "American Grain Trade," part 5, p. 250. The tonnage of individual steamboats arriving at Cincinnati during 1850–1851 varied from 61 to 478. *HMM,* 25 (July–December 1851), 506–508.

154. Soap is the only commodity in table A.26 other than iron for which the majority of shipments did not go to New Orleans. The low percentage for pork shipments by the pound is more than balanced by the much higher percentage for pork shipments in large containers. In fact, if the four pork freight categories in table A.26 are converted to a common base, it becomes evident that no less than 68.63 percent of all Cincinnati pork shipments initially went to New Orleans.

155. Clark, *Grain Trade,* pp. 229–230 (quotation). For additional data see Kohlmeier, *Old Northwest,* pp. 117–118; Berry, *Western Prices,* p. 168.

156. *HMM,* 22 (January–June 1850), 362; Andrews, *Report . . . of the Trade and Commerce,* pp. 705–707; Scheiber, *Ohio Canal Era,* p. 223. In terms of value, in 1850–1851 the importance of sugar as a Cincinnati import was surpassed only by hogs ($2.17 million vs. $2.51 million). At the end of the 1850s, Cincinnati took about one-sixth of all the sugar made in Louisiana, and about one-fifth of all the molasses. *WJ,* 7 (1851), 43; *DBR,* 14 (1853) 183; *HMM,* 42 (January–June 1860), 60.

157. Derived from Cincinnati Chamber of Commerce statistics reproduced in Leonard P. Curry, *Rail Routes South: Louisville's Fight for the Southern Market, 1865–1872* (Lexington: University of Kentucky Press, 1969), pp. 14–15.

158. Bishop, *History of American Manufactures,* III, 462; *DBR,* 9 (1850), 648; Berry, *Western Prices,* pp. 221 (quotation), 258.

159. Curry, *Rail Routes South,* pp. 14–15 (see note 157 above for original source). Pork shipments to New Orleans during 1858–1859 accounted for 35.6 percent of Cincinnati's shipments of that commodity by all modes of transportation (see note 154).

160. *WJ*, 7 (1851), 43; Berry, *Western Prices*, pp. 43, 204, 258, 310, 318, 336. Apparently, the Ohio and Mississippi Rail Road did not have any real impact on goods flows between Cincinnati and St. Louis until 1859. Wyatt Winton Belcher, *The Economic Rivalry between St. Louis and Chicago, 1850–1880* (New York: Columbia University Press, 1947), pp. 93–94.

161. Scheiber, *Ohio Canal Era*, p. 222; Andrews, *Report . . . on the Trade and Commerce*, p. 708; Kohlmeier, *Old Northwest*, p. 149; Berry, *Western Prices*, pp. 87, 256. Seven regularly scheduled packets transported almost 217,-000 tons of freight between Pittsburgh and Cincinnati in 1852. Elisabeth M. Sellers, "The Pittsburgh and Cincinnati Packet Line: Minute Book, 1851–1853," *Western Pennsylvania Historical Magazine*, 19 (1936), 245.

162. Pred, *Urban Growth*, pp. 132–134; Berry, *Western Prices*, p. 318.

163. *HMM*, 31 (July–December 1854), 556; *ARJ*, 24 (1851), 187; Scheiber, *Ohio Canal Era*, pp. 322–323; Kohlmeier, *Old Northwest*, pp. 119, 156. Subsequent to 1856, Cleveland's importance as an outlet for Cincinnati pork products was reduced by an increasing use of the Pennsylvania Railroad via Pittsburgh.

164. *NWR*, 68 (Aug. 16, 1845), 384. (Intraregional large-city interdependencies between Cincinnati and Buffalo were discussed earlier in conjunction with Toledo-to-Buffalo commodity flows.)

165. Groceries and manufactures are among the items known to have moved by water from Cincinnati to Detroit. *HMM*, 31 (July–December 1854), 556.

166. See chap. 3 at note no. 20.

167. Berry, *Western Prices*, pp. 51, 85–86, 92–93; Edward K. Muller, "Selective Urban Growth in the Middle Ohio Valley, 1800–1860," *Geographical Review*, 66 (1976), 193. Prior to 1853, comparatively small quantities of foodstuffs moved occasionally from Cincinnati to Philadelphia and New York via Pittsburgh and the Pennsylvania Main Line of canals and railroads.

168. See table A.2 and data in this chapter at note no. 155.

169. Clark, *Grain Trade*, p. 226 (quotation). See discussion of Boston flour receipts via Baltimore and Philadelphia in this chapter at note no. 55. When the four pork categories in table A.26 are converted to a common base, it is evident that 4.92 percent of Cincinnati's pork exports moved by rail and canal in 1850–1851. A similar conversion of the two freight categories for lard in the same table reveals that 10.1 percent of the exports of that commodity went by rail and canal.

170. Scheiber, *Ohio Canal Era*, p. 325; Berry, *Western Prices*, p. 318 (quotation). See table A.21 and the discussion of industrial raw materials shipped from Pittsburgh to Philadelphia via the Pennsylvania Railroad, in this chapter at note no. 121.

171. Berry, *Western Prices*, pp. 327 (quotation), 328–329; Scheiber, *Ohio Canal Era*, p. 350; Andrews, *Report . . . on the Trade and Commerce*, p. 712; *Cincinnati Enquirer*, Jan. 31, June 12, Oct. 3, 1860.

172. Berry, *Western Prices*, p. 227; *BM*, 6 (1852), 1,007.

173. Columbus, Ohio, Indianapolis, Ind., Lexington, Ky., and the lower end of the Kanawha River valley are mentioned frequently as points on, or near, the periphery of Cincinnati's antebellum trading hinterland. See *HMM*, 42 (January–June 1860), 56; *DBR*, 3 (1847), 583; Kohlmeier, *Old Northwest*, pp.

117–118, 203; Muller, "Selective Urban Growth," pp. 181–182; Scheiber, *Ohio Canal Era,* p. 224.

174. *HMM,* 12 (January–June 1845), 456; 22 (January–June 1850), 468–469; *NWR,* 67 (Jan. 18, 1845), 310; Clark, *Grain Trade,* pp. 135–224; Scheiber, *Ohio Canal Era,* p. 202. The Whitewater Canal, which in 1845 began to tap eastern Indiana for Cincinnati, also lost its significance during the 1850s due to railroad competition.

175. *HMM,* 14 (January–June 1846), 484; 24 (January–June 1851), 363; Clark, *Grain Trade,* p. 224.

176. Muller, "Selective Urban Growth," pp. 188–198; Scheiber, *Ohio Canal Era,* pp. 203, 222.

177. *HMM,* 37 (July–December 1857), 633; 42 (January–June 1860), 56; *DBR,* 9 (1850), 648; Bishop, *American Manufactures,* III, 462; Scheiber, *Ohio Canal Era,* p. 339; Berry, *Western Prices,* pp. 258, 318. For 1860 populations of Memphis, Nashville, Keokuk, and Evansville, see table A.8.

178. *DBR,* 12 (1852), 70; Clark, *Grain Trade,* pp. 224, 226; Berry, *Western Prices,* p. 43. Note the volume of goods destined for "other downriver ports" in 1850–1851, as indicated in table A.26, keeping in mind that St. Louis and Louisville are included in that port category.

179. *Cincinnati Enquirer,* Jan. 31, June 12, Oct. 3, 1860; *ARJ,* 24 (1851), 693; *HMM,* 42 (January–June, 1860), 59.

180. Muller, "Selective Urban Growth," pp. 189, 197–198; Berry, *Western Prices,* pp. 18–19, 226; Clark, *Grain Trade,* pp. 127, 141–142, 227–228; Scheiber, *Ohio Canal Era,* pp. 335, 337–338.

181. Robert Royal Russel, *Economic Aspects of Southern Sectionalism, 1840–1861,* Illinois Studies in the Social Sciences, vol. XI, nos. 1–2 (Urbana: University of Illinois Press, 1923), pp. 111–112; Robert Greenhalgh Albion, *Square Riggers on Schedule: The New York Sailing Packets to England, France, and the Cotton Ports* (Princeton: Princeton University Press, 1938), p. 229.

182. *HMM,* 13 (July–December 1845), 572; *DBR,* 24 (1858), 110. In 1857, exports from Charleston to foreign ports amounted to $16,006,425, and direct imports from such ports totaled $2,046,734.

183. Russel, *Economic Aspects,* p. 12.

184. *Eighth Census, 1860, Mortality and Miscellaneous Statistics,* p. xviii.

185. *Eighth Census, Manufactures of the United States in 1860,* p. 553; Leonard Price Stavisky, "Industrialism in Ante Bellum Charleston," *Journal of Negro History,* 36 (1951), 316, 320; *DBR,* 10 (1851), 347; Alfred Glaze Smith, Jr., *Economic Adjustment of an Old Cotton State: South Carolina, 1820–1860* (Columbia: University of South Carolina Press, 1958), pp. 131–133. By 1860, a few more ambitious plants, such as a cotton textile mill and a shoe factory, had failed. *DBR,* 7 (1850), 398; 10 (1851), 682; Smith, *Economic Adjustment,* pp. 131–133.

186. Russel, *Economic Aspects,* pp. 50–51 (quotation), 62–63, 111, 174, 206, 222; Stavisky, "Industrialism," pp. 304–305, 308, 315, 319; Smith, *Economic Adjustment,* pp. 119, 122–124, 127–129, 134; Eugene D. Genovese, *The Political Economy of Slavery: Studies in the Economy and Society of the Slave South* (New York: Vintage Books, 1967), pp. 158–159, 162, 164–165, 173, 184, 186, 224, 227; Ulrich Bonnell Phillips, *A History of Transportation in the*

Eastern Cotton Belt to 1860 (New York: Columbia University Press, 1908), p. 9 (quotation); Robert W. Fogel and Stanley Engerman, *Time on the Cross: The Economics of American Negro Slavery* (Boston: Little, Brown, 1974), pp. 247–257; David R. Goldfield, *Urban Growth in the Age of Sectionalism: Virginia, 1847–1861* (Baton Rouge: Louisiana State University Press, 1977), pp. xvii, 123. There is a varying degree of scholarly disagreement as to the validity of these and other proposed reasons for Charleston's weak manufacturing sector. For example, although there is some consensus that attutudes of the planter aristocracy retarded the availability of manufacturing investment capital, it is still acknowledged by some that the "roster of planter-industrialists in South Carolina" contained "the names of the biggest plantation families." Genovese, *Political Economy of Slavery,* p. 188. Also note Charleston's bank capital situation as given in table A.37.

187. Stavioky, "Industrialism," p. 303 (quotation).

188. See Russel, *Economic Aspects,* pp. 100–102; Albion, *New York Port,* pp. 95–96.

189. See note e, table A.29.

190. Ralph H. Brown, *Historical Geography of the United States* (New York: Harcourt, Brace, 1948), pp. 36–37, 63, 140–143; Sam B. Hilliard, "Antebellum Tidewater Rice Culture in South Carolina and Georgia," in James R. Gibson, ed., *European Settlement and Development in North America* (Toronto: University of Toronto Press, 1978), pp. 91–115.

191. Whereas the tonnage of rice annually shipped from Charleston to U.S. destinations during the 1850s ranged between 17.3 and 27.7 thousand short tons (table T.30), the corresponding figures for the early and mid-1820s—the earliest dates for which statistics are available—never exceeded 5.4 thousand tons. J. B. DeBow, *Encyclopedia of the Trade and Commerce of the United States* (London, 1854), p. 250.

192. Berry, *Western Prices,* p. 320.

193. Almost all of the "other U.S. ports" listed in table A.30 must have been smaller nonhinterland ports. The small South Carolina ports within Charleston's hinterland themselves sent rice to Charleston, and with the exception of Mobile and Richmond, every major port on or near the Atlantic and Gulf coasts is accounted for explicitly in the table. For possible shipments to Mobile, see note f to table A.30.

194. *DBR,* 7 (1850), 93; and sources listed in table A.31.

195. *DBR,* 21 (1856), 508–509; Genovese, *Political Economy of Slavery,* p. 227; John G. B. Hutchins, *The American Maritime Industries and Public Policy, 1789–1914* (Cambridge: Harvard University Press, 1941), pp. 190–191. In connection with the limited shipbuilding of the South it also should be noted that almost all of the small quantity of turpentine and other naval stores domestically exported from Charleston went to major northeastern centers. For example, during 1855–1856 more than 96 percent of Charleston's domestic shipments of naval stores moved to New York, Boston, and Philadelphia. *DBR,* 21 (1856), 517.

196. The "other U.S. ports" indicated in table A.31 are very unlikely to have included the hinterland ports of Georgetown and Beaufort, which probably had easy access to lumber from their own subhinterlands. Nor were "other U.S. ports" apt to include either New Orleans, which normally was

listed separately in other Charleston staple-export statistics, or Mobile, which was more than self-sufficient with respect to lumber. Because of this, and the explicit inclusion in the table of all other major Atlantic and Gulf ports, it is assumed that the category consists of nonhinterland ports of intermediate and small size.

197. By 1858–1859, coastwise shipments from Charleston had plummeted to 70,924 bushels; and by 1859–1860 they had almost disappeared, having fallen to 3,764 bushels. *DBR,* 29 (1860), 526.

198. Andrews, *Report . . . on the Trade and Commerce,* p. 133.

199. Once again, the "other U.S. ports" indicated in Table A.32 are quite unlikely to have included New Orleans, which usually was listed separately in other Charleston export data. The category may have included Mobile, but that place is not likely to have received much, given New Orleans's dominant position as its supplier. Diane Lindstrom, "Southern Dependence upon Inter-regional Grain Supplies: A Review of the Trade Flows," *Agricultural History,* 44 (1970), 102–103. Some of the coastwise shipments from Charleston must have gone to hinterland ports, which normally acquired supplies either directly from other sources, or from Philadelphia and Baltimore via Charleston. Thus, it is not possible to estimate how much of Charleston's wheat and flour shipments to other U.S. ports went to nonhinterland cities of intermediate and small size.

200. Russel, *Economic Aspects,* p. 97 (quotation); Stavisky, "Industrialism," p. 321 (quotation).

201. The tonnage capacity (1,627) of Charleston–New Orleans packets was about one-seventh that of Charleston–New York packets and one-half that of Charleston-Philadelphia packets. Furthermore, packets as well as other vessels going to and from New York, Boston, Philadelphia, Baltimore, and Providence could make a greater number of trips per year than those plowing back and forth to New Orleans, since the latter had to sail greater distances because of the lengthy detour around Florida. *HMM,* 22 (January–June 1850), 503.

202. Lindstrom, "Southern Dependence," pp. 104–105; *DBR,* 13 (1852), 511; 23 (1857), 374; 25 (1858), 566; 28 (1859), 479; 29 (1860), 784; 31 (1861), 455; *HMM,* 31 (July–December 1854), 477; 33 (July–December 1855), 604. Between 1855 and 1859, exporters in New Orleans were able to provide Charleston grain merchants with only 1.5 percent of their supplies. Lindstrom, "Southern Dependence," p. 107.

203. *HMM,* 22 (January–June 1850), 503; 40 (January–June 1859), 62.

204. *DBR,* 25 (1858), 225–226; Lindstrom, "Southern Dependence," pp. 102–110.

205. *DBR,* 26 (1859), 328; *HMM,* 39 (July–December 1858), 485; Goldfield, *Urban Growth,* pp. 94, 237.

206. In 1860, only 2.61 percent of Mobile's population was engaged in manufacturing. *Eighth Census, 1860, Mortality and Miscellaneous Statistics,* p. xviii.

207. *DBR,* 9 (1850), 659; 20 (1856), 446; 29 (1860), 666; *HMM,* 5 (July–December 1841), 471; 13 (July–December 1845), 422; 40 (January–June 1859), 182.

208. *HMM,* 13 (July–December 1845), 425; 32 (January–June 1855), 97.

209. In 1860 rapidly growing Memphis supplanted Savannah as the South's fifth largest city, reaching a population of 22,623, or just slightly more than the Georgia city's 22,292.

210. A mere 2.87 percent of Savannah's population held manufacturing occupations in 1860. *Eighth Census, 1860, Mortality and Miscellaneous Statistics,* p. xviii.

211. Not unrepresentatively, 1.43 percent of Savannah's domestic rice shipments were bound for Charleston in 1853–1854. In 1859–1860, the corresponding figure was 0.41 percent. *DBR,* 19 (1855), 461; 29 (1860), 669. The available data reveal no shipments of lumber from Savannah to Charleston for reexport.

212. See discussion, in chapter 2, concerning the second group of cities in tables 2.1 and 2.2.

213. For more general remarks on the interdependencies of cities that act as colonial outliers of a city-system based in another region or country, see Pred, *City-Systems,* pp. 14–15; C. A. Vapnarsky, "On Rank-Size Distributions of Cities: An Ecological Approach," *Economic Development and Cultural Change,* 17 (1969), 594–595. For extensive documentation of Richmond's position as a colonial outlier of the northeastern regional city-system, see Goldfield, *Urban Growth.*

214. See James A. Ward, "A New Look at Antebellum Southern Railroad Development," *Journal of Southern History,* 39 (1973), 409–420; Phillips, *History of Transportation,* pp. 8, 20, 388.

215. See Rothstein, "Antebellum Wheat," pp. 93–94.

216. Percentage derived from U.S. Bureau of the Census, *Census of Population: 1970, Number of Inhabitants—United States Summary* (Washington, D.C., 1971), p. 1–68. See chap. 2 at note no. 6, on the reasonableness of the 2,-500 cut-off level.

217. The Georgia Railroad reached Atlanta in 1845. During that same year 120,000 bales of cotton went from Augusta to Savannah, while only 20,000 went from Augusta to Charleston. After a bridge was completed over the Savannah River from Augusta to Hamburg in 1853, a larger share of the Georgia Railroad's traffic was steered toward Charleston. Phillips, *History of Transportation,* pp. 208, 216, 300.

218. Ibid., p. 8.

219. *DBR,* 25 (1858), 226; *ARJ,* 23 (1850), 687; Lindstrom, "Southern Dependence," pp. 108, 110.

220. *DBR,* 7 (1850), 267; 27 (1859), 236; Russel, *Economic Aspects,* p. 110; Porter and Livesay, *Merchants and Manufacturers,* pp. 90–91, 110; Genovese, *Political Economy of Slavery,* p. 169; Goldfield, *Urban Growth,* p. 246.

221. Conzen, "Maturing Urban System," p. 108. Conzen's observation is based solely on the analysis of data pertaining to correspondent banking relationships, or situations in which a bank (usually in a small community) maintained a deposit account with another bank (usually in a large city). Also note idem, "Capital Flows and the Developing Urban Hierarchy: State Bank Capital in Wisconsin, 1854–1895," *Economic Geography,* 51 (1975), 321–338, esp. 328–331.

5. *Growth and Development within the U.S. City-System, 1840–1860: A Model*

1. See chap. 3 at note nos. 15 and 33.

2. After the reorientation of agricultural flows from the West brought about by the railroad construction of the 1850s, New Orleans's interdependencies with Cincinnati and other midwestern major centers no longer loomed so large. However, down to the outbreak of the Civil War, the domestic interdependencies arising from the selling activities of New Orleans's cotton, tobacco, sugar, and molasses middlemen primarily involved New York, Boston, Providence, Philadelphia, and Baltimore. See, e.g., data in *DBR,* 31 (1861), 455–456.

3. By way of comparison, Conzen's analysis shows that major centers did not have important horizontal correspondent banking relations with more than two or three other major centers until after 1880. Michael P. Conzen, "The Maturing Urban System in the United States, 1840–1910," *Annals of the Association of American Geographers,* 67 (1977), 96–97.

4. Major-center interdependencies also must have led on occasion to reflexive nonlocal employment multipliers, or situations in which the employment multipliers engendered by a major center (A) at another major center (B) in turn precipitated increased demand at center B for some goods normally obtained for center A.

5. See the discussion of hinterland relationships in the models proposed by Muller and Lindstrom, in chap. 3 at note nos. 36 through 51.

6. This generalization holds even if the flows to and from less populous urban places within areas of fuzzy hinterland overlap are ignored. On the lack of clear hinterland boundaries between major centers during the antebellum period, see Michael P. Conzen, "A Transport Interpretation of the Growth of Urban Regions: An American Example," *Journal of Historical Geography,* 1 (1975), 380. See also chap. 4 at note no. 44; and notes 67 and 145 to chap. 4.

7. See Buffalo evidence in chap. 4 at note no. 147. Washington, D.C., is another major center whose linkages were not in keeping with this generalization. However, the Washington exception is quite different from the Buffalo and Providence cases because the capital city's functions were primarily political rather than truly economic and it therefore lacked an economic hinterland in the normal sense of the term.

8. Allan Pred, *City-Systems in Advanced Economies: Past Growth, Present Processes and Future Development Options* (London: Hutchinson University Library, 1977), pp. 127–166; idem, "The Interurban Transmission of Growth in Advanced Economies: Empirical Findings versus Regional Planning Assumptions," *Regional Studies,* 10 (1976), 151–171.

9. The urban places to which an important hinterland city wholesaled or forwarded goods, and the lower-order collection points from which such a city secured agricultural commodities or natural resources, usually were not confined to those places found within its immediate central-place subhinterland. See Edward K. Muller, "Regional Urbanization and the Selective Growth of Towns in North American Regions," *Journal of Historical Geography,* 3 (1977), 26.

10. Evidence for Philadelphia as of 1840 suggests, in general, that "relative

to capital invested or output" the local employment multipliers of manufacturing activities were greater than those of wholesaling-trading activities. Diane Lindstrom, *Economic Development in the Philadelphia Region, 1810–1850* (New York: Columbia University Press, 1978), p. 47.

11. Between 1840 and 1860 most urban manufacturers did not directly market their own products.

12. The initial multipliers that affected retailing and service activities also may be described in terms of threshold fulfillment. Regardless of sector, new establishments or additions sometimes could appear considerably before or after the fulfillment of theoretical threshold conditions because of entrepreneur-to-entrepreneur variations in perception of demand and in level of profit aspiration.

13. Changing levels of real income per capital also could affect the operation of this circular and cumulative feedback sequence. See Lindstrom, *Economic Development,* p. 180.

14. Glenn Porter and Harold C. Livesay, *Merchants and Manufacturers: Studies in the Changing Structure of Nineteenth-Century Manufacturing* (Baltimore: Johns Hopkins University Press, 1971), pp. 72 (quotation), 115, 229. See Victor S. Clark, *History of Manufactures in the United States* (New York: McGraw-Hill, 1929), I, 368–369. Note, however, that antebellum urban banks themselves were for the most part run by officers and directors who were or had been merchants. Porter and Livesay, *Merchants and Manufacturers,* p. 72.

15. See Clark, *History of Manufactures,* I, 466.

16. The feedbacks between manufacturing expansion, specialized information circulation, and inventions or innovations became more important to the process of major-center local growth in the decades after 1860. During the immediate postbellum period, however, wholesaling-trading activities fell back to a position of secondary importance in the local-growth process of major centers. For more details on the manufacturing feedbacks contained in figure 5.2, see the discussion of a local-growth model for the period 1860–1910 in Allan Pred, *The Spatial Dynamics of U.S. Urban-Industrial Growth, 1800–1914: Interpretive and Theoretical Essays* (Cambrdige: MIT Press, 1966), pp. 24–41. For more details on the wholesaling-trading feedbacks shown in figure 5.2, see the local-growth model for mercantile cities in idem, *Urban Growth and the Circulation of Information: The United States System of Cities, 1790–1840* (Cambridge: Harvard University Press, 1973), pp. 191–194.

17. For a description of the four components of the wholesaling-trading complex, see chap. 1 at note no. 19.

18. See, e.g., Almon Ernest Parkins, *The Historical Geography of Detroit* (Chicago: University of Chicago Libraries, 1918), pp. 291–293; Peter G. Goheen, "Industrialization and the Growth of Cities in Nineteenth-Century America," *American Studies,* 14 (Spring 1973), 49; John B. Sharpless, "The Economic Structure of Port Cities in the Mid-Nineteenth-Century: Boston and Liverpool, 1840–1860," *Journal of Historical Geography,* 2 (1976), 132; Edward K. Muller, "Selective Urban Growth in the Middle Ohio Valley, 1800–1860," *Geographical Review,* 66 (1976), 199; Diana Klebanow, Franklin L. Jonas, and Ira M. Leonard, *Urban Legacy: The Story of America's Cities*

(New York: New American Library, 1977), pp. 59–60; Davis M. Gordon, "Capitalist Development and the History of American Cities," in William K. Tabb and Larry Sawers, eds., *Marxism and the Metropolis: New Perspectives in Urban Political Economy* (New York: Oxford University Press, 1978), p. 37. See also chap. 1 at note no. 24.

19. See Conzen, "Maturing Urban System," pp. 94–95; Hugh T. Rockoff, "Varieties of Banking and Regional Economic Development in the United States, 1840–1860," *Journal of Economic History,* 35 (1975), 160–181; Joseph A. Swanson and Jeffrey G. Williamson, "A Model of Urban Capital Formation and the Growth of Cities in History," *Explorations in Entrepreneurial History,* 8 (1970–1971), 216. Because of the importance of mercantile investments made with nonbank capital, there is no significant correlation between relative capital availability, as reflected in table A.37, and the 1840–1860 urban growth rates.

20. See Richard C. Wade, *Slavery in the Cities: The South, 1820–1860* (New York: Oxford University Press, 1964); Claudia Dale Goldin, *Urban Slavery in the American South, 1820–1860: A Quantitative History* (Chicago: University of Chicago Press, 1976). Slaves also made up somewhat less than 8 percent of the 1860 populations of New Orleans and Louisville. Whatever retarding effects slavery had on New Orleans's growth, they must have been greater during the 1840s, since enslaved blacks formed roughly 23 percent of the Crescent City's 1840 population.

21. *HMM,* 42 (January–June 1860), 325 (quotation); 39 (July–December 1858), 429–430. The lower construction expenditures of Chicago may have been due to the more widespread use in that city of relatively cheap balloon building frames.

22. George Rogers Taylor, "The Beginnings of Mass Transportation in Urban America," *The Smithsonian Journal of History,* 1 (Summer 1966), 35–50; 1 (Fall 1966), 31–54; Arthur J. Krim, "The Innovation and Diffusion of the Street Railway in North America" (M.A. thesis, University of Chicago, 1967), pp. 38, 56–64; David R. Goldfield, *Urban Growth in the Age of Sectionalism: Virginia, 1847–1861* (Baton Rouge: Louisiana State University Press, 1977), p. 199; Charles J. Kennedy, "Commuter Services in the Boston Area, 1835–1860," *Business History Review,* 36 (Summer 1962), 153–170. All twenty-eight major centers had horse-drawn street railways by 1865. Cleveland and Buffalo had also had such facilities for a brief time during the 1830s, but they collapsed during the panic of 1837.

23. Evidence for Philadelphia indicates that real-estate and street-railway speculation sometimes went hand in hand. *HMM,* 44 (January–June 1861), 146. Also see note c, table A.39, on New York.

24. Because the fares for omnibuses, commuter trains, and horse-drawn street railways corresponded to a significant percentage of the daily wages of members of the working and lower-middle classes, frequent usage of these means of transportation was confined to riders from the upper-middle and upper classes. The different levels of passenger usage per mile of street railway shown in table A.39 presumably mean that different levels of transportation-related employment could arise from similar levels of route development.

25. Goldfield, *Urban Growth,* pp. 174–175; *HMM,* 14 (January–June 1846), 431; Edwin T. Freedley, *Philadelphia and Its Manufactures* (Philadelphia,

1859), p. 64. In comparison, the per-capita government expenditures of New York in 1850 were $6.53. Charles N. Glaab and A. Theodore Brown, *A History of Urban America* (New York: Macmillan, 1967), p. 180.

26. See Thomas C. Cochran, "The Business Revolution," *American Historical Review,* 79 (1974), 1,449–1,466.

27. Implicit locational decisions (which involve the purchase of goods or services, miscellaneous capital allocations, and, under modern circumstances, the awarding of contracts and subcontracts), are to be contrasted with explicit locational decisions (which involve the establishment or physical expansion of job-providing facilities). The implicit decisions are not usually regarded by their perpetrators as being locational in character, but they are locational insofar as they involve some nonlocal places rather than others.

28. With some modifications, both the business-opportunity and innovation-diffusion feedback loops may be seen as having helped to reinforce the growth of major centers from the early nineteenth century to the present in both the United States and other currently advanced economies. Allan Pred, "The Location of Economic Activity since the Early Nineteenth Century: A City-Systems Perspective," in Bertil Ohlin, ed., *The International Allocation of Economic Activity: Proceedings of a Nobel Symposium* (London: Macmillan, 1977), pp. 127–147. Muller has suggested (in "Regional Urbanization," p. 37) that the diffusion of innovations contributes most to the "stability of growth in an established regional system *after the initial period of settlement"* (italics added).

29. No distance factor is explicitly included in either (5.1) or (5.2) since it is assumed that trade flows already reflect any influence exerted by distance costs. Equation 5.2 could be made more complicated by the inclusion of a factor for place-to-place variations in prevailing entrepreneurial attitudes toward risk taking. With or without such an additional factor, equation 5.2 allows initial innovation adoptions to be concentrated at major centers without falling back on the rigid hierarchical diffusion interpretations criticized in chap. 3 at note nos. 52–54.

30. *WJ,* 6 (1851), 35; James E. Vance, Jr., *The Merchant's World: The Geography of Wholesaling* (Englewood Cliffs, N.J.: Prentice-Hall, 1970), pp. 152, 156.

31. See Eric E. Lampard, "The Evolving System of Cities in the United States: Urbanization and Economic Development," in Harvey S. Perloff and Lowdon Wingo, Jr., eds., *Issues in Urban Economics* (Baltimore: Johns Hopkins University Press, 1968), p. 82; Goheen, "Industrialization," pp. 62–63.

32. See Edgar S. Dunn, "A Flow Network Image of Urban Structures," *Urban Studies,* 7 (1970), 239–258.

33. Here too, with appropriate modifications, the feedbacks described may be seen as having some applicability to both the U.S. economy and other currently advanced economies for different periods of time ranging from the early nineteenth century to the present. Pred, "Location of Economic Activity," p. 136.

34. See Muller, "Regional Urbanization," pp. 24–27. See also chap. 3 between note nos. 37 and 40.

35. See Lindstrom, *Economic Development,* pp. 8–18. See also chap. 3 between note nos. 46 and 51.

36. However, through the very operation of the model, or through the occurrence of low or intermediate probability events permitted by equation (5.2), some of the older hinterland interdependence dyads of major centers could gain in weight. See comments on urban growth and manufacturing investments made during the 1840s from New York and Philadelphia in hinterland places within thirty-five miles' distance, in Simeon J. Crowther, "Urban Growth in the Mid-Atlantic States, 1785–1850," *Journal of Economic History,* 36 (1976), 638–639.

37. See John Burk Sharpless, *City Growth in the United States, England and Wales, 1820–1861: The Effects of Location, Size and Economic Structure on Inter-Urban Variations in Demographic Growth* (New York: Arno Press, 1977), esp. pp. 188–189.

38. As might be expected from the operation of these feedbacks, once places reached the top of the intermediate size ranks they tended to function as subregional dominants and to maintain regional rank stability throughout the remainder of the nineteenth century and into the twentieth century. See Edward K. Muller, "Selective Urban Growth in the Middle Ohio Valley, 1800–1860," *Geographical Review,* 66 (1976), 199.

39. *HMM,* 8 (January–June 1843), 512 (quotation). See also *DBR,* 13 (1852), 88.

40. The same can be said of the canal construction of the 1840s.

41. See chap. 1 at note no. 13. See also note 43 below. The empirical evidence regarding these seven points is so abundant for such major centers as New York, Boston, Philadelphia, Chicago, and Richmond that it is impractical to document it here. For general and theoretical arguments relating to individual points, see such widely ranging works as the following: Karl Marx, *Capital* (New York: International Publishers, 1967), II, 121–128, 149–152; idem, *Grundrisse* (Harmondsworth: Penguin Books, 1973), pp. 524–525; Charles H. Cooley, *The Theory of Transportation* (Baltimore, 1894); Allan Pred, *The External Relations of Cities during 'Industrial Revolution,'* University of Chicago, Department of Geography Research Paper no. 76 (Chicago, 1962), pp. 29–43; John R. Borchert, "American Metropolitan Evolution," *Geographical Review,* 57 (1967), 301–332.

42. This positive feedback sequence is consistent with more general models developed by Janelle and Pottier in which the provision of transportation improvements between major centers aids both the concentration of population and economic activities in those centers and the eventual appearance of further transportation improvements that favor highly nodal major centers. See Donald G. Janelle, "Spatial Reorganization: A Model and Concept," *Annals of the Association of American Geographers,* 59 (1969), 348–364; P. Pottier, "Axes de communication et développement économique," *Revue économique,* 13, no. 1 (1963), 70–128.

43. When the nodality of a medium- or small-sized urban place was improved because it had become the intersection of a major route and a feeder line, the major center within whose hinterland it was located often profited through hinterland expansion, or piracy, and the development of new interdependence dyads. For a model covering this type of hinterland expansion see Edward J. Taaffe, Richard L. Morrill, and Peter R. Gould, "Transport Expansion in Underdeveloped Countries," *Geographical Review,* 53 (1963), 503–519.

44. For empirical evidence on the growth of urban places bypassed by transportation improvements, see, e.g., Harry N. Scheiber, *Ohio Canal Era: A Case Study of Government and the Economy, 1820–1861* (Athens: Ohio University Press, 1969), pp. 336–337; Muller, "Selective Urban Growth," pp. 185–199.

6. Spatial Biases in the Antebellum Circulation of Specialized Economic Information

1. In 1843, steamboats between New York and Albany supposedly could run at eighteen miles per hour. One year later trains on the rail segments of the New York–Boston route averaged about twenty-four miles per hour. *HMM,* 9 (July–December 1843), 184; 11 (July–December 1844), 371.

2. For maps, data, and further details illustrating spatial biases in the availability of published specialized information during 1840 and 1841 see Allan Pred, *Urban Growth and the Circulation of Information: The United States System of Cities, 1790–1840* (Cambridge: Harvard University Press, 1973), pp. 48–63, 73–77.

3. For documentation, further postal receipt data, and a more precise depiction of variations in the speed and frequency of postal services around 1840, see Pred, *Urban Growth,* pp. 82–103. Note that postal service in the South was poor compared to other regions. Also, because a large share of the mailings from southern major centers were assessed the maximum distance rate (for 400 miles and over), those cities almost certainly sent a relatively small number of letters per $1,000 of receipts.

4. For more specifics on interurban travel costs, volumes, and times at the end of the pretelegraphic period, see Pred, *Urban Growth,* pp. 143–185.

5. For a discussion of the diffusion of the Panic of 1837 and other innovations during the 1830s see Pred, *Urban Growth,* pp. 239–262. Contrast the summarized diffusion attributes with those called for by proponents of strictly hierarchical diffusion models based on Christaller's central-place theory (see chap. 3 at note no. 52).

6. *HMM,* 23 (July–December 1850), 697.

7. Edward T. Freedley, *Philadelphia and Its Manufactures* (Philadelphia, 1857), p. 70; Frank Luther Mott, *American Journalism: A History of Newspapers in the United States through 250 Years, 1690 to 1940* (New York: Macmillan, 1941), pp. 283, 285, 291.

8. Mott, *American Journalism,* p. 316; Alfred McClung Lee, *The Daily Newspaper in America: The Evolution of a Social Instrument* (New York: Macmillan, 1937), pp. 116–117; S. N. D. North, *History and Present Condition of the Newspaper and Periodical Press of the United States* (Washington, D.C., 1884), pp. 101–102.

9. By 1860, weekly editions of the *New York Tribune* reached 286,750 subscribers in twenty states, including about 7,400 in California (*New York Times,* Aug. 22, 1860). The nonlocal circulation of major-center newspapers was facilitated by special postage rates. For example, the Post Office Act of 1852 reduced postage charges on newspapers by 50 percent, if prepaid, thus often allowing major-center dailies to undersell the local papers of lesser

urban places. See Robert Sobel, *Machines and Morality: The 1850s* (New York: Thomas Crowell, 1973), p. 154; Lee, *Daily Newspaper*, pp. 302–304.

10. See David R. Goldfield, *Urban Growth in the Age of Sectionalism: Virginia, 1847–1861* (Baton Rouge: Louisiana State University Press, 1977), pp. 104–105.

11. For amplification, see the discussion accompanying the content analysis of selected major-center dailies in the third section of this chapter.

12. Representatively, by 1849 the Mercantile Library Association of Boston was making twenty-eight dailies and sixty-one weeklies and semiweeklies available to its more than 1,100 members. *HMM*, 21 (July–December 1849), 135.

13. Pred, *Urban Growth*, pp. 51–53; Robert Luther Thompson, *Wiring a Continent: The History of the Telegraph Industry in the United States, 1832–1866* (Princeton: Princeton University Press, 1947), pp. 140–166; John Langdale, "The Impact of the Telegraph on the Buffalo Agricultural Commodity Market: 1846–1848" (Paper prepared at Macquarie University, North Ryde, Australia, 1978), p. 4; *ARJ*, 20 (1847), 27; *New York Daily Tribune*, May 24, 1851.

14. See e.g., *Cleveland Plain Dealer*, Oct. 6, 1860; *New Orleans Daily Picayune*, Aug. 2, 1860. San Francisco was the only major center where daily newspapers could not exploit the telegraph in this manner; the transcontinental telegraph line was not put into operation until late in 1861.

15. Mott, *American Journalism*, pp. 251–252; Lee, *Daily Newspaper*, pp. 496–503; Alexander Jones, *Historical Sketch of the Electric Telegraph* (New York, 1852), pp. 90–91, 136; Thompson, *Wiring a Continent*, pp. 217–239.

16. For further details on postage rates during the 1840s and 1850s, see U.S. Bureau of the Census, *Historical Statistics of the United States: Colonial Times to 1957* (Washington, D.C., 1960), p. 498; *HMM*, 10 (January–June 1844), 27–28; Pliny Miles, "The Post Office in the United States and England," *Bulletin of the American Geographical and Statistical Society*, 2 (1857), 174–175.

17. The costliness of antebellum postal services to people outside the business world is to be judged from average daily wages for nonfarm labor, which stood at $0.85 in 1840, $0.90 in 1850, and $1.04 in 1860. (The average earnings of nonslave farm labor were much lower at each of these dates.) Stanley Lebergott, "Wage Trends, 1800–1900," in National Bureau of Economic Research, *Trends in the American Economy in the Nineteenth Century* (Princeton: Princeton University Press, 1960), p. 462.

18. Miles, "Post Office," p. 188 (quotation); *BM*, 12 (1857), 438.

19. *HMM*, 38 (January–June 1858), 112–113; U.S. Senate, *History of the Railway Mail Service*, Executive Document no. 40, 48th Cong., 2d sess., 1885; *DBR*, 9 (1850), 530; *ARJ*, 32 (1859), 497; *BM* 12 (1857), 439. Even the opening in 1860 of the short-lived Pony Express to and from St. Joseph, Mo., can be seen as a service-improvement effort that informationally benefited San Francisco more than any other urban place west of the Rockies.

20. *HMM*, 22 (January–June 1850), 50; 36 (January–June 1850), 758; 38 (January–June 1858), 112; U.S. Senate, *Report of the Postmaster General*, Executive Document no. 2, part 3, 36th Cong., 1st sess., 1860, II, 1,474.

21. Thompson, *Wiring a Continent,* pp. 52, 220, 234; *NWR,* 67 (Feb. 5, 1845), 384; U.S. Senate, Executive Document no. 373, 29th Cong., 1st sess., 1846, p. 1; *HMM,* 12 (January–June 1845), 122; *BM,* 12 (1857), 289–307.

22. *BM,* 12 (1857), 290–303; Lee, *Daily Newspaper,* p. 302; J. Thomas Sharf, *The Chronicles of Baltimore* (Baltimore, 1874), p. 510; Robert Greenhalgh Albion, *The Rise of New York Port, 1815-1860* (New York: Scribner's, 1939), pp. 354–369.

23. *Cincinnati Enquirer,* Jan. 31, June 12, 1860; *New Orleans Daily Picayune,* Aug. 2, 1860.

24. George Rogers Taylor, *The Transportation Revolution, 1815-1860* (New York: Holt, Rinehart and Winston, 1951), p. 144; *ARJ,* 31 (1858), 466. See note 1 to this chapter. See also Erik F. Haites, James Mak, and Gary M. Walton, *Western River Transportation: The Era of Early Internal Development, 1810-1860* (Baltimore: Johns Hopkins University Press, 1975), pp. 59–73.

25. James Robertson, *A Few Months in America: Containing Remarks on Some of Its Industrial and Commercial Interests* (London, 1855), p. 159. See note 17 to this chapter.

26. Taylor, *Transportation Revolution,* p. 144. For additional data on interurban passenger fares and rates by rail and other means see, for example, John Disturnell, *Disturnell's American and European Railway and Steamship Guide* (New York, 1853); John Lee Williams, *The Traveller's and Tourist's Guide through the United States, Canada, Etc.* (Philadelphia, 1855); Eugene Alvarez, *Travel on Southern Antebellum Railroads, 1828-1860* (University: University of Alabama Press, 1974); *HMM,* 9 (July–December 1843), 389; *DBR,* 6 (1848), 62–64; 12 (1852), 572.

27. See chap. 5 at note no. 44, and note 42 to chap. 5.

28. *ARJ,* 19 (1846), 234, 250; 31 (1858), 466; 32 (1859), 386, 435.

29. Robert Greenhalgh Albion, *Square-Riggers on Schedule: The New York Sailing Packets to England, France, and the Cotton Ports* (Princeton: Princeton University Press, 1938), pp. 253–258.

30. Robertson, *Few Months in America,* pp. 14, 18.

31. Albion, *New York Port,* p. 164.

32. During the 1840s and 1850s business travel between major southern centers, except New Orleans and Mobile, was still hampered by poor connections and was secondary to the business travel between those places and New York and the other major centers of the Northeast.

33. Israel Andrews, *Report . . . on the Trade and Commerce of the British North American Colonies,* U.S. Senate Document no. 112, 32nd Cong., 1st sess., 1853, p. 739; Pred, *Urban Growth,* p. 158.

34. Robertson, *Few Months in America,* p. 118; Haites, Mak, and Walton, *Western River Transportation,* pp. 71, 161.

35. *ARJ,* 25 (1852), 357. Prior to railroad construction, the most frequent overland passenger services available to business travelers in the western portion of the Midwest were the daily stagecoaches connecting Detroit, Chicago, Milwaukee, St. Louis, Cincinnati, Louisville, and the rapidly rising intermediate-sized city of Indianapolis (1860 population 18,611). Michael P. Conzen, "A Transport Interpretation of the Growth of Urban Regions: An American Example," *Journal of Historical Geography,* 1 (1975), 367.

36. Wyatt Winton Belcher, *The Economic Rivalry between St. Louis and Chicago, 1850–1880* (New York: Columbia University Press, 1947), p. 70; *ARJ,* 32 (1859), 185, 646. The volume of Milwaukee-Chicago traffic is particularly impressive because only 9 percent of the passengers had special low-price emigrant tickets. The Chicago-Pittsburgh traffic corresponded to 162 one-way trips per thousand persons for the combined 1860 population of the two major centers.

37. Although most domestic and foreign migrants arriving at midwestern major centers had rural destinations, and although many of the Europeans had little or no command of English, a few of them contributed to the availability of specialized economic information in those major centers, especially when they carried some technological know-how.

38. *DBR,* 8 (1850), 447.

39. As the construction of telegraph lines was pushed westward and southward from the major centers of the Northeast, new investment funds were sought from businessmen in other major centers, such as Cincinnati, St. Louis, Louisville, and New Orleans. Thompson, *Wiring a Continent,* pp. 135, 150–151.

40. Ibid., pp. 174, 243–245, 347; Jones, *Electric Telegraph,* pp. 189–194; U.S. Senate, *Report of the Superintendent of the Census,* Dec. 1, 1852, Executive Document no. 1, 32nd Cong., 2nd sess., I, 568–569.

41. *HMM,* 39 (July– December 1858), 243; 43 (July–December 1860), 492; *ARJ,* 31 (1858), 405; George B. Prescott, *History, Theory and Practice of the Electric Telegraph* (Boston, 1860), p. 214.

42. Marshall Lefferts, "The Electric Telegraph: Its Influence and Geographical Distribution," *Bulletin of the American Geographical and Statistical Society,* 2 (1857), 258–259. Also see Thompson, *Wiring a Continent,* pp. 242–243, on the dominance of business messages on the telegraph line connecting New York, Albany, and Buffalo.

43. Thompson, *Wiring a Continent,* p. 47; Lefferts, "Electric Telegraph," p. 259; Jones, *Electric Telegraph,* pp. 87–88, 105, 110; James D. Reid, *The Telegraph in America and Morse Memorial* (New York, 1886), p. 142; *HMM,* 12 (January–June 1845), 151; 39 (July–December 1858), 333; *DBR,* 4 (1847), 138; U.S. Senate, *Report of the Superintendent of the Census,* I, 569.

44. Message transmission could require hours rather than minutes when it was necessary to have transfers made from one independently owned line to another. For further comments on transmission speed and the capital accumulation process see David Harvey, "The Geography of Capitalist Accumulation: A Reconstruction of the Marxian Theory." *Antipode,* 7 (September 1975), 12.

45. See chap. 5 at note no. 15.

46. Thompson, *Wiring a Continent,* pp. 38–39; Alvin F. Harlow, *Old Wires and New Waves: The History of the Telegraph, Telephone, and Wireless* (New York: D. Appleton-Century, 1936), p. 148.

47. Details of antebellum telegraph-line development are given in Thompson, *Wiring a Continent;* Reid, *Telegraph in America;* and Harlow, *Old Wires and New Waves,* pp. 100–171. Comparatively few feeder lines were constructed prior to 1854, despite the relatively low capital requirements of

new telegraph lines (an average of about $150 per mile). Also note that San Francisco was the nodal focus of the first telegraph lines of California, which were not tied into the national network until 1861.

48. Thompson, *Wiring a Continent,* pp. 173–174; Jones, *Electric Telegraph,* pp. 102, 104, 109–110, 112–113, 115, 129; Harlow, *Old Wires and New Waves,* p. 162; Gardiner G. Hubbard, *Union of the Post-Office and Telegraph: Letter to the Postmaster General on the European and American Systems of Telegraph, with Remedy for the Present High Rates* (Boston, 1868), pp. 13–15; *HMM,* 27 (July–December 1852), 168.

49. On operational difficulties see, for example, Jones, *Electric Telegraph,* pp. 91–92, 94, Lefferts, "Electric Telegraph," p. 259; Thompson, *Wiring a Continent.*

50. Thompson, *Wiring a Continent,* p. 68; Harlow, *Old Wires and New Waves,* pp. 150–151 (quotation).

51. Reid, *Telegraph in America,* p. 189 (quotation); *Wiring a Continent,* p. 248. Although some long-distance transmission improvements had been made prior to the late 1850s, message retapping could be avoided between New York and Mobile (or other distant points) "only in good weather and under ideal conditions." Thompson, *Wiring a Continent,* p. 248.

52. Jones, *Electric Telegraph,* p. 87; Lefferts, "Electric Telegraph," p. 251. Another 1857 source reported 1,029 stations in the United States; however, since many major centers were served by more than one company, and since auxiliary stations were common at hotels, railway depots, and other intraurban locations, the figure of over 800 places given by Lefferts appears to be reasonable. *HMM,* 37 (July–December 1857), 624.

53. Lefferts, "Electric Telegraph," pp. 259–260; Jones, *Electric Telegraph,* pp. 105, 108; Thompson, *Wiring a Continent,* p. 446.

54. The representativeness of the November 1856 total given by Lefferts ("Electric Telegraph," p. 259) appears to be validated by indications that by 1852 New York–Boston telegraphic traffic had already averaged between 500 and 600 messages per day. Jones, *Electric Telegraph,* p. 110.

55. See note 41.

56. Based on data presented in *DBR,* 4 (1847), 138.

57. U.S. Senate, *Report of the Superintendent of the Census,* p. 567. The company dividends generated by New York–Buffalo traffic were one of the two highest such dividends in the country in the early 1850s. Jones, *Electric Telegraph,* pp. 93–94.

58. Harlow, *Old Wires and New Waves,* p. 177.

59. Jones, *Electric Telegraph,* pp. 93–94.

60. The microfilm newspaper holdings of the library at the University of California, Berkeley, somewhat restricted the choices that could be made in selecting nine major centers for analysis.

61. In the eighth and ninth 1851 cases, the *New Orleans Times Picayune* and the *Cleveland Plain Dealer,* nonlocal place mentions in an economic context were so abundant that a sample of two issues more than sufficed.

62. For comments concerning the advantages and disadvantages of using content analysis in the social sciences in general, and in historical and geographical inquiries in particular, see, e.g., Ole R. Holsti, *Content Analysis for*

the Social Sciences and Humanities (Reading, Mass.: Addison-Wesley, 1969);
Richard L. Merritt, *Symbols of American Community, 1735–1775* (New
Haven: Yale University Press, 1966), pp. xii–xvi; Alan R. H. Baker, "Histori-
cal Geography," *Progress in Human Geography,* 1 (1977), 470. For related
place-mention studies see J. P. Cole, *Places in Pravda,* Department of Geography, University of Nottingham, Mini Bulletin no. 22 (Nottingham, 1969; J.
P. Cole and P. Whysall, *Places in the News: A Study of Geographical Information,* Department of Geography, University of Nottingham, Bulletin of
Quantitative Data for Geographers, no. 17 (Nottingham, 1968); Paul G.
Kariel, "Parochialism among Canadian Cities," *Professional Geographer,* 30
(1978), 37–41.

63. See Elihu Katz, "The Two-Step Flow of Communications: An Up-to-
Date Report on an Hypothesis," *Public Opinion Quarterly,* 21 (1957), 61–78;
Everett M. Rogers and F. Floyd Shoemaker, *Communication of Innovations:
A Cross-Cultural Approach* (New York: Free Press, 1971), pp. 198–225.

64. The Boston hinterland is liberally defined in maps 6.2 and 6.3 inasmuch as it includes locations both in the Connecticut River valley and along
Long Island Sound that actually were within the overlapping economic
spheres of influence of New York and Boston. (See notes 30, 44, and 67 to
chap. 4 and the sources cited therein.) Cincinnati's hinterland is liberally defined in maps 6.4 and 6.5: it extends well beyond the points usually mentioned
as being on, or near, the outer rim of that city's antebellum trading area; i.e.,
it extends beyond Columbus, Ohio, Indianapolis, Ind., Lexington, Ky., and the
lower end of the Kanawha River valley into the hinterlands of Cleveland,
Pittsburgh, and Louisville. (See sources cited in note 173, chap. 4.)

65. See comments in chap. 4 at note no. 71.

66. Similar evidence is found consistently in other 1851 and 1860 content
analyses not discussed in detail here. For example, Cedar Rapids, Iowa, and
Quincy, Ill., were the hinterland places mentioned most often in the 1860 Chi-
cago content analysis, but their mentions were behind those for New York,
St. Louis, Cincinnati, Boston, Buffalo, Milwaukee, and Louisville. *Chicago
Daily Democrat,* Mar. 1, July 12, Oct. 5, 1860.

67. In the few additional instances where hinterland and nonhinterland
mentions were separated, the results were similar to those obtained for Boston and Cincinnati. For example, in the 1860 content analyses for Chicago
and Philadelphia, nonhinterland lesser cities, towns, and settlements answered for 19.48 and 17.64 percent respectively of all nonlocal place mentions
made in an economic context. *Chicago Daily Democrat,* Mar. 1, July 12, Oct.
5, 1860; *Philadelphia Public Ledger,* Jan. 10, May 24, Nov. 14, 1860.

68. From what is known of present-day decision-making, it may be assumed that the higher the level of uncertainty about a business opportunity
involving a place, the greater the quantity of new or redundant information
that had to be actively obtained or unintentionally encountered before new
action was undertaken.

69. Also note that, in the case of Cincinnati, the altered role of Memphis
was the most significant element in the relative frequency-mention gain made
by nonhinterland places other than major centers. In 1851, Memphis was responsible for just over 1 percent of the nonlocal economic place mentions

made in the sampled Cincinnati newspapers, whereas by 1860 the share for Memphis in the sampled Cincinnati dailies had grown to 3.56 percent.

7. Some Closing Words

1. For but one suggestion of the relationships between the economics of slavery and urban growth, see the discussion of Charleston's economy during the 1840s and 1850s in chap. 4 at note nos. 181–187. Also see chap. 5 at note no. 20; and Claudia Dale Goldin, *Urban Slavery in the American South, 1820–1860: A Quantitative History* (Chicago: University of Chicago Press, 1976).

2. The newly combining midwestern regional city-system involved the previously separate Lake Erie regional city-system and the Ohio and upper Mississippi valley regional city-system, as well as Chicago, Milwaukee, and a number of other urban newcomers.

3. Susan E. Hirsch, *Roots of the American Working Class: The Industrialization of Crafts in Newark, 1800–1860* (Philadelphia: University of Pennsylvania Press, 1978), p. 89. Compare and contrast this with the comments appearing in David M. Gordon, "Capitalist Development and the History of American Cities," in William K. Tabb and Larry Sawers, eds., *Marxism and the Metropolis: New Perspectives in Urban Political Economy* (New York: Oxford University Press, 1978), esp. pp. 29–32 and 36–43; and Richard A. Walker, "The Transformation of Urban Structure in the Nineteenth Century and the Beginnings of Suburbanization," in Kevin R. Cox, ed., *Urbanization and Conflict in Modern Societies* (Chicago: Maaroufa, 1978), pp. 165–212.

4. See chap. 6 at note no. 44; Allan Pred, "The Impact of Technological and Institutional Innovations on Life Content: Some Time-Geographic Observations," *Geographical Analysis*, 10 (1978), 365–367.

5. *HMM*, 39 (July–December 1858), 333.

6. Only a small percentage of the inventions patented between 1840 and 1860 actually were implemented and diffused as innovations. Antebellum investment practices suggest that most implemented inventions were initially put to use in the inventor's city or town of residence. Preliminary analysis for some, but not all, major centers indicates that patents, or potential innovation-diffusion origins, were concentrated disproportionately in those major centers in 1840 as well as 1860. Allan Pred, *Urban Growth and the Circulation of Information: The United States System of Cities, 1790–1840* (Cambridge: Harvard Univesity Press, 1973), pp. 265–269; idem, *The Spatial Dynamics of U.S. Urban-Industrial Growth, 1800–1914: Interpretive and Theoretical Essays* (Cambridge, MIT Press, 1966), p. 106.

7. See chap. 4 at note nos. 187, 200, and chap. 5 at note no. 19; and the discussion of pre-1840 place-to-place variations in business attitudes and behavior in Pred, *Urban Growth*, pp. 277–283.

8. A study conceptually vital to any historical investigation of the influence of information circulation upon migration is Torsten Hägerstand, "Migration and Area: Survey of a Sample of Swedish Migration-Fields and Hypo-

thetical Considerations on Their Genesis," in David Hannerberg, Torsten Hägerstrand, and Bruno Odeving, eds., *Migration in Sweden,* ser. B, no. 13 (Lund: Gleerup, 1957), pp. 27–158.

9. Allan Pred, "The Location of Economic Acitivity since the Early Nineteenth Century: A City-Systems Perspective," in Bertil Ohlin, ed., *The International Allocation of Economic Activity: Proceedings of a Nobel Symposium* (London: Macmillan, 1977), pp. 127–147.

Index

Harvard Studies in Urban History